The Bare Essentials

Form B
Second Edition

Sarah Norton/Brian Green

English Writing Skills

Holt, Rinehart and Winston of Canada, Limited
Toronto

Canadian Cataloguing in Publication Data

Norton, Sarah, date–
    The bare essentials

2nd ed.
ISBN 0-03-922022-2

1. English language – Rhetoric.   2. English language –
Grammar – 1950 –   .   I. Green, Brian. II. Title.

PE1408.N67 1988   808'.042   C87-094362-6

Publisher: Susan Lilholt
Editor: Tessa McWatt
Publishing Services Manager: Karen Eakin
Editorial Co-ordinator: Edie Franks
Copy Editor: Franca Cesario
Production Assistant: Cindy Cianciolo
Interior and Cover Design: Annette Tatchell, Daniel Perrault
Typesetting and Assembly: Q Composition Inc.
Printing and Binding: Metropole Litho Inc.

Printed in Canada

2 3 4 5   92 91 90 89

Preface

The second edition of Form B of *The Bare Essentials* maintains the approach of the first edition but replaces about one-third of the exercises. We have increased the proportion of paragraph exercises, as opposed to sets of discrete items, since finding and correcting errors in continuous prose is more closely analagous to the student's "real-life" editing experience. Also, we have added throughout the book a number of exercises to which answers are not provided (except in the *Instructor's Manual*) so that an accurate test of the student's achievement may be measured.

The Bare Essentials is designed for Canadian college students taking a first-semester or first-year writing course. The concise explanations, numerous exercises and answers, however, make it as suitable for individualized, self-paced learning programs as it is for conventional composition classes.

As the title suggests, *The Bare Essentials* covers only those points of grammar, usage, and mechanics that are indispensable to clear expository writing: organization of ideas, sentence structure, grammar, spelling, diction, and punctuation.

Each "essential" is presented in a discrete unit. A glance at the table of contents will show that we have arranged the units in what might be called the "order of visibility" of composition errors — starting with spelling and ending with organization and diction — but the instructor may introduce the units in any order. The chapters within a unit should, however, be covered in the order in which they appear.

We begin most chapters with a few words about the practical significance of the material. A short, nontechnical explanation of the writing principle appears next, followed by examples. Where the material is complex, we've broken it down into several easy-to-follow steps. Most of each chapter is devoted to practice exercises of gradually increasing difficulty, and the student is directed to do as many as necessary to master the rule. Taken sometimes from student work, sometimes from professional writing, the exercises are all designed to appeal to the interests of Canadian college students. Each unit ends with one or more answerless exercises and a writing assignment that tests the student's mastery of all the principles in the unit.

Several features of the book make it especially helpful and easy to use. First, the student can do most of the exercises right in the book. Second, the answers are printed on detachable pages at the back of the book, so students can easily correct their own work, getting immediate feedback about their errors. Finally, on the inside of the back cover is a Revision Guide, which can be used both as a checklist for revision and rewriting and as a subject index to the book. Teachers may wish to duplicate the Revision Guide, attach it to a student's paper, and use it to guide and explain grading.

We wish to express our appreciation to those who reviewed the manuscript and offered wise suggestions for its improvement: Patricia M. Conway, Vanier College; Michael H. Shields, the University of Alberta; and Jean F. Smyth, Humber College. In particular, we thank Centennial's Beth Clelland and Nell Waldman, who developed and class-tested many of the exercises.

Sarah Norton
Centennial College
Scarborough, Ontario

Brian Green
Niagara College
Welland, Ontario

introduction

Why You Need This Book

Who needs to write well, anyway? If I get a factory or general labour job, I won't ever need to write, and if I'm in management, a secretary will fix all my mistakes.

college student

We can train a person on the job to do the specific tasks we require in about two weeks . . . maximum. What we need you people at the colleges to do is teach them to communicate — with other workers, with their supervisors — orally and in memos, reports, and letters.

president of a steel-
fabricating firm speaking
to the technical faculty
at an Ontario community
college

You look at the guys who move up in this industry. They're the ones who can write intelligently and who can read and understand other people's writing. Hard work helps, and so does being the owner's nephew . . . but you've got to be able to read and write reasonably well to move past manual labour — and the guys who can't do it know that better than anyone. Ask them.

former employee in the
Canadian mining industry

To an employer, any employee is more valuable if he or she is able to write correctly and clearly. No one can advance very far in a career without the ability to construct understandable sentences. It's that simple. Fairly or unfairly, employers and others will judge your intelligence and ability on the basis of your use of English. If you want to communicate effectively and earn respect, both on and off the job, you need to be able to write clearly.

That's the bad news. The good news is that *anyone who wants to* can achieve the standards of written English that are acceptable anywhere. All that is needed from you, really, is *caring*. If you care enough — about what others think of you, about advancement in a career — then you'll put out the effort necessary, whether that means looking up spelling, rereading what you've written, or doing all the exercises in this book twice!

How to Use This Book

In each chapter, we do three things: explain a point, illustrate it with examples, and give exercises to help you master it. The exercises are arranged in **groups of 10-item sets** that get more difficult as you go along. By the end of the last set in a chapter, you should have a good grasp of the skill.

Here's how to proceed:

1. Read the explanation. Do this even if you think you understand the point being discussed.
2. Study the examples carefully.
3. Now turn to the exercises. If you've found an explanation easy and feel you have no problems with the skill, try an exercise (10 sentences) near the end of the group of exercises following the explanation. If you get all 10 sentences right, do one more set. If you get that one all right too, skip the rest and go on to the next point. Skip ahead only if you're really confident, though.

   If you don't feel confident, don't skip anything. Start with the first set and work through all the exercises until you're sure you understand the point.
4. ALWAYS CHECK YOUR ANSWERS TO ONE EXERCISE (10 sentences) BEFORE GOING ON TO THE NEXT. If you ignore this instruction, we can't help you. Only if you check after every 10 sentences can you avoid repeating your mistakes and possibly reinforcing your error.
5. When you discover a mistake, go back to the explanation and examples and study them again. Make up some examples of your own to illustrate the rule. When you're sure you understand, continue with the exercises.

Finally, on the inside of the back cover you'll find the Revision Guide. Use it to check over your papers before handing them in. This book is meant to be a practical tool, not a theoretical reference. Apply the lessons in the writing assignments we've included and in all the writing you do. Explanations can identify writing problems and show you how to solve them, exercises can give you practice in eliminating errors, but only writing and revising can bring real and lasting improvement.

contents

spelling

chapter

Three Suggestions for Quick Improvement

We will deal with spelling first because, of all the errors you might make in writing, spelling is the one that is noticed by everyone, not just English teachers. No piece of writing that is full of misspellings can be classified as good. Misspellings can cause misunderstanding, as when the communications teacher promised his students a course with "a strong *vacational* emphasis." (Those students who weren't misled wondered what he was doing teaching communications.)

Sometimes misspellings cause confusion. Take this sentence, for example:

Mouse is a desert with a base of wiped cream.

It takes a few seconds to "translate" the sentence into a definition of *mousse,* a dessert made with whipped cream.

Most often, though, misspellings are misleading, in that they spoil the image you want to present. You want, naturally, to be seen as intelligent, careful, and conscientious. But, if your writing is riddled with spelling errors, your reader will think you careless, uneducated, or even stupid. It is not true, by the way, that intelligence and the ability to spell go hand in hand. It *is* true, though, that people generally think they do. So, to prevent both confusion and embarrassment, it is essential that you spell correctly.

There are three things you can do to improve your spelling almost instantly:

> 1. Buy and use a good dictionary.

A good dictionary is the one indispensable tool of the writer. You will need it *every time* you write. Most of your doubts about spelling can be answered if you take the time to check in your dictionary. The time you spend looking up words will not be wasted; your rewards will be the increased accuracy of your writing and the increased respect of your reader. Two useful dictionaries are Holt, Rinehart and Winston's *Compact Dictionary of Canadian English* (a light, easy-to-carry dictionary, convenient for school) and *The Gage Canadian Dictionary* (a complete, up-to-date Canadian reference, ideal for use at home or in the office).

If you wonder how it's possible to look up a word that you can't spell, look at the two dictionaries we've recommended. At the front of each is a "Guide to the Dictionary," and in the Guide is a chart showing the common spellings for all the sounds in the English language. If you know only how to pronounce a word, the chart will help you find its spelling.

---

2. Ask a good speller.

Most good spellers are secretly proud of their talent and pleased to demonstrate it. Don't be afraid to ask. Remember, they probably aren't as good as you are at something else; you may have a talent they could use in exchange.

---

3. Learn three basic spelling rules.

English spelling is frustratingly irregular, and no rule holds true in *all* cases. But there are three simple rules that do hold for most words, and mastering these rules will help you avoid many common errors.

Before learning the three rules, you need to know the difference between **vowels** and **consonants**. The vowels are **a, e, i, o,** and **u** (and sometimes y). All the other letters are consonants.

Rule I: Dropping the Final e

The first rule tells you when to drop the final, silent *e* when adding an ending to a word.

Drop the final, silent *e* when adding an ending beginning with a vowel.
Keep the final, silent *e* when adding an ending beginning with a consonant.

Keeping the rule in mind, look at these examples:

Endings Beginning with a Vowel	Endings Beginning with a Consonant
-ing: amuse + ing = amusing	*-ment:* amuse + ment = amusement
-ed: live + ed = lived	*-ly:* live + ly = lively
-able: like + able = likable	*-ness:* like + ness = likeness
-ible: force + ible = forcible	*-ful:* force + ful = forceful
-er: use + er = user	*-less:* use + less = useless

Exercises

Combine each word with the ending to form a new word. When you have finished, check your answers in the back of the book. (Answers begin on p. 240. You can tear the pages out if you want to.) If you miss even one answer, go over the rule and the examples again to find out why. If you get all the answers to exercises I and 2 correct, skip ahead to exercise 4.

I

1. desperate + ly =

2. crackle + ing =

3. conceive + able =

4. atone + ment =

5. mate + ing =

6. rare + ly =

7. elevate + or =

8. emerge + ing =

9. positive + ly =

10. apologize + ing =

2

1. grave + ly =

2. heave + ing =

3. defuse + ible =

4. generate + or =

5. shape + ly =

6. excite + ment =

7. release + ing =

8. remove + able =

9. consummate + ly =

10. assure + ing =

3

1. operative + ly =

2. interfere + ence =

3. desire + able =

4. continue + ance =

5. abridge + ing =

6. mange + y =

7. dissolute + ly =

8. acquire + ing =

9. shake + able =

10. aerate + ing =

4

Add *e* in the blank space wherever it's needed to complete the spelling of these words. If no *e* is needed, leave the space blank.

1. apologiz____ing
2. encourag____ment
3. nois____y
4. issu____able
5. fam____ous

6. abridg____ment
7. mov____able
8. officiat____ing
9. valu____ation
10. valu____less

5

Add *e* in the blank space wherever it's needed.

1. imagin____ary
2. wrangl____ing
3. advers____ity
4. pranc____ing
5. blam____less

6. blam____ing
7. wav____y
8. obtus____ness
9. realiz____able
10. oblig____ing

6

Make up sentences, using all of the words you got wrong in exercises 1 through 5.

Exceptions to Rule I

Three common words do not follow the rule. Here they are:

argue + ment = argument
nine + th = ninth
true + ly = truly

There is one more exception to rule 1: after soft *c* (as in *notice*) and soft *g* (as in *change*), keep the final, silent *e* when adding an ending beginning with *a* or *o*. Here are two examples:

notice + able = noticeable
outrage + ous = outrageous

Rule 2: Doubling the Final Consonant

The second rule tells you when to double the final consonant when adding an ending to a word.

> When adding an ending beginning with a vowel (such as *-able, -ing, -ed,* or *-er*), double the final consonant of the root word if the word
> 1. ends with a *single* consonant preceded by a *single* vowel AND
> 2. is stressed on the last syllable.

Notice that a word must have *both* characteristics for the rule to apply. Let's look at a few examples.

begin + er	ends with a single consonant (*n*) preceded by a single vowel (*i*) and is stressed on the last syllable (*begín*), so the rule applies, and we double the final consonant:	**beginner**
control + ed	ends with a single consonant (*l*) preceded by a single vowel (*o*) and is stressed on the last syllable (*contról*), so the rule applies:	**controlled**
drop + ing	ends with a single consonant (*p*) preceded by a single vowel (*o*) and is stressed on the last syllable (there is only one: *dróp*), so the rule applies:	**dropping**
appear + ing	ends with a single consonant (*r*) preceded by *two* vowels (*ea*), so the rule does not apply, and we do not double the final consonant:	**appearing**
turn + ed	ends with *two* consonants (*rn*), so the rule does not apply:	**turned**
open + er	ends with a single consonant (*n*) preceded by a single vowel (*e*) but is *not* stressed on the last syllable (*ópen*), so the rule does not apply:	**opener**

(In words such as *equip, quit,* and *quiz,* the *u* should be considered part of the *q* and not a vowel. These words then follow the rule: *equipping, quitter,* and *quizzed.*)

Exercises

Combine each word with the ending to form a new word. Check your answers to each set of ten before going on. If you make no mistakes in exercises 7 and 8, skip ahead to exercise 11. If you make even one mistake, do exercises 9 and 10.

7

1. blot + ing =
2. span + ing =
3. submit + ed =
4. fail + ing =
5. blur + ed =

6. plump + er =
7. admit + ing =
8. abate + ing =
9. beg + ing =
10. entail + ed =

8

1. fat + er =
2. get + ing =
3. stop + ed =
4. persist + ing =
5. blot + er =

6. maul + ed =
7. pin + ed =
8. lengthen + ing =
9. knit + er =
10. enlist + ed =

9

1. beguile + ing =
2. demur + ed =
3. refer + ing =
4. strip + ed =
5. shoot + ing =

6. expel + ing =
7. grab + ed =
8. jar + ing =
9. knit + ing =
10. hinder + ed =

10

1. defer + ing =
2. remit + ance =
3. regret + able =
4. cuddle + ed =
5. acquit + al =

6. concur + ed =
7. flag + ing =
8. abet + or =
9. shine + ing =
10. refer + ed =

11

1. tip + able =

2. wonder + ing =

3. regret + ful =

4. reject + ed =

5. corrupt + ible =

6. whip + ing =

7. detain + ed =

8. extol + ing =

9. reappear + ance =

10. regret + able =

12

1. equip + ing =

2. repel + ing =

3. trap + er =

4. remit + ed =

5. smear + ing =

6. blur + ing =

7. occur + ing =

8. allot + ing =

9. access + ible =

10. petition + er =

13

1. occur + ence =

2. persist + ence =

3. emerge + ence =

4. recur + ence =

5. persevere + ance =

6. consist + ency =

7. suffer + ance =

8. resist + ance =

9. concur + ence =

10. deter + ence =

When it comes to adding *-ence,* three words are especially troublesome. *Prefer, refer,* and *confer* all appear to require a doubled final consonant. But they don't, because, when you add *-ence,* the stress shifts to the *first* syllable of the word. So you write

prefér	preférring	preférred	but	*préference*
refér	reférring	reférred	but	*réference*
confér	conférring	conférred	but	*cónference*

Exercises

14

Make up sentences in which you use the words you got wrong in exercises 7 through 13.

Rule 3: Words Containing *ie* or *ei*

There are almost a thousand common English words containing *ie* or *ei*, so remembering the rule that governs them is worthwhile. It helps to keep in mind that *ie* occurs roughly twice as often as *ei*.

The old rhyme tells you most of what you need to know to spell these words:

> Write *i* before *e*, except after *c*
> Or when sounded like $\bar{a}$, as in *neighbour* and *weigh*.

If you remember this rhyme, you'll have no difficulty in spelling words like *belief, piece, ceiling, receive,* and *freight.*

Unfortunately, the rhyme covers only two of the cases in which we write *e* before *i*: after *c*, and when the syllable is pronounced with a long $\bar{a}$ sound. So an addition to the rule is necessary:

> If short $\breve{e}$ or long $\bar{\imath}$ is the sound that is right,
> Write *e* before *i*, as in *their* or in *height.*

This rule covers such words as *Fahrenheit, seismic, heir,* and *leisure* (pronounce it to rhyme with *pleasure*). *Either* and *neither* can be pronounced "eye-ther" and "nye-ther," so they, too, require *ei*.

There are, of course, exceptions. This silly sentence contains the most common ones:

The *friend* of a *weird species* of *sheik seized caffeine, codeine,* and *protein.*

Exercises

Fill in the blanks with *ie* or *ei*. After you finish each set, check your answers.

15

1. br____f

2. w____ld

3. dec____ve

4. ach____ve

5. rel____ve

6. retr____val

7. c____ling

8. bes____ge

9. rec____pt

10. gr____ve

16

1. p____r

2. hyg____ne

3. h____rarchy

4. dec____t

5. f____rce

6. p____ced

7. t____r

8. conc____vable

9. rec____ve

10. h____roglyph

17

1. The quick, masked th____f jumped over the lazy pr____st.

2. The surv____llant supervisor s____zed the somnolent shipworker.

3. The fr____ght in the ship's hold w____ghed less than five tons.

4. N____ther of these great musicians is conc____ted about her

   accomplishments.

5. With v____ns standing out on his forehead and eyes bulging, he watched the

   G____ger needle reach its limit.

18

1. At the front____r, we will be entering for____gn territory.

2. However, that shouldn't concern you, since a king, fr____ndly to our nation,

   r____gns.

3. On the other hand, he is being challenged by a f____rce rebel ch____f, who

   is loyal to no one but himself.

4. At last report, the capital was under s____ge, and the h____r to the throne

   was a hostage of the rebels.

5. We will avoid the trouble, though, by staying away from the h____ghts, and

   remaining in our resort on the beach, where our l____sure should be undisturbed.

19

1. Can we really trust _____ther of them, when we know th_____r bel_____fs to be so similar?

2. After all, anyone who thinks that we are dec_____ved by everything we perc_____ve must be a couple of grams short of a full kilo!

3. If we can't trust our own senses, what conc_____vable information is there that we can rec_____ve with confidence?

4. Frankly, it would be a great rel_____f if n_____ther of them ever appeared in my life again.

5. My n_____ghbour is so conc_____ted, she speaks to no one on our block. It's mere conc_____t.

There are three or four more spelling rules we could explain here, but we won't — for two reasons. First, there are many exceptions to the remaining "rules" for English spelling. And, second, you don't need to memorize more rules *if you use your dictionary.* Now is the time to read the "Guide to the Dictionary" in the front of your dictionary. Reading it won't be very entertaining, but it will be well worth your while. The Guide outlines the kinds of information given for each word in the dictionary and explains the abbreviations and symbols that are used. You will discover, for example, that you don't need to memorize long lists of irregular plurals: your dictionary provides the irregular plurals of the nouns you look up. It also gives the irregular forms of verbs, adjectives, and adverbs. (If you've forgotten how *regular* plurals, verb forms, adjectives, and adverbs are formed, the Guide will remind you.) Your dictionary will also tell you how to add various endings to root words and even where you can divide a word when you need to hyphenate it at the end of a line. Take half an hour to read the Guide in your dictionary; then do the following exercises.

Exercises

Use your dictionary to do these exercises. Check your answers to each set of ten before going on to the next.

20

Write the plural form of each word.

1. potato
2. mystery
3. business
4. ghetto
5. leaf

6. thesis
7. sheep
8. criterion
9. larva
10. index

21

Combine each root word with the ending given.

1. lonely + ness =
2. money + ed =
3. lazy + ness =
4. hazy + er =
5. likely + est =

6. deny + s =
7. deny + ing =
8. twenty + eth =
9. healthy + ly =
10. subtle + ly =

22

Using hyphens, show where each word could be divided at the end of a line. (Some words can be divided in two or more places — for example, *ice-break-er*.)

1. better
2. comprise
3. patience
4. acknowledgment
5. rehearse

6. whipping
7. diphtheria
8. thrown
9. distribution
10. succeed

chapter 2

Sound-Alikes, Look-Alikes, and Spoilers

Using a dictionary, asking a good speller for help, and applying the three spelling rules will make an immediate improvement in your spelling. By following two additional suggestions you will further increase your spelling accuracy, but the skills involved will take longer to master. First, learn to tell apart words that are often confused because they sound or look alike. Second, learn to spell the words that most people find difficult — words we have called Spelling Spoilers. Don't try to master all of these words at once. Instead, memorize a few each week, and review them frequently. In two or three months, you could be one of the people poor spellers turn to for help!

Sound-Alikes and Look-Alikes

Some of your spelling troubles are probably caused by your using words that either sound or look like the words you really want. Careful pronunciation sometimes helps to correct this problem. For example, if you pronounce the words *accept* and *except* differently, you'll be less likely to confuse them in your writing. It is also useful to make up memory aids to help yourself remember the difference between words that sound alike but have very different meanings.

accept
except
: *Accept* means "take." It is always a verb. *Except* means "excluding." Everyone *except* Brian *accepted* my explanation.

advice
advise
: The difference in pronunciation makes the difference in meaning clear. *Advise* (rhymes with *wise*) is a verb. *Advice* (rhymes with *nice*) is a noun. I *advise* you not to listen to free *advice*.

affect
effect
: *Affect* is a verb meaning "influence." *Effect* is a noun meaning "result." If you can substitute *result*, then *effect* is the word you need. (Occasionally *effect* can be a verb — meaning "bring about" — but you probably won't need to use it that way.)
Learning about the *effects* of caffeine *affected* my coffee-drinking habits.

a lot
allot
: *A lot* (often misspelled *alot*) should be avoided. Use *many* or *much* instead. *Allot* means "distribute" or "assign."

         many   *much*
He still has ~~a lot of~~ problems, but he's coping ~~a lot~~ better.
The teacher will *allot* the assignments according to the student's interests.

are   *Are* is a verb. *Our* shows ownership.
our

        Pierre Berton and Margaret Atwood *are* two of Canada's best-known writers.
        Canada is *our* home and native land.

choose   Pronunciation gives the clue here. *Choose* rhymes with *booze* and
chose   means "select." *Chose* rhymes with *rose* and means "selected."

        Please *choose* a topic.
        I *chose* film making.

coarse   *Coarse* means "rough, unrefined." (Remember that the word ***arse*** is
course   coarse.) For all other meanings, use *course.*

        That sandpaper is too *coarse.*
        You'll enjoy the photography *course.*
        Of *course* you'll do well.

complement A *complement* completes something. A *compliment* is a gift of praise.
compliment

        A glass of wine would be the perfect *complement* to the meal.
        Some people are embarrassed by *compliments.*

conscience Your *conscience* is your sense of right and wrong. *Conscious* means
conscious   "aware" or "awake" — able to feel and think.

        After Katy cheated on the test, her *conscience* bothered her.
        Katy was *conscious* of having done wrong.
        The injured man was *unconscious* for an hour.

consul   A *consul* is a government official stationed in another country. A
council   *council* is an assembly or official group. Members of a council are
counsel   *councillors. Counsel* can be used to mean both "advice" and "to advise."

        The Canadian *consul* in Mexico was very helpful.
        The Women's Advisory *Council* meets next month.
        Maria gave me good *counsel.*
        She *counselled* me to hire a lawyer.

desert   A *désert* is a dry, sandy place. As a verb, *desért* means "leave behind."
dessert   *Dessert* is "double good," the kind of food you'd like two servings of, so give it *two s's.*

        The tundra is Canada's only *desert* region.
        My neighbour *deserted* her husband and children.
        Dessert is my favourite part of the meal.

dining   You'll spell *dining* correctly if you remember the phrase "wining and
dinning   dining." You'll probably never use *dinning.* It means "making a loud noise."

        The children are in the *dining* room.
        We are *dining* out tonight.
        The sounds from the disco next door were *dinning* in my ears.

does   Pronunciation provides the clue. *Does* rhymes with *buzz* and is a verb.
dose   *Dose* rhymes with *gross* and refers to a quantity of medicine.

        John *does* drive fast, *doesn't* he?
        My grandmother gave me a *dose* of cod liver oil.

forth
fourth

Forth means "forward" or "onward." ***Fourth*** contains the number **four**, which gives it its meaning.

Please stop pacing back and *forth*.
The B.C. Lions lost their *fourth* game in a row.

hear
here

Hear is what you do with your **ears**. *Here* is used for all other meanings.

Now *hear* this!
Ray isn't *here*.
Here is your assignment.

it's
its

It's is a shortened form of *it is*. The apostrophe takes the place of the *i* in *is*. If you can substitute *it is*, then *it's* is the form you need. If you can't substitute *it is*, then *its* is the correct word.

It's really not difficult. (*It is* really not difficult.)
The book has lost *its* cover. ("The book has lost *it is* cover" makes no sense, so you need *its*.)

later
latter

Later refers to time and has the word ***late*** in it. *Latter* means "the second of two" and has two *t*'s. It is the opposite of *former*.

It is *later* than you think.
You take the former, and I'll take the *latter*.

loose
lose

Pronunciation is the key to these words. *Loose* rhymes with *goose* and means "not tight." *Lose* rhymes with *ooze* and means "misplace" or "be defeated."

A *loose* electrical connection is dangerous.
Some are born to win, some to *lose*.

miner
minor

A **miner** works in a **mine**. *Minor* means "lesser" or "not important." For example, a *minor* is a person of less than legal age.

Liquor can be served to *miners*, but not if they are *minors*.
For me, spelling is a *minor* problem.

moral
morale

Again, pronunciation provides the clue you need. *Móral* refers to the understanding of what is right and wrong. *Morále* refers to the spirit or mental condition of a person or group.

People often have to make *moral* decisions.
The low *morale* of the workers prompted the strike.

peace
piece

Peace is what we want on **earth**. *Piece* means "a part or portion of something," as in "a **pie**ce of **pie**."

Everyone hopes for *peace* in the Middle East.
A *piece* of the puzzle is missing.

personal
personnel

Personal means "private." *Personnel* refers to the group of people working for a particular employer or to the office responsible for maintaining employees' records.

The letter was marked "*Personal* and Confidential."
We are fortunate in having hired highly qualified *personnel*.
Nellie works in the *Personnel* Office.

principal
principle

Principal means "main." A *principle* is a rule.

A *principal* is the main administrator of a school.
Oil is Alberta's *principal* industry.

The *principal* and the interest totalled more than I could pay.
(In this case, the principal is the main amount of money.)
One of the teacher's *principles* is to refuse to accept late assignments.

quiet
quite

If you pronounce these words carefully, you won't confuse them. *Quiet* has two syllables; *quite* has only one.

The librarian asked us to be *quiet*.
We had not *quite* finished our homework.

stationary
stationery

Stationary means "fixed in place." *Stationery* is writing paper.

Did you want a portable or a *stationary* computer?
Please order a new supply of *stationery*.

than
then

Than is used in comparisons. Pronounce it to rhyme with *can*. *Then* refers to time and rhymes with *when*.

Peter is a better speller *than* I.
He made his decision *then*.
Ted withdrew from the competition; *then* he realized the consequences.

their
there
they're

Their indicates ownership. *There* points out something or indicates place. It includes the word *here*, which also indicates place. *They're* is a shortened form of *they are*. (The apostrophe replaces the *a* in *are*.)

It was *their* fault.
There are two weeks left in the term.
You should look over *there*.
They're late, as usual.

too
two
to

The *too* with an extra *o* in it means "more than enough" or "also." *Two* is the number after one. For all other meanings, use *to*.

He thinks he's been working *too* hard. She thinks so, *too*.
There are *two* sides to every argument.
The *two* women knew *too* much about each other *to* be friends.

were
where
we're

If you pronounce these three carefully, you won't confuse them. *Were* rhymes with *fur* and is a verb. *Where* is pronounced "hwear," includes the word *here*, and indicates place. *We're* is a shortened form of *we are* and is pronounced "weer."

You *were* joking, *weren't* you?
Where did you want to meet?
We're on our way.

who's
whose

Who's is a shortened form of *who is* or *who has*. If you can substitute *who is* or *who has* for the *who's* in your sentence, then you are using the right spelling. Otherwise, use *whose*.

Who's coming to dinner? (*Who is* coming to dinner?)
Who's been sleeping in my bed? (*Who has* been sleeping?)
Whose calculator is this? ("*Who is* calculator" makes no sense, so you need *whose*.)

woman

Confusing these two is guaranteed to irritate your women readers.

women *Woman* is the singular form; compare *man. Women* is the plural form; compare *men.*

A *woman's* place is wherever she chooses to be.
The *women's* movement promotes equality between *women* and men.

you're *You're* is a shortened form of *you are.* If you can substitute *you are* for
your the *you're* in your sentence, then you're using the correct form. If you can't substitute *you are,* use *your.*

You're welcome. (*You are* welcome.)
Unfortunately, *your* hamburger got burned. ("*You are* hamburger" makes no sense, so *your* is the word you want.)

Exercises

Choose the correct word in each pair. If you don't know an answer, go back and reread the explanation. Check your answers after each set of ten questions (answers begin on p. 243). When you get five sets entirely correct, you may skip ahead to exercise 11.

1

1. Limiting (coarse course) selection so drastically will (affect effect) students' academic development and subsequent job opportunities.
2. (Are Our) you going to (accept except) the offer?
3. Eat your vegetables; (than then) you can have your (desert dessert).
4. If (your you're) overweight by fifty pounds, (loosing losing) the excess will be a long-term proposition.
5. It's (quiet quite) true that they did not get (hear here) until two in the morning.
6. Ironically, it is the saint, not the sinner, (who's whose) (conscience conscious) troubles him.
7. After her (forth fourth) child left home, she looked younger (than then) before the birth of her first.
8. (Its It's) hard to tell the dog from (its it's) owner.
9. To (choose chose) a (coarse course) of action contrary to your lawyer's (advice advise) would be foolish.
10. Constant (dining dinning) out (does dose) become boring after awhile.

2

1. The (principal's principle's) high (principals principles) constrained him to request the offending teacher's resignation.
2. They (choose chose) the (forth fourth) house that the real estate agent showed them.
3. (Accept Except) for one Italian dish, the (deserts desserts) served were all French.

4. (Your You're) being (conscience conscious) and in the classroom is a prerequisite, though not a guarantee, of learning.
5. To be (quiet quite), even to listen, is not necessarily to (hear here).
6. (Accept Except) for (miner minor) bruises, passengers wearing seat belts sustain fewer injuries in accidents than those who do not buckle up.
7. (Morales Morals) that have been judged as being (to too two) (loose lose) are reputed to have caused the downfalls of great empires.
8. Oh, take it! (Your You're) not going to let (your you're) (conscience conscious) keep you from a chocolate chip cookie, (are our) you?
9. (Its It's) a shame that the (stationary stationery) has the old address printed on it.
10. A (woman women) (who's whose) been out of the work force for fifteen years (does dose) need some help in planning career choices.

3

1. Bartender, do you (hear here)? Over (hear here), we want beer.
2. (To Too Two) be (stationary stationery) for that long is to be dead.
3. (Loosing Losing) or winning is not important in the early stages of learning a sport; (its it's) the development of skills and attitudes that really matters.
4. Gretzky, (your you're) being sent to the (miner minor) leagues!
5. I can't stand city noise; maybe in the Sahara (Desert Dessert) I'll find (peace piece).
6. The (Consul Council Counsel) for the Defence of the Miniscule Tsetse Fly failed to meet at nine this morning; (accept except) for one, all the members slept in.
7. He is handsome, clever, and talented, but his (coarse course) language entirely spoils the (affect effect) at his interviews.
8. (Peace Piece) and (quiet quite) are the wistful illusions of the media-bombarded 1980s mind.
9. (Woman Women) working in traditionally male areas of employment are the ones (who's whose) competence is most often questioned.
10. War and (peace piece): back and (forth fourth) the pendulum swings.

4

1. The young girls took the babies for a walk without permission, but (than then), when they heard the police sirens, they became frightened and (deserted desserted) them.
2. At the dinner hour, it was (quiet quite) and peaceful in the park (were we're where) the infants had been left in (their there they're) carriages.
3. The (to too two) children may have imagined that they (were we're where) kidnapping dolls or that they (were we're where) teenage baby-sitters on duty; (later latter) the babies' mothers realized the girls' innocent motives.

4. The father of one child is the Swedish (consul council counsel) in Canada and the father of the second is a county court judge; both presumably have high (principals principles).
5. (A lot of   Allot of   Many) parents would (loose lose) their composure, not to mention their tempers, in this embarrassing situation.
6. You don't deal out family justice like a (does dose) of medicine; after all, (your you're) responsibilities don't begin and end with a pill or a teaspoon.
7. In the (quiet quite) of (their there they're) homes, the families carefully explained some (principals principles) of family love and private ownership; (than then) the young girls understood.
8. (Its It's) the (later latter) of the (to too two) ideas that the children actually grasped.
9. (Later Latter) the babies' mothers were able to (accept except) the young girls.
10. It is (quiet quite) often thought that (woman women) forgive more readily than men, although they also (loose lose) their tempers more frequently.

5

1. We (a lot   allot) $200 of our monthly budget to (dining dinning) out.
2. To keep the (peace piece) with (are our) small children, we will eat twice a month at McDonald's.
3. (Woman Women) have (deserted desserted) their families for less.
4. I've decided (were we're where) not going to eat more than once a month at a restaurant (were we're where) I do not want to eat.
5. Last month, after our (forth fourth) hamburger dinner, I (choose chose) to remain (stationary stationery) in my own kitchen until things changed.
6. "(Are Our) you even (conscience conscious) of what (your you're) eating?" I cried in desperation.
7. (Their There They're) reply astonished me. "Of (coarse course)! We (choose chose) the restaurants we do because they cook exactly the way you do (hear here) at home."
8. My family's judgment on my cooking profoundly (affected effected) my culinary pride and (moral morale).
9. (Who's Whose) (advice advise) should I take?
10. On (principal principle), we'll eat twice at French restaurants and two (peace-piece-) keeping meals at burger palaces.

6

1. Increasingly violent crime and nationwide industrial strikes seem to be some of the (affects effects) and symptoms of society's (moral morale) decline.
2. If we (complement compliment) ourselves on social progress, (than then) we deceive ourselves.

3. Some social reformers and therapists (advice advise) that society will progress only as individuals make (personal personnel) progress.
4. The coal (miner minor) (does dose) as much to help or hinder his society as the country's minister of natural resources.
5. (Their There They're) seems to be no way to boost (their there they're) (morale moral).
6. To (hear here) the manager speak was the best thing that could happen to (your you're) employees.
7. The company (personal personnel) (who's whose) job it was to print the (stationary stationery) were on strike.
8. They (choose chose) the (later latter) (coarse course) of action rather than (accept except) management's offer.
9. They (deserted desserted) their posts (quiet quite) hopefully, looking for a quick settlement.
10. (To   Too   Two) many social prophets and (to too two) many politicians want to tell us (were we're where) our society is headed.

7

1. (Its It's) (quiet quite) true that the (personal personnel) department will influence the (coarse course) of strike action, however inadvertently.
2. You see, it was (their there they're) decision to (hear here) the union's legal (consul council counsel) inside the plant.
3. Once before, they (choose chose) to listen to such (advice advise) inside the plant.
4. (Than Then) they should have known this time that an inside meeting would ensure total management control of the issues rather (than then) allow for representative opinions of both managers and labourers.
5. Neutral territory for the negotiations would have provided an atmosphere (were we're where) judgment of the issues could be (affected effected).
6. (Who's   Whose) (moral   morale) values could possibly have been offended if the meeting had been held in Miss Bundy's Nursery School?
7. (Who's   Whose) (conscience   conscious) has been (affected   effected) the most by the railroading of a proposal no one can (accept except)?
8. That (coarse course) of action (does dose) offend (your you're) own plant managers.
9. It also (deserts desserts) and discounts completely any (personal personnel) values the employees may have.
10. (To Too Two) bad!

8

(Accept Except) my (advice advise): go immediately (to too two) Weight Watchers! Do not pass (your you're) home; do not collect one last (desert dessert).

Of (coarse course), (its it's) all a matter of (conscience conscious) — (your you're) (conscience conscious). Whether you (choose chose) (to too two) think of yourself as pleasingly plump or (to too two) fat is your business. (Their There They're) (are our) always those friends without (principal principle) who will tell you anything you want to (hear here) — for instance, how your gently curving middle (read, bulging stomach) (complements compliments) your tall frame and large bones. But (than then), (are our) those friends? I'm (your you're) friend, so please believe me: (dining dinning) heavily six or seven times daily is not only not for you, (its it's) not for anyone. You really must (loose lose) weight. Two hundred pounds on a five-foot-two frame is big-league fat. I beg you, join the (miners minors)!

9

(Their They're There) must be a better way to cope with house renovations. If I were to describe my (personal personnel) agony during the months it took for the construction workers and contractors to (acheive achieve) their final (affect effect), (you're your) heart would bleed. Plaster dust was the worst problem, because it gets into everything, making even (dinning dining) an uncomfortable experience. As the walls were torn (lose loose) and the house was gradually reduced to (it's its) skeleton, plaster dust found (its it's) way into every crack and corner. The noise and confusion (affected effected) my (moral morale), and I became inclined to use (course coarse) language, particularly with those who insisted on giving me (advice advise). (Later Latter), when my (conscience conscious) got the better of me, my feeble attempts at apology (were we're) not (accepted excepted). In the end, the renovations cost me my (peace piece) of mind, my (friends freinds), and more money (than then) I dreamed possible.

10

By the time we discovered that (there they're their) was (too to two) much cholesterol in fried foods, we (were we're where) already addicted. French fries and chicken wings, battered fish and doughnuts were an (excepted accepted) part of our diet. The (affect effect) that (dinning dining) on such foods has on us is evident in both our (waste waist)lines and in the nation's heart disease statistics. The (desserts deserts) we tend to (chose choose) are the worst offenders, according to diet (councillors counsellors), but (our are) main (course coarse) can be equally dangerous if (its it's) cholesterol count is high. Experts now (advice advise) us (too to two) be guided by the (principle principal) that "less is more." But this (advice advise) is more difficult to follow than one might expect in a society that has been conditioned to (believe beleive) "bigger is better." The (moral morale) seems to be that we must (chose choose) between foods that taste good and foods that do good.

11

Your own writing is the best test of your spelling accuracy. Write ten sentences using sound-alikes and look-alikes. Try to use those words that cause you the most difficulty.

12

Write a short paragraph on any topic you choose. In your paragraph, use at least five of the sound-alikes and look-alikes you have had trouble with. Refer to the explanations, if necessary, and don't forget to use your dictionary!

Spelling Spoilers

Here is a list of words that are frequently misspelled. Have someone dictate the list to you. Circle the ones you misspell, and memorize them, a few at a time. Try to learn ten each week. Review your list often, until you have mastered every word. Making up memory aids for especially troublesome words will help you conquer them. Here are some examples to get you started:

accommodate: It means "make room for," and the word itself makes room for two c's and two m's.

business: Business is no **sin**.

environment: The word *environment,* like the earth, has *iron* in it.

friend: He is a fri**end** to the **end**.

grammar: Poor gra**mmar** will **mar** your writing.

absence	business	development
accommodate	careful	disappear
achievement	category	disappoint
acknowledge	clothes	discipline
across	committee	dissatisfied
adolescence	conscious	doesn't
among	criticism	eighth
answer	definitely	embarrassed
argument	dependent	environment
beginning	desperate	exercise

existence	mentally	safety
explanation	necessary	schedule
extremely	ninety	separate
familiar	ninth	shining
February	occasionally	similar
finally	omission	somewhat
forty	opinion	speech
friend	opportunity	studying
gauge	paid	succeed
government	parallel	superintendent
grammar	perform	surprise
guarantee	planned	technique
guidance	possess	thorough
height	prejudice	tragedy
hoping	privilege	truly
hypocrisy	procedure	unnecessary
immediately	proceed	until
independent	professor	unusual
laboratory	psychology	usually
license (*or* licence)	recommend	vacuum
likely	relevant	Wednesday
loneliness	repetition	writing
lonely	restaurant	written
maintenance	rhythm	
marriage	ridiculous	

Exercise

13

Make up sentences containing the words you misspelled when the list of Spelling Spoilers was dictated. Underline the Spelling Spoiler(s) in each sentence. (If you do this exercise once a week, you will master the list very quickly.)

One final suggestion. You may find that, despite all your efforts, there are a few words you just cannot spell correctly. The solution? Either write them out on the inside cover of your dictionary or, even simpler, don't use them. Look in your dictionary or thesaurus to find synonyms (different words with the same or similar meanings), and use those instead. Two thesauruses are available in inexpensive paperback editions: *Roget's Thesaurus* and Soule's *Dictionary of English Synonyms*.

chapter 3

The Apostrophe

Although it is very easy to use correctly, the apostrophe is one of the most misused gadgets in English. In fact, correct use of apostrophes is one of the best indicators of a careful writer. One large government corporation gives prospective employees a five-part grammar test, and three of the sections test the applicant's ability to use the apostrophe correctly. Clearly this employer doesn't consider the apostrophe a frill.

In many sentences, an apostrophe is needed to enable the reader to understand what you're trying to say. Here's an example:

> The teacher began class by calling the students names.
> The teacher began class by calling the students' names.

The apostrophe is used for two distinct purposes: to indicate contraction and to indicate possession.

Contraction

The rule about where to put apostrophes in contractions is one of the rare rules to which there are no exceptions. It *always* holds.

> When two words are shortened into one, and a letter (or letters) is left out, the apostrophe goes in the place of the missing letter(s).

they are ⟶ they're

there is ⟶ there's

we are ⟶ we're

we will ⟶ we'll

it is, it has ⟶ it's

you would ⟶ you'd

cannot ⟶ can't

is not ⟶ isn't

who is, who has ⟶ who's

will not ⟶ won't (Note the slight spelling variation here.)

Exercises

Check your answers to each set of ten before going on to the next. Answers for this chapter begin on p. 245.

1

Make these sets of words into contractions.

1. it is
2. has not
3. they are
4. there is
5. will not

6. it will
7. he has
8. we will
9. you are
10. she is

2

Make these sets of words into contractions.

1. he will
2. you have
3. I am
4. do not
5. who has

6. would not
7. we are
8. who will
9. you will
10. did not

3

Place apostrophes correctly in these words.

1. cant
2. youre
3. theyre
4. shouldnt
5. wholl

6. dont
7. youll
8. were
9. theyve
10. itll

4

Correct these sentences by placing apostrophes where needed.

1. Yes, its a long way from Halifax to Vancouver, but weve been in training for three months.

2. Were taking the train to Antigonish and were biking to Halifax; then well begin the big trip west.
3. Cant you stop your poodle from chasing its tail?
4. Dont the maps youve packed show secondary roads?
5. Lets get some others; I havent the courage for highways.
6. Whats the plan for the rest of the club?
7. Whos detouring through Manitoulin? Shouldnt the officials know?
8. Id prefer my own bike for the trip; wouldnt you?
9. There isnt a dry eye in the theatre when Spielbergs film reaches its climax.
10. Wont we take our down jackets? Well still be travelling in October and its quite cool then.

5

If you've had no difficulty with exercises 1 through 4, skip this exercise and go on to "Possession." If you have had problems, review the rule for contraction, study your errors carefully to be sure you understand why you were wrong, and do exercise 5. Then check your answers.

Make the bracketed words into contractions.

The loudest complainer about smoking (is not) the person who never started; (it is) the person (who has) recently quit. There are many reasons for this phenomenon, including the fact that recent non-smokers (are not) really convinced that (they have) kicked the habit. They (do not) want temptation blown in their faces. (You have) probably noticed that someone (who has) never smoked can refuse an offered cigarette with "No thanks," while the recent convert (cannot) resist adding "No, (I have) given them up," or "No thanks, I (do not) touch them; (they are) bad for you!" Reformed smokers are surprisingly unsympathetic toward others (who are) still addicted, providing little support for those who (cannot) break the habit as (they have) been able to do. On the other hand, (there is) no one as belligerent and full of excuses as a person (who has) fallen off the wagon and resumed smoking after a short period of "reformation." (We would) do well to remember the words of Mark Twain: "(It is) easy to stop smoking; (I have) done it dozens of times."

Possession

The apostrophe also shows ownership or possession: *'s* is added to the *owner* word.

>the book's cover (The cover belongs to the book.)
>the students' names (The names belong to the students.)
>an arm's length (The length is of, or belonging to, an arm.)

As you can see, possession does not have to be literal. The owner does not have to be a person or thing; ideas or concepts can be owners, too.

>day's work (the work of, or belonging to, a day)
>hour's pay (the pay of, or belonging to, an hour)
>danger's thrill (the thrill of danger)
>Saturday's child (the child of Saturday)

When you want to show possession, *first identify the owner word;* then apply this simple rule.

---

1. Add *'s* to the owner word, regardless of what letter it ends in.
2. If the resulting word ends in a double or triple *s*, erase the last one, leaving the apostrophe in place.[1]

Examples:

car + 's = car's	clerks + 's = clerks's
ball + 's = ball's	Dickens + 's = Dickens's
women + 's = women's	Pam + 's = Pam's
boss + 's = boss's	Les + 's = Les's

It doesn't matter whether the owner word is singular or plural; the rule is the same.

There are several exceptions to the possession rule. The following words show possession by their spelling and don't need the *'s*.

---

[1]*Alternatives: Some grammarians retain the -ss's endings for 1) all singular one-syllable words of this kind (e.g., the* class's *work), and for 2) any word of this kind whose plural form adds an extra syllable (e.g., singular* congress → *plural* congresses; congress → *possessive* congress's). *Also in the case of names, some grammarians prefer to retain* 's *on multiple* s *endings — e.g.,* Dickens's *novels, Lake* Kennisis's *pollution count,* Jesus's *life.*

my	her	its
mine	hers	whose
your	our	their
yours	ours	theirs
his		

As you learned in chapter 2, in the section on sound-alikes and look-alikes, four of these words are often confused with contractions that sound like them. The possessives are at the left in the following list, the contractions at the right. Remember, when you need to decide which word to use, you can separate the contraction into its two words and try them out in the sentence. Better yet, you can memorize these words.

their:	they own something	they're = they are
your:	you own something	you're = you are
whose:	"who" owns something	who's = who is, who has
its:	it owns something	it's = it is, it has

They're going to try *their* luck at cards.
You're losing *your* hair.
Who's been sleeping in *whose* bed?
It's obvious the car has a hole in *its* muffler.

Exercises

6

Make the following words possessive (owner words).

1. tractor
2. Lee
3. somebody
4. dove
5. Beatrice

6. course
7. Norsemen
8. loss
9. glass
10. bandits

7

If you got any of the words in exercise 6 wrong, go back over the possession rule. Make sure you fully understand what you're doing, because the exercises are going to get harder. When you're satisfied you know the rule and how to apply it, make these words possessive.

1. salesmen
2. purses
3. our
4. yesterday
5. no one

6. Hopkins
7. Fenelon Falls
8. man
9. actress
10. Judy

8

Make the following words possessive.

1. their
2. Chris
3. her
4. gentlemen
5. strawberries

6. mystery
7. one
8. Burgess
9. chairmen
10. ladies

9

Make the bracketed words in the sentences possessive.

1. One (week) work under (he) supervision is enough.

2. This strange (fish) breathing apparatus is also (it) dorsal fin.

3. By the (day) end, our (dogs) coats were matted with burrs.

4. That (church) contributions to the Relief Fund were very generous, thanks to (it) (minister) hard work.

5. (Sandy) exam got a better mark than (Lewis).

6. The (children) temperaments are not like (he); they're like (they) (mother).

7. The (hoses) nozzles were all defective; however, the (salesmen) discount pleased (they) clients very much.

8. (Todays) television stars seem unable to resist (producers) temptations to make them into (tomorrows) film idols.

9. In a (minute) expression of anger, she destroyed a (year) painstaking work.

10. The (United States) action against (terrorists) training bases may bring reprisals from some (countries) radical elements.

10

Correct these sentences by adding apostrophes where necessary. This is the last exercise on possession, so be sure you understand possession before going on to the next exercises.

1. A floppy disks quality is measured by its ability to store information without error.

2. Expo 86 owed much of its success to Vancouvers natural beauty and its citizens natural friendliness.

3. Diplomatic ambassadors wives or husbands are often as important to a missions success as the ambassadors themselves.
4. Near Chicoutimi is one of the countrys most beautiful parks, where the skills of canoeists, fishermen, and wildlife photographers can all be put to the test on a summers day.
5. The Leafs forward and the Oilers defenceman were exchanged during the last days trading at the NHL meetings.
6. Womens clothing styles have changed more than mens over the last thirty years, but mens fashions are becoming more interesting as we enter the twentieth centurys last decade.
7. The Metro Toronto Zoos care for its animals is world famous; it was the first zoo to employ a nutritionists services for the maintenance of the animals diets.
8. My grandparents wedding picture sits on the desk next to my computer manuals to help me keep a perspective on lifes changes and challenges.
9. Janis career got its start when she sang fishermens songs in the yacht clubs dining lounge.
10. Many movies plots are criticized for violence, but our censors scissors are usually reserved for scenes involving sex.

Review Exercises

The following exercises will test and reinforce your understanding of both contraction and possession.

11

Choose the correct word from those in brackets. Check your answers before going on.

1. (Its It's) going to run (its it's) laps faster than yours, but I bet my (turtles turtle's) legs are shorter than your (turtles turtle's) legs.
2. (Its It's) strange what creatures people choose to race; (their there they're) going to have the national championship cricket race in Japan next week.
3. Where (your your're) going, (your you're) biggest problem will be maintaining (your you're) health.
4. (Joan's Joans') career goals involve the Humane (Society's Societies) plan to extend this (provinces province's) lost-animal services into their Manitoba and Saskatchewan facilities.
5. (Someones Someone's) got to take responsibility for the large numbers of domestic animals (whose who's) owners have abandoned them.
6. (Their There They're) isn't much chance that the (Jones's Jones') animals will find (their there they're) way home, since (its it's) five hundred desolate miles from Moose Factory to Cochrane.
7. (Countries Country's Countries') that maintain (their there they're) neutrality find (their there they're) under pressure from super(power's powers powers') delegations.

8. The Ringling (Brothers Brother's Brothers') circus animals were well cared for compared to the animals of (todays today's todays') circuses.
9. My (fathers father's fathers') (uncles uncle's) hound could scent a (foxes fox's) ten-day-old trail even in dense (woods woods') teeming with other wildlife.
10. Contrary to some (people's peoples) opinions, postal (workers worker's workers') contracts are most often settled by both (sides side's sides') willingness to bend long before a (strikes strike's) necessary.

12
Correct the following sentences where necessary.

1. Garlics effects should not be forgotten by those who's aim is to impress they're friends with close-up wit.

2. Noticing the customers' suspicious behaviour, David questioned her about her purses' contents.

3. Your playing well already, with only a years' study.

4. Fort Garys history is revealed in the book's, document's, and historical artifacts' on display at the Art Galleries special show.

5. Admissions to the journalism program are down this term, but its not the director's fault; she toured the citys high schools to find interested students.

6. Your not going to improve your playing beyond this point unless you concentrate on making the most of youre instrument's projection capabilities.

7. After all, audiences shouldnt have to strain to hear what theyve paid good money to hear with ease and pleasure; its a different matter if the concert halls acoustics are at fault.

8. The concertmasters patience gave out when his two solo's were suddenly cut from the score; hed been practising them daily for several weeks.

9. Jerry Smith built a house that became known to our areas residents as Smiths Folly, thanks to it's strange design and it's owners even stranger decorations.

10. Canadas opportunities for it's professional musicians are numerous.
From coast to coast their are symphony orchestras, opera and ballet
companies, rock groups, pop groups, and music-teaching facilities, all requiring
talented professionals.

13

Make words 1 through 5 possessive. Give the contraction for words 6 through 10.

1. girls

2. life

3. fence

4. it

5. activities

6. we are

7. who is

8. it is

9. they are

10. should not

Now write five sentences, each containing one of the possessives and one of the
contractions.
Example: The *girls'* game is still on, but *we're* not playing.

14

Make words 1 through 5 possessive. Give the contraction for words 6 through 10.

1. women

2. violinist

3. someone

4. intermediary

5. intermediaries

6. cannot

7. he has

8. there is

9. could not

10. have not

Now write five sentences, each containing one of the possessives and one of the
contractions.

unit

2

sentence structure

chapter 4

Cracking the Sentence Code

There is nothing really mysterious or difficult about the sentence itself; you've been speaking sentences successfully since you were two. The difficulty arises when you go to write — not sentences, oddly enough, but paragraphs. Almost all college students, if asked to write ten sentences on ten different topics, could do so without an error. But, if those same students were to write paragraphs, sentence fragments and run-on sentences would creep in — errors that confuse or annoy readers.

The solution to fragment and run-on problems has two parts:

> Be sure every sentence you write
> 1. sounds right and
> 2. has a subject and a verb.

Your ear is the best instrument with which to test your sentences. If you read your sentences aloud, you'll probably be able to tell by the sound whether they are complete, clear, and satisfactory. A complete sentence is one that makes sense by itself.

Read these sentences aloud:

> Windsurfing is one of the world's newest sports.
> Although windsurfing is still a young sport.

The second "sentence" doesn't sound right, does it? It does not make sense on its own and is in fact a sentence fragment.

Testing your sentences by reading them aloud won't work if you read your paragraphs straight through from beginning to end. The trick is to read from end to beginning. That is, read your last sentence aloud, and *listen* to it. If it sounds all right, then read aloud the next-to-last sentence, and so on, until you have worked your way back to the first sentence you wrote.

Now, what do you do with the ones that "sound funny"? Before you can fix them, you need to be able to "decode" each sentence to find out whether it has a subject and a verb. The subject and the verb are the bare essentials of the sentence; every sentence you write must have both. (The only exception is the *command*, in which the subject is understood rather than expressed. Consider this command: "Put your signature here." The subject *you* is understood.)

Finding Subjects and Verbs

A sentence is about *someone* or *something*. That someone or something is the **subject**. The word (or words) that tells what the subject *is* or *does* is the **verb**. The verb will express some sort of action, or condition, or occurrence.

Find the verb first. One way is by finding the word or group of words whose form can be changed to indicate a change in time. In the sentence

The prime minister has called an election.

has called (in the past) can be changed to *is calling* (present) or *will call* (future), so *has called* is the verb.

Once you have found the verb, find the subject, by asking *who* or *what* the verb is referring to.

Look at these examples. We have underlined the subjects once and the verbs twice.

Jean helped me.
(Helped expresses an action and is the verb.
Who or what helped? Jean helped, so Jean is the subject.)

Finding verbs is relatively easy.
(Is expresses a condition and is the verb.
Who or what is [easy]? Finding, which is the subject.)

How you do it remains a mystery to me.
(Remains expresses a condition and is the verb.
Who or what remains [a mystery]? How you do it, which is the subject.
Notice that the subject can be more than one word.)

David Crombie was called Toronto's tiny perfect mayor.
(Was called expresses an occurrence and is the verb.
Who or what was called? David Crombie.)

Their rehabilitation program seems successful.
(Seems expresses a condition and is the verb.
Who or what seems successful? Program.)

Exercise

I

Find the subject and the verb in each of the following sentences. Underline the subject with one line and the verb with two. When you have finished, check your answers on p. 248. If you make even one mistake, carefully reread "Finding Subjects and Verbs." Be sure you understand this material thoroughly before you go on.

1. Marie types slowly.
2. Her essays are always late.
3. Marie's essays usually get high marks, though.
4. Henri is a fast typist.

5. His marks, however, are disappointing.
6. Henri asked Marie for a date.
7. Finally she agreed to go out with him.
8. Suddenly, Henri's marks improved dramatically.
9. Coincidentally, Marie began to submit her work on time.
10. How these events relate to one another is fairly obvious.

Usually the subject comes before the verb in a sentence, but not always. Occasionally we find it after the verb:

Back to the refreshment stand for the fourth time stumbled the weary father.
(Who or what stumbled? The father.)

At the bottom of the page, in red ink, was my grade.
(Who or what was? My grade.)

In sentences beginning with *There* + some form of the verb *to be,* or with *Here* + some form of the verb *to be*, the subject is always found after the verb.

There are three good reasons for learning to write well.
(Who or what are? Reasons.)

There will be a test next week.
(Who or what will be? A test.)

Here are the solutions to last week's problem set.
(Who or what are? Solutions.)

In questions, the subject often follows the verb:

Are you sure about this?   Is he late again?
(Who or what are? You.)   (Who or what is? He.)

But notice that, in questions beginning with *who, whose, what,* or *which,* the subject and verb are in "normal" order:

Who met the bear?   What happened to Algy?
Whose belly was bulgy?   Which grizzly ate Algy?

Exercises

Find the subject and the verb in each of the following sentences. Underline the subject with one line, the verb with two. Check your answers to each set of ten sentences before you go on.

2

1. Canoeing the old voyageurs' route was exciting.
2. More than the common cold and car accidents, sugar is your body's worst enemy.

3. Was that nice?
4. Up on the display wall was the famous blue bicycle.
5. Here is the officer from Station 52.
6. Are the other teachers as helpful?
7. On every weekend in the summer, Québec's highways are crowded.
8. On Hallowe'en, soaping windows is mischievous but not destructive.
9. Please write in the spaces provided.
10. Saskatoon almost became the home of a National Hockey League team a few years ago.

3

1. Pierre Trudeau, like Jack Benny, is perennially middle-aged.
2. Here is an idea to consider.
3. Lucy Maud Montgomery was born in Ontario's Durham County before Confederation.
4. Who will eat the last pickle?
5. Eat slowly.
6. Physical activity builds strong bodies and healthy minds.
7. Keep your body fit.
8. Far behind the Liberals and New Democrats trailed the Conservatives, bringing up the rear.
9. Pride goes before a fall. (Biblical proverb)
10. Only in Canada is a so-called lack of national identity a distinctive national characteristic.

4

1. Toronto is a metropolitan centre with scores of distinct neighbourhoods.
2. The word "Toronto" is the Anglicization of the Indian term for "meeting place."
3. The Toronto Islands were originally a part of the mainland.
4. Are you a year-round island resident?
5. At a joint meeting of the councils, the city mayor opposed the Metro Council on behalf of island residents.
6. No evictions occurred last year.
7. The islanders' cohesiveness is the product of both genuine neighbourliness and common community concerns.
8. There is surprisingly little vandalism, the plague of other downtown areas.
9. For the average visitor to the Toronto Islands, the combination of private and public properties is acceptable and even enjoyable.
10. Minutes from the middle of the city nestles my sunny, serene island retreat.

More about Verbs

The verb in a sentence may be a single word, as in most of the exercises you've just done, or it may be a group of words. **Helping verbs** are often added to main verbs, so that an idea can be expressed precisely. The words *shall, should, may, might, can, could, must, ought, will, would, have, do,* and *be* are helping verbs.

> The complete verb in a sentence consists of the main verb + any helping verbs.

Here are a few of the forms of the verb *write*. Notice that in questions the subject may come between the helping verb and the main verb.

You <u>may write</u> now.	He <u>had written</u> his apology.
He certainly <u>can write</u>!	You <u>ought to write</u> to him.
We <u>should write</u> home more often.	We <u>will have written</u> by then.
I <u>shall write</u> tomorrow.	I <u>will write</u> to the editor.
He <u>could have written</u> yesterday.	The proposal <u>has been written</u>.
She <u>is writing</u> her memoirs.	Orders <u>should have been written</u>.
<u>Did</u> he <u>write</u> to you?	<u>Could</u> you <u>have written</u> it in French?

One verb form, in particular, always takes a helping verb. Here is the rule:

> A verb ending in *-ing* MUST have a helping verb (or verbs) before it.

Here are a few of the forms an *-ing* verb can take:

I <u>am writing</u> the report.	She <u>must have been writing</u> all night.
You <u>will be writing</u> a report.	You <u>are writing</u> illegibly.
He <u>should have been writing</u> it.	I <u>was writing</u> neatly.
<u>Is</u> she <u>writing</u> the paper for him?	<u>Have you been writing</u> on the wall?

Beware of certain words that are often confused with helping verbs:

> Words such as *not, only, always, sometimes, never, ever,* and *just* are NOT part of the verb.

These words sometimes appear in the middle of a complete verb, but they are modifiers, not verbs. Do not underline them:

I <u>have</u> just <u>won</u> the lottery!
He <u>is</u> almost always <u>chosen</u> first.
Most people <u>do</u> not <u>welcome</u> unasked-for advice.

Exercises

Underline the subject once and the complete verb twice. Correct each set of ten sentences before you go on to the next.

5

1. He has talked nonstop for three hours.
2. She should have been examining each package.
3. Could they return the goods tomorrow?
4. In the winter, the car starts more easily inside the garage than outside.
5. Where is the nearest gas station?
6. He is not going to drive.
7. Which horse does she prefer?
8. Parents will always perceive their offspring as small children.
9. The barometer has just fallen alarmingly.
10. Patiently and painstakingly, against all odds, struggled the little army.

6

1. In a couple of years, you will be a professional dancer.
2. By noon, he will have been sleeping for eighteen hours.
3. How are the different cycling clubs' members identified?
4. The police will certainly stop all yellow cars on the road tonight except their own.
5. Salad suppers were sometimes supplied secretly to the sufferers.
6. To some small degree at least, accidentally or purposely, in the schools personal opinion is often presented as fact.
7. Could you have taught your personal philosophy objectively and without prejudice?
8. Have you ever been seen at the Zanzibar tavern?
9. Little is known about his past, except that he visited here twice.
10. Isn't she going to go home now?

7

1. The new member's idea was accepted eagerly by the committee.
2. How should the committee introduce this concept to management?
3. Management is increasingly concerned with income over product quality.
4. Time and time again had they demonstrated that fact.
5. The committee cannot make things true, but it must prove things true.
6. There have been several unconvincing presentations.
7. Management must become convinced; superior product quality will ultimately ensure greater income and profit.
8. Why could he convince management? The committee could not do it.
9. Has the committee completely understood his idea?
10. Only through his presentation did management understand and accept the new program.

More about Subjects

Very often, groups of words called **prepositional phrases** come before the subject in a sentence, or between the subject and the verb. When you're looking for the subject in a sentence, prepositional phrases can trip you up unless you know this rule:

The subject of a sentence is never in a prepositional phrase.

You have to be able to identify prepositional phrases, so that you will know where *not* to look for the subject. A prepositional phrase is a group of words that begins with a preposition and ends with the name of something or someone (a noun or a pronoun). Often a prepositional phrase will indicate the direction or location of something. Here are some prepositional phrases:

about the book	between the desks	near the wall
above the book	by the book	on the desk
according to the book	concerning the memo	onto the floor
after the meeting	despite the book	of the typist
against the wall	down the hall	over a door
along the hall	except the staff	to the staff
among the books	for the manager	through the window
among them	from the office	under the book
around the office	in the book	until the meeting
before lunch	inside the office	up the hall
behind the desk	into the elevator	with a book
below the window	in front of the door	without the book
beside the book	like the book	without them

When you're looking for the subject in a sentence, you can make the task easier by crossing out any prepositional phrases. For example,

The keys ~~of the typewriter~~ should be cleaned frequently.
What <u>should be cleaned</u>? The <u>keys</u> (not the typewriter).

~~In case of an emergency~~, one ~~of the group~~ should go ~~to the nearest ranger station~~ ~~for help.~~
Who <u>should go</u>? <u>One</u> (not the group).

Exercises

First cross out the prepositional phrase(s) in each sentence. Then underline the subject once and the verb twice. Check your answers to each set of ten sentences before going on. When you get three sets entirely correct, skip ahead to Exercise 13.

8

1. Charlie Chaplin on film is funnier than Eddie Murphy is in person.
2. Some of them are staying for the matinée on Saturday.

3. All of your friends are welcome here.
4. Can you use either of these two ingredients in the recipe?
5. Follow me out to the highway.
6. A couple of pounds of bananas now costs more than a dollar.
7. A dozen cigarette butts of several kinds littered the floor of the burnt-out room.
8. Here is an example of successful career change at mid-life.
9. Creative thought without action is not productive.
10. Two occurrences of vandalism in three years do not constitute a crime wave.

9

1. According to the old proverb, a stitch in time saves nine.
2. I have had a stitch in my side, and I have often been in stitches.
3. Stitching, in my opinion, is best left to tailors and surgeons.
4. For today's prices, clothing manufacturers should be sewing triple seams in their clothing, all by hand.
5. From the beginning, each item of clothing should be separately designed.
6. After that, every pattern piece should be hand cut.
7. Each piece of cloth should then be sewn with great care to the other appropriate pieces, by one person.
8. The same craftsperson should then pay attention to double seaming and to details of hand finishing.
9. Items of clothing produced in this way might justify today's high prices.
10. In this kind of manufacturing procedure, the individual maker of the item should receive a specified percentage of the wholesale price.

10

1. After years of arguing politics over a few beers, I started campaigning for the NDP.
2. The idea of actually fighting the issues originated with you.
3. Around my right ankle, on the palms of both hands, and in my left ear, the dreaded green pox appeared.
4. Over a period of three months, most of the springs dried up.
5. During the winter months, every weekend, this sportsman curled up at the fireside with a book.
6. His wife's ideas of winter fun are skiing, skiing, and skiing.
7. Despite their differences of temperament and interest, their marriage is quite stable.
8. At the time of Marco Polo's explorations, vast China was ruled by its warlords.
9. Why wouldn't you ride with him in the Jaguar?
10. One of Alcoholics Anonymous' members, a distinguished show business personality, will speak on television on Tuesday night about the organization.

11

1. In the cage next to my dog's at the kennel lay the saddest-looking basset hound in dogdom.
2. Having realized the dangers, Rudolf, along with the rest of the club members, requested a change in the route of the race.
3. Please send me the quotations on the construction of sprung floors for the three studios.
4. In the past, barefoot and pregnant in the kitchen, women's only authority was over their stoves and sinks.
5. Experiments in consciousness-raising sadly demonstrated some women's preference for the status quo.
6. On the seventeenth hole, at the right edge of the fairway, there is a marshy spot as big and inviting as ten bathtubs.
7. Here is a list of the public schools in the area.
8. According to the LaMarsh Commission's report, children already predisposed to violent behaviour are incited to increased violent behaviour by its portrayal on television.
9. There, on an island off Scotland's rocky coast, the Canadian with the dark auburn hair traced her immediate and ancient family tree.

12

1. In the next twenty years, the average age of the Canadian population will increase significantly.
2. For those of us now in our forties, this trend is good news.
3. For those in their teens, however, the news is not so good. They will have to carry the burden of caring for the increasing numbers of elderly persons in society.
4. On the positive side, the leaders of tomorrow will have the experience and wisdom of a large segment of the population to draw on in their planning and decision making.
5. Throughout history, cultures around the world have traditionally associated age with wisdom.
6. Ironically, however, this assumption is not always supported by the evidence.
7. There are many examples from the past and in the present of young leaders with more wisdom and maturity than their aged counterparts.
8. Consider, for example, Alexander the Great. He had conquered the known world by the age of 19.
9. For a contemporary example, consider the success stories of youthful entrepreneurs like Bill Gates. Many young people, just out of college, have launched hi-tech ventures to compete with old, established companies.

10. Over the next two decades, with the maturing of the "baby boom," Canadians will encounter changes in lifestyle, in political focus, and in cultural attitudes toward the "young" and the "old."

13

Write ten sentences of your own. Cross out all the prepositional phrases, and underline the subject once and the complete verb twice.

Multiple Subjects and Verbs

So far you have been working with sentences containing only one complete subject and one complete verb. Sentences can, however, have more than one subject and verb. Here is a sentence with a multiple subject:

Southlands and West Point Grey are suburbs of Vancouver.

This sentence has a multiple verb:

He elbowed and wriggled his way along the aisle of the bus.

And this sentence has a multiple subject and a multiple verb:

The psychiatrist and the police officer leaped from their chairs and seized the woman.

The elements of a multiple subject or verb are usually joined by *and* (but sometimes by *or*). Multiple subjects and verbs may contain more than two elements, as in the following sentences:

Clarity, brevity, and simplicity are the basic qualities of good writing.
I finished my paper, put the cat outside, took the phone off the hook, and crawled into bed.

Exercises

Find and underline the subjects once and the verbs twice. Be sure to underline all the elements in a multiple subject or verb. Check your answers after completing each set of ten sentences.

14

1. The prime minister and the provincial premiers met at Meech Lake.
2. They debated and drafted amendments to the Constitution.
3. The anaesthetist and the surgeon scrubbed for surgery and hurried to the operating room.
4. Blue spruce and hemlock are both northern imports to southern Ontario.
5. I tried and failed once, and then later tried again and succeeded.
6. My son or my daughter will drive me home.
7. The two dogs and the cat travelled a thousand miles in three months.

8. My retired father reads, travels, golfs, walks the dog, and loves all these activities.
9. Knock three times and ask for Joe.
10. Sight reading and improvising are necessary skills of the small-band musician.

15

1. Fortunately for Sean, Dan listened sympathetically and understood clearly.
2. During his bouts of drunkenness, Sean talked compulsively and complainingly about everything under the sun.
3. In response, Dan sometimes just put up with the whining and sometimes suggested a visit to AA.
4. Drunk and depressed one night, Sean phoned Dan and asked him to go drinking.
5. Dan and his friend Robert answered ''No'' to the request and suggested AA to Sean.
6. On this occasion, Sean actually listened to his friend and thought, ''Maybe I should give it a try.''
7. Sean's new friends encouraged and helped him: "Live one day at a time, and let the higher power help you."
8. His special sponsor had entered the program five years earlier and had been dry for the same amount of time.
9. Stay dry: don't take the first drink.
10. The suggestion of one friend, the support of new friends, his own determination and, according to him, a higher power, all helped Sean in the climb back to sobriety and sanity.

16

1. Consider the lilies of the field. (Biblical proverb)
2. Melanie and Morris adjusted their chains, checked their earrings, and patted their spiked hair into place before stomping off to their job interviews.
3. I asked the necessary questions and recorded the householders' answers but was puzzled by one most unusual response.
4. In my house live my wife and I, our two teenagers, two dogs, one cat, and one ghost.
5. No other researcher got such a startling answer or finished a questionnaire so quickly.
6. On King Street, between St. Andrew's Church on the east and assorted small buildings on the west, lies Toronto's Roy Thomson Hall.
7. Ragweed, goldenrod, and twitch grass formed the essential elements in the bouquet for his English teacher.
8. He spun around the corner, whirled into a doorway, and careened up the stairs, with the police in hot pursuit.

9. Today's artists must mirror the real world rather than create an ideal one.
10. This theory of art produces "slice-of-life" drama, encourages representational painting and visual art, engenders atonal music, and sells computers.

17

This exercise is a review.[1] Find and underline the subjects once and the verbs twice. Be sure to underline all the elements in a multiple subject or verb. No answers are given for this exercise.

1. A plain shaft of composition stone with the simple inscription "Here Lies Sarah Binks" marks the last resting place of the Sweet Songstress of Saskatchewan.
2. This monument was erected by the citizens of the Municipality of North Willows and was unveiled on July 1, 1931, by the Hon. Augustus E. Windheaver in the presence of the Reeve and Council.
3. Halfway between Oak Bluff and Quagmire in Saskatchewan lies the little town of North Willows.
4. A post office, two general stores, Charlie Wong's restaurant and billiard parlour, two United churches, the Commercial House (Lib.), the Clarendon Hotel (Cons.), a drug store, a consolidated school, and eighteen filling stations make up the east side of Railway Avenue, North Willows' chief commercial street.
5. Into this free and untrammelled country came Jacob Binks and his wife Agathea (née Agathea Thurnow), the parents of Sarah.
6. Here the chickens were plucked and the eggs were collected. Here slept Rover, the dog, and Ole, the hired man.
7. Neither Rover the dog nor Ole the hired man actually wrote any poetry. However, together they first taught Sarah the singing quality of verse.
8. Those poignant lines of Sarah's poem *Calf* could not have been written before this date and were probably written soon after.
9. O calf, I sit and languish, calf.
   With sombre face, I cannot laugh.
   Can I forget thy playful bunts?
   O calf, calf, you loved me once!
10. Why would Sarah Binks, Poetess, not win the Wheat Pool Medal? Nominating her for this honour was the unanimous decision of the Reeve and Councillors of the Municipality of North Willows and the Associated Boards of Trade of Quagmire and Pelvis. Who could refuse such a nomination?

[1] *Adapted from* Sarah Binks *by Paul Hiebert. Reprinted by permission of the Canadian Publishers, McClelland and Stewart Limited, Toronto.*

chapter 5

Still More about Verbs (For Those Who Need It)

Every verb has four forms:

1. the base form: used by itself or with *can, may, might, shall, will, could, would, should, must*;
2. the past tense form: used by itself;
3. the -ing form: used with *am, is, are, was, were*; and
4. the past participle form: used with *have, has, had* or with *am, is, are, was, were.*

These forms are the **principal parts** of a verb. Here are some examples:

Base	Past Tense	-ing Form	Past Participle
walk	walked	walking	walked
learn	learned	learning	learned
seem	seemed	seeming	seemed
enjoy	enjoyed	enjoying	enjoyed

To use verbs correctly, you must know their principal parts. Knowing two facts will help you. First, your dictionary will give you the principal parts of certain verbs (irregular ones). Just look up the base form, and you'll find the past tense and the past participle beside it, usually in parentheses. If the past tense and past participle are *not* given, the verb is **regular**. So, the second thing you need to know is how to form the past tense and the past participle of regular verbs: by adding -*ed* to the base form. The examples listed above — *walk, learn, seem,* and *enjoy* — are regular verbs.

Many of the most common verbs are **irregular**. Their past tense and past participle are formed in a variety of ways. Following is a list of the principal parts of some of the most common irregular verbs. (We have not included the -*ing* form, because it never causes any difficulty. It is always made up of the base form + *ing*.)

The Principal Parts of Irregular Verbs

Base (Use with *can, may,* *might, shall, will, could,* *would, should, must.*)	Past Tense	Past Participle (Use with *have, has,* *had* or with *am, is, are,* *was, were.*)
be (am, is, are)	was, were	been
bear	bore	borne
become	became	become
begin	began	begun
bid (offer to pay)	bid	bid
bite	bit	bitten
blow	blew	blown
break	broke	broken
bring	brought	brought
build	built	built
burst	burst	burst
buy	bought	bought
catch	caught	caught
choose	chose	chosen
come	came	come
cost	cost	cost
deal	dealt	dealt
dive	dived/dove	dived
do	did	done
draw	drew	drawn
drink	drank	drunk
drive	drove	driven
eat	ate	eaten
fall	fell	fallen
feel	felt	felt
fight	fought	fought
find	found	found
fling	flung	flung
fly	flew	flown
forget	forgot	forgotten/forgot
forgive	forgave	forgiven
freeze	froze	frozen
get	got	got/gotten
give	gave	given
go	went	gone (*not* went)
grow	grew	grown
hang (suspend)	hung	hung
hang (put to death)	hanged	hanged
have	had	had
hear	heard	heard
hide	hid	hidden
hit	hit	hit
hold	held	held

Base	Past Tense	Past Participle
hurt	hurt	hurt
keep	kept	kept
know	knew	known
lay	laid	laid
lead	led	led
leave	left	left
lend	lent	lent
lie	lay	lain
lose	lost	lost
make	made	made
mean	meant	meant
meet	met	met
pay	paid	paid
put	put	put
ride	rode	ridden
ring	rang	rung
rise	rose	risen
run	ran	run
say	said	said
see	saw (*not* seen)	seen
sell	sold	sold
set	set	set
shake	shook	shaken
shine	shone	shone
sing	sang	sung
sit	sat	sat
sleep	slept	slept
slide	slid	slid
speak	spoke	spoken
speed	sped	sped
spend	spent	spent
stand	stood	stood
steal	stole	stolen
strike	struck	struck
swear	swore	sworn
swim	swam	swum
swing	swung	swung
take	took	taken
teach	taught	taught
tear	tore	torn
tell	told	told
think	thought	thought
throw	threw	thrown
wear	wore	worn
win	won	won
wind	wound	wound
write	wrote	written

Exercises

In the blank, write the correct form (either the past tense or the past participle) of the verb shown to the left of the sentence. Do not add or remove helping verbs. Answers begin on p. 253.

I

1. be   Before the race, all the horses _____ inside the gate.

2. strike   His remarks should have been _____ from the record.

3. sell   We could have _____ the house last year.

4. hide   You _____ the children's gifts, didn't you?

5. swim   Ignoring the sign on the buoy, they _____ past the reef.

6. forgive   Without fail, over and over again, the father _____ his son's behaviour.

7. ride   We have _____ at Redstone Equestrian Centre before.

8. build   To keep up with the neighbours, they _____ an expensive patio and barbecue in the tiny yard!

9. swear   Once more, he _____ off wine, women, and song.

10. pay   After calling the tune, he _____ the piper.

2

1. come   Down from the high mountain that lay beyond the little town _____ the strangest creature they had ever seen.

2. spend   Appearing in the city square in the morning, he had apparently _____ the night crouched in a handy tree.

3. make   Odd-looking, but not frightening or ugly, he _____ even the early-morning dogs look his way.

4. be   He could have _____ a Hobbit, so much like Frodo did he look.

5. lose   Apparently he had _____ his way while picnicking with his friends in the foothills.

6. speak   The children from Miss Bundy's Nursery School _____ to

    find   him first and _____ him friendly and intelligent.

7. know   The townspeople all _____ the legend of a mountain

            kingdom of little people.

8. have   Now they _____ evidence before their eyes for the truth of

            the story.

9. choose   They could have _____ to ignore or do away with the

            friendly little fellow.

10. tell   Instead, he stayed and _____ them more about the mountain

    lead   kingdom and eventually _____ them there to see it for

            themselves.

The sentences in exercises 3 through 10 require both the past tense and the past participle of the verb shown at the left. Write the required form in each blank. Do not add or remove helping verbs.

3

1. slide   Nick _____ his essay under the teacher's door at 5 P.M.; Judy

            had _____ hers under just ten minutes before.

2. tear   He _____ down the road in his hot rod just as he had

            _____ down the sidewalk on his tricycle.

3. shine   The sun had once _____ brightly on this beautiful valley

            where not even the moon _____ through the dense brush

            now.

4. throw   No horse had ever _____ him before; this one _____

            him in three seconds flat.

5. draw   A skilled child could have _____ the pictures he _____

            for the book.

6. hurt   At Christmastime in Edmonton, her arthritic knee _____ as

it had never _____ before.

7. eat   Having _____ three of the four cherry pies, he decided it

wouldn't matter if he _____ the fourth one, too.

8. sleep   Once I cleared my conscience, I _____ as I had never

_____ before.

9. sit   Jim _____ patiently waiting for her for two hours, and he

would have _____ for two more.

10. think   I would have _____ you _____ that way, too.

4

1. win   Tom had _____ the long-distance run many times before he

_____ his first sprint.

2. wear   The white tuxedo had been _____ by Tom's brother, but

at yesterday's presentation Tom _____ it with more pizzazz.

3. do   Tom _____ what he had never _____ before: he

made a speech.

4. forget   It was amazing: all his notes were _____ and he even

_____ to be nervous.

5. become   Tom _____ quite good at speech-making on behalf of the

fitness cause; having _____ proficient, he was asked to speak

at many other meetings and banquets.

6. see   Having been _____ and mobbed on the street outside, Tom

then _____ that he would have to avoid recognition.

7. set   Having _____ a world record for the mile when he was twenty, Tom _____ another one for the decathlon when he was twenty-five.

8. fall   Tom had _____ and broken an ankle when he was twelve; he _____ again and broke his arm a year later.

9. meet   I was _____ at the door by this medical and athletic miracle; he surely _____ all my expectations.

10. keep   Now sixty, he had _____ himself in top condition over the years and still _____ up a daily exercise routine.

5

1. burst   The crate could have _____ in the freight car on the way, but it really looks as though it _____ as the receivers moved it into the stockyard.

2. sing   The "Hymn to Joy" is really supposed to be _____ as the finale to Beethoven's Symphony Number Nine, but the Mendelssohn Choir _____ it last night as a single selection.

3. run   He would have _____ in this month's marathon, but he _____ last month and the rules permit only two races per year per person.

4. shake   Philosophically, he was _____ by their arguments, just as he _____ my beliefs when I was a first-year student.

5. bring   We _____ the same dishes to their barbecue last night that we had _____ the year before.

6. wind We _____ up the old victrola again; it had to be

_____ up for every record and sometimes in between.

7. hit The girl said her brother had _____ her three times before

she finally _____ him in retaliation.

8. rise The sun must have _____ only seconds before I

_____ to go fishing with Dad.

9. blow He _____ up twenty balloons in two minutes; he could not

have _____ up another one to save his life.

10. choose The other captain would never have _____ the tiny boy; Tom

_____ him right away, and he turned out to be the team's

best batter.

6

1. hear I _____ that she could have _____ about it indirectly.

2. come The Nolans had just _____ downstairs in the morning when

their son _____ in from the party.

3. get She seems to have _____ younger over the years; we all

definitely _____ older.

4. hang She hasn't _____ her herbs on the rafters to dry yet; we

_____ ours up last week.

5. steal David should've _____ third base when Amber _____

second.

6. mean I _____ exactly what I said, but he couldn't possibly have

_____ what he said.

7. ring   My brothers should have ——————— to tell you whether they were coming to your party; everyone else ———————, I know.

8. put   She ——————— the coat on over all the clothes she had ——————— on earlier.

9. bear   Dan ——————— Sean's drunken insults as tolerantly as if he hadn't ——————— them a thousand times before.

10. stand   He had been ——————— up, just as he ——————— her up the night before.

7

1. lie   The puppy ——————— down to sleep in exactly the same spot where his old dog had ———————.

2. say   The old man ——————— he would never get another dog, but his son ——————— he would.

3. leave   The pup had been ——————— in the old man's barn, tied to a post; whoever ——————— him there obviously hoped the old man would care for him.

4. write   Having ——————— to two of my aunts, to keep the peace I also ——————— to the other three.

5. lend   I know you haven't ——————— him any money, but I ——————— him $100 last night.

6. fling   Dan ——————— Sean's bottle down the garbage chute the way he would have ——————— a rat out of the kitchen.

7. fly   We hadn't ——————— before, but we ——————— all the way to New Zealand last winter.

8. give   Having _____ his employee the responsibility for the project,

he also _____ him the authority necessary to carry it

through.

9. catch   Timmy hasn't _____ nearly as many fish as he _____

last summer.

10. buy   Hadn't you _____ anything in Chinatown before you

_____ your jade pendant there?

8

1. deal   Jane could not have _____ with the builders the way Jerry

_____ with them.

2. drive   Because she is a woman, they would have _____ a much

harder bargain than they _____ with Jerry.

3. fight   It was a crucial match; Rocky _____ as he never had

_____ before.

4. grow   They could have _____ an excellent kitchen garden in the

yard, but they _____ flowers instead.

5. bid   She would have _____ ten times more than he _____

last night at the auction.

6. begin   As they _____ to pick the cotton crop, they prayed that the

weevils had not already _____ their harvest.

7. feel   She could have _____ cheated, but instead she _____

elated at being relieved of the responsibility.

8. cost   The effort to speak at his first AA meeting _____ Sean

dearly, but his alcoholism had almost _____ him his life.

9. leave   Having _____ their place so early the last time, this time she _____ later, when everyone else did.

10. swing   The dancer was supposed to have _____ his partner into a stationary pose, but he _____ her into a pirouette instead.

9

1. teach   He had _____ the course for three consecutive years, but this year he _____ it so differently that it seemed like a new course.

2. hang   In Canada, convicted murderers were _____ until the 1950s; many still believe that murderers should be _____.

3. hold   According to her sentence, Sophia could have been _____ as a prisoner for thirty days; they _____ her for only thirteen days.

4. drink   Sean would have _____ several bottles of wine at one party in the old days; at last night's party, he _____ only soda water.

5. speed   He _____ out of the choppy, open water as quickly as he had _____ into it from the bay.

6. lay   Phyllis _____ the brake cables on the repair bench where the bicycle salesman had _____ them when the bike fell off the wall.

7. go   Having _____ home very late on Thursday, Robert _____ home at 4:30 P.M. on Friday.

8. freeze   They could have _____ four gallons of strawberries, but they

              gave away two gallons and _____ two.

9. dive   For safety's sake, he should have _____ from beyond the

              reef,,but he _____ on the shallow west side instead.

10. break   He _____ his nose; he's lucky not to have _____ his

              neck.

10

This exercise reviews the same principles as exercises 3 through 9, but there are no answers for it at the back of the book.

1. bite   Though Trish wasn't _____ by the dog, the cat _____

             her on the hand.

2. pay   The job _____ very poorly, but the experience has

             _____ off many times.

3. put   Having _____ the hat on his head, Duncan then _____

             his head out into the rain.

4. sit   We _____ for as long as we could, but by the time we had

             _____ for an hour, we were sore.

5. fling   Susan _____ her paper to the floor; she might as well have

             _____ her books as well.

6. hold   Once they had _____ the fortress for a week, they knew

             they _____ the key to victory.

7. wear   Kevin _____ his best clothes to church, but having

             _____ them once, he gave them away.

8. hide   We would have _____ the children in the loft, but Bill

_____ the money there last week.

9. wind   They _____ the clock daily until it was discovered that it

had been _____ too tight.

10. grow   In soil where nothing ever _____, the beanstalk had

_____ fifty feet overnight!

chapter

Solving Sentence-Fragment Problems

Any group of words that is punctuated as a sentence but that does not have a subject or a complete verb is a **sentence fragment.** Fragments are perfectly appropriate in conversation and in some kinds of writing, but normally they are unacceptable in college, technical, and business writing. You've already learned how to spot a sentence fragment: read the words aloud, and check to see whether the subject or the verb (or both) is missing. Let's look at a few examples:

Now, as always, is greatly influenced by her willful neighbour.
(Who or what <u>is influenced</u>? The sentence doesn't tell you. The subject is missing.)

Historians attempting to analyse Canada's role in WW II.
(Part of the verb is missing. Remember that a verb ending in -*ing* must have a helping verb in front of it.)

For motorcycle riders in every province but Manitoba.
(Subject and verb are both missing.)

Regarding the student we discussed last week.
(Subject and verb are both missing.)

Now, what do you do with the fragments you've found?

> To change a sentence fragment into a complete sentence, add whatever is missing: a subject, a verb, or both.

You may need to add a subject:

Now, as always, <u>Canada</u> is greatly influenced by her willful neighbour.

You may need to add part of a verb:

Historians <u>are attempting</u> to analyse Canada's role in WW II.

Sometimes it's better to change the form of the verb:

Historians <u>attempt</u> to analyse Canada's role in WW II.

You may need to add both a subject and a verb:

<u>Helmets</u> <u>are required</u> for motorcycle riders in every province but Manitoba.

And sometimes you need to add more than just a subject and a verb:

<u>I</u> <u>have written</u> to the registrar regarding the student we discussed last week.

Don't let the length of a fragment fool you. Students often think that if a string of words is long it must be a sentence. Not so. No matter how long the string of words is, if it doesn't have both a subject and a verb, it is not a sentence. Here is an example, taken from "The Men of Moosomin," by Sara Jeannette Duncan:

Here and there a ruddy little pond, like a pocket looking glass dropped on the prairie, with a score or so of wild ducks swimming in it, or a slight round hollow where a pond used to be, with the wild ducks flying high.

Do you know what's missing? Can you change the fragment into a sentence?

Exercises

Read each "sentence" aloud. Put *S* before each complete sentence and *F* before each sentence fragment. Make each fragment into a complete sentence by adding whatever is missing: a subject, a verb, or both. After you complete each set of ten sentences, check your answers. If you get three sets of ten entirely correct, you may skip the rest. Answers begin on page 254.

I

1. _____ Regarding myths and fairy tales.

2. _____ To decide on the basis of rumour, not facts.

3. _____ Sad to hear of the many occurrences of vandalism.

4. _____ Writing exams all evening, after working all day.

5. _____ The party members gathering in the campaign office.

6. _____ Anyone goes who so desires.

7. _____ Air attack cancelled because of cloud cover.

8. _____ Painting in a studio with bad lighting.

9. _____ Having worked outdoors all his life.

10. _____Wanting to please them, she had tea ready on their arrival.

2

1. _____ Far too much to learn in a two-day conference.

2. _____ Dogs being both intelligent and affectionate.

3. _____ Always wanted to travel to northern British Columbia.

4. _____ Knowing how to proceed in any case.

5. _____ The earliest explorations by Vikings of Canada's coastal lands and waters.

6. _____ Miss Ditchburn, formerly of the National Ballet of Canada.

7. _____ Is he actually sober?

8. _____ Much of which has been discussed in previous meetings.

9. _____ Events cancelled because of the equipment they require.

10. _____ Sufficient for the day is the evil thereof. (Biblical proverb)

3

1. _____ As he sees it, the world is a dark and miserable place.

2. _____ Her idea of it being "the best of all possible worlds."

3. _____ Do you remember Dixie cups?

4. _____ Why he thinks he will return home to Cayuga.

5. _____ Reliable in all respects.

6. _____ The directions that were printed in the pamphlet included with the kit.

7. _____ Know that you aren't holding a grudge.

8. _____ The confidence to speak for herself.

9. _____ These along with similar examples of ESP.

10. _____ To have been forced to attend her wedding, which was an irony in itself.

4

1. __F__ To exaggerate for the sake of personal image and for monetary gain.

2. _____ Hyperbole is an extravagant exaggeration used as a figure of speech.

3. __F__ *He is* Exaggerating his own influence being of great importance to him.

4. __F__ *They* Because they know what is true, *they went to the coach.* *He come*

5. __F__ As usual, with some twisting of the truth.

6. __F__ Speakers and listeners *are* recognizing the tall tale for what it is.

7. __S__ Let's hear it.

8. __F__ *While* Realizing their incredulity, she stopped speaking.

9. __F__ Another name for it, this exaggerating and extending of the truth.

10. __S__ Oh, what a tangled web we weave, when first we practise to deceive!

5

1. __F__ *He won't go to the field;* Unless he knows someone in the field.

2. __F__ She is educated and intelligent but *she has* no social graces.

3. __S__ The sweet smell of success is often mixed with less desirable aromas.

4. __F__ J. Paul Getty *is* speaking on financial success.

5. __F__ Because financial gain is, for most people, synonymous with success.

6. __F__ The saying, "Nothing succeeds like success."

7. _____ For the moment, not looking at the money and power aspects of the question.

8. _____ To bring to actualization the best human instincts in oneself and others?

9. _____ The more personal aspects usually not considered when the topic comes up in ordinary conversation.

10. _____ In our culture, the tendency to equate financial worth with personal success.

Independent and Dependent Clauses

A group of words containing a subject and a verb is a clause. There are two kinds of clauses. An **independent clause** is one that makes complete sense on its own. It can stand alone, as a sentence. A **dependent clause,** as its name suggests, cannot stand alone as a sentence; it *depends* on another clause to make complete sense.

Dependent clauses are easy to recognize, because they begin with words such as these:

Dependent-Clause Cues

after	so that
although	that
as, as if	though
as soon as	unless
as long as	until
because	what, whatever
before	when, whenever
even if, even though	where, wherever
if	whether
in order that	which, whichever
provided that	while
since	who, whom, whose

Whenever a clause begins with one of these words or phrases, it is dependent.

> A dependent clause must be attached to an independent clause. If it stands alone, it is a sentence fragment.

Here is an independent clause:

I am a poor speller.

If we put one of the dependent-clause cues in front of it, it can no longer stand alone:

Because I am a poor speller

We can correct this kind of fragment by attaching it to an independent clause:

Because I am a poor speller, I have chained my dictionary to my wrist.

Exercises

Put an *S* before each clause that is independent and therefore a sentence. Put an *F* before each clause that is dependent and therefore a sentence fragment. Underline the dependent-clause cue in each sentence fragment.

6

1. _F_ What parents don't know.

2. _F_ As she was led to believe.

3. _F_ Where three roads meet.

4. _F_ If he decides on that basis.

5. _F_ So that the children could see the performance with no difficulty.

6. _F_ Although she practised it constantly.

7. _F_ Since the bicycle fell on her.

8. _S_ As soon as the troops arrived, the fighting stopped.

9. _F_ Whichever route the cyclists choose.

10. _F_ Before Phyllis bought her racer.

7

1. _F_ Who is going to the camp this summer.

2. _F_ Unless they pass the swimming test for their age group.

3. _F_ When David connects with the Grey Coach bus in Orillia.

4. _F_ Even if Wendy has never gone anywhere without her family.

5. _S_ Because of a polluted water supply, the camp had to be closed.

6. _S_ Since last summer, Camp Iona's facilities have improved.

7. _____ Whatever canoe they want.

8. _F_ Because the children had a campfire every night.

9. _F_ The campers who kept the cleanest unit.

10. _S_ After the last canoe was put in the boathouse and the last tent was aired and rolled up for another year.

Exercises

**Identify the sentence fragments in the following passages by under-
lining the dependent-clause cue in each fragment you find.**

8

Before the curtain went up on the lavishly decorated and beautifully lit set, The
actor playing Frankie could be seen pacing up and down nervously. Although he
was a veteran of many stage performances, and several popular movies, and was
accustomed to appearing before large audiences. Which made it very strange that
he would demonstrate the symptoms of stage fright so clearly. Looking closely, a
careful observer might have noticed, however, that he wasn't studying his lines or
rehearsing his role. In fact, unless one were right beside him and watching very
closely. The real purpose of his pacing could easily be missed. Although he appeared
to be alone. He was, in reality, exercising his pet cockroach.

9

Our fishing trip turned out to be a huge success. Although it started out very
poorly, After awakening to an overcast, blustery day, We left the house at 6 A.M.
to be the first on the lake. After four hours of driving in weather which alternated
between heavy rain and wet snow, We concluded that we were lost. We tried to fix
the blame on each other and quarrels soon broke out in the car, almost leading to a
fist fight. Even before the first morning of the week was over, We were at each
other's throats! Which of my friends it was, I don't know. One of them began
laughing, and soon we were all helpless with laughter. That broke the ice. From
then on, whenever things looked their worst, and we were on the edge of disaster,
Someone would recall that moment.

10

Photographing wildlife can be a rewarding and entertaining experience. Provided that one is very careful and has the right photographic equipment. Where some photographers try to capture the essence of a bowl of fruit, and others aim for a spiritual quality in family portraits or wedding pictures. I prefer to capture on film an accurate reflection of true wildlife. So that I can achieve this goal, I follow some of my crazy friends around from party to party, recording their antics with my pocket camera. Since so many of my friends are, by any definition, wild, The reproduction of wildlife in my photo albums is quite remarkable. Whether it is Jayne trying to play baseball in an evening gown, or Tessa going to a ballet opening in her jeans. As long as I have friends like Terry, who carries a pair of scissors to cut off people's ties, or Phyllis, who insists that she is Princess Di. I will always have plenty of subject matter for wildlife photography.

Most sentence fragments are dependent clauses punctuated as sentences. Fortunately, this is the easiest kind of fragment to recognize and fix. All you need to do is join the dependent clause either to the sentence that comes before it or to the one that comes after it — whichever linkage makes better sense.

One final point: if you join your clause fragment to the independent clause that follows it, you must separate the two clauses with a comma (see chapter 17, p. 157).

Read the following example to yourself; then read it aloud (remember, last sentence first).

Montreal is a sequence of ghettos. Although I was born and brought up there. My experience of French was a pathetically limited and distorted one.

The second "sentence" sounds incomplete, and the dependent-clause cue at the beginning of it is the clue you need to identify it as a sentence fragment. You could join the fragment to the sentence before it, but then you would get "Montreal is a sequence of ghettos, although I was born and brought up there," which doesn't make sense. Clearly the fragment should be linked to the sentence that follows it, like this:

Montreal is a sequence of ghettos. Although I was born and brought up there, my experience of French was a pathetically limited and distorted one. (Mordecai Richler, "Quebec Oui, Ottawa Non!")

Exercises

11

Correct the sentence fragments in Exercises 6 through 10. Make each fragment into a complete sentence by adding an independent clause either before or after the dependent clause. Remember to punctuate correctly: if a dependent clause comes at the beginning of your sentence, put a comma after it. When you have completed this exercise, exchange with another student and check each other's work.

12

This paragraph contains both independent clauses and dependent clauses (fragments), all punctuated as if they were complete sentences. Letting meaning be your guide, join each fragment to the most appropriate independent clause. Remember to punctuate correctly. Then turn to the answer section to compare your sentences with the author's. (Adapted from Pierre Berton's introduction to Henri Rossier's collection of photographs called *The New City: A Prejudiced View of Toronto*, published 1961, cited in Alan Dawe's *Profile of A Nation,* Macmillan, 1969.)

The attitude to Toronto takes two forms. There is first the attitude of the non-Torontonians, Who live in places like St. John's, Maple Creek and Vancouver.

Then there is the attitude of the Torontonians themselves.

The attitude of the outsider is compounded of envy, malice and pity. In about equal quantities. It is admitted that Torontonians make large sums of money. But not much else. Certainly they never have any fun. There is none of the leisurely gracious living that is to be found in Montreal, say. Or Halifax, or Okotoks, Alberta. When a young man sets out for Toronto, He is surrounded by a covey of friends, all commiserating with him and whispering to him, To look about for a job for them in the big city. It is generally acknowledged that the bereaved young man will return, but he rarely does. If he sees his friends again, he sees them in Toronto, Where they all have a good cry, and talk over the grand old days. When they were poor in Pelvis or West Webfoot.

The attitude of the Torontonians is that they simply do not care. What people think of them. They live in Toronto and that is good enough for them. For years a host of magazine articles, newspaper editorials and commentators have baited Toronto. Toronto refuses to swallow the bait. One mayor tried to launch a campaign. To make the city popular but it fizzled out after a few days. Torontonians do not really care about being popular; in fact, about half the criticism about the city comes from its own people. Nobody baits Toronto quite as much as those who live there.

13

Below are ten independent clauses. Make each into a dependent clause by adding one of the dependent-clause cues. Then add an independent clause to make a complete sentence.
Example: He felt very nervous.
Add a dependent-clause cue: *Although* he felt very nervous.
Now add an independent clause: Although he felt very nervous, *he gave a good speech.*

1. They are hopeful.

2. He ate the cold leftover pizza.

3. She won't know immediately.

4. I want to see the new house.

5. There are eleven now.

6. Nothing ever goes right.

7. He is usually more careful.

8. She washed it thoroughly.

9. According to those in the media, the parties' opinions vary greatly.

10. Everyone knows something about computers' probable impact on future employment.

14

Using the following dependent-clause cues, write ten dependent clauses of your own. Then make each into a complete sentence by adding an independent clause. Watch your punctuation!

1. as long as

2. even though

3. until

4. in order that

5. whatever

6. though

7. whether

8. whom

9. which

10. after

15

As a final test of your skill in correcting sentence fragments, try this exercise. Put S before each complete sentence and F before each sentence fragment. Make each fragment into a complete sentence. No answers are given for this exercise.

_____ 1. Although the class was long, boring, and frustrating for me because I hadn't read the assignment and couldn't understand the discussion.

_____ 2. Pierre Berton's famous definition of a Canadian: "Someone who knows how to make love in a canoe."

_____ 3. The point being that hard work, intelligence, and dedication are not always rewarded.

_____ 4. Getting promoted is often a matter of knowing the right people and of being in the right place at the right time.

_____ 5. Probably the fastest growing but least publicized of modern crimes being data theft, sometimes known as computer tapping.

_____ 6. Help me figure this one out, would you please?

_____ 7. As long as I've known you, an honest, patient, loyal friend.

_____ 8. There are several things you should think about first.

_____ 9. Goodman Ace's famous quip that television was called a "medium" because things on it were rarely well done.

_____ 10. The problem resulting from our stumbling blindly into the future, ignorant of the harm technological advances can bring.

chapter 7

Solving Run-On Problems

Just as a sentence can lack certain elements and thus be a fragment, so can it contain too many elements. A sentence with too much in it is a **run-on.** Run-ons most often occur when you write in a hurry or when you're disorganized and not thinking clearly. If you think about what you want to say, and proceed slowly and carefully, you shouldn't have any problems with them.

There are two varieties of run-on sentence: the comma splice and the true run-on.

The Comma Splice

As the name suggests, the **comma splice** occurs when two complete sentences (independent clauses) are joined together, with only a comma between them. Here's an example:

> That dog's obedient, it's been well trained.

> The easiest way to fix a comma splice is to replace the comma with a semicolon.

> That dog's obedient; it's been well trained.

To be sure you understand how to use semicolons correctly, read chapter 18, page 164.

> Another way to fix a comma splice is to add an appropriate linking word between the two clauses.

Two types of linking words will work.

1. You can insert one of these words: *and, but, or, nor, for, so, yet.* These should be preceded by a comma.

> That dog's obedient, for it's been well trained.

2. You can insert one of the dependent-clause cues listed on page 63.

> That dog's obedient because it's been well trained.

> The third way to fix a comma splice is to make the run-on sentence into two short sentences.

That dog's obedient. It's been well trained.

All three solutions to the comma splice problem require that you replace the comma with a word or punctuation mark strong enough to come between two independent clauses.

Exercises

Correct the following sentences where necessary. Then check your answers. (Answers begin on p. 257.) If you find that you're confused about when to use a semicolon and when to use a period, be sure to read p. 164 before going on.

I

1. The teacher's late, let's go!
2. Just let me do the talking, you'll get us a ticket if you open your mouth.
3. I keep buying lottery tickets, but I've only won once.
4. My parents golf and swim every day, they're both quite fit, they're only in their fifties.
5. As long as you smile when you speak, you can say almost anything.
6. Montreal used to be called *Ville Ste. Marie*, I think, but before that it had an Indian name.
7. Students today need summer jobs, tuition and living costs are too much for most families.
8. Bryan will be going to college if he is accepted, his parents have lots of money.
9. My word processor makes writing much easier, though it doesn't seem to spell any better than I do.
10. I am seeking a hero after whom I can model my life, so far I've rejected Sly Stallone, Madonna, and Hulk Hogan.

2

1. The comma splice gets its name from the film splice, two pieces of film are taped, or spliced, together.
2. Old movies are sometimes choppy and disconnected, they have been spliced badly or too often.
3. Two sentences cannot be spliced together with a comma, you need to use a semicolon or a period or a linking word between them.
4. You should be particularly careful when using linking words like "however," "consequently," "therefore," and "moreover," these words need a semicolon before them and a comma after.
5. This isn't a very difficult rule, in fact, it's one of the easiest rules to learn because it has no exceptions.

6. With one minute to go, the opposing team scored the winning goal, consequently no one on our team felt much like celebrating the end of the season.
7. The anti-smoking bylaw doesn't seem to have done much good, I often see people smoking in restaurants, stores, and even elevators.
8. One of the things I hope to learn at college is French, however I doubt if I'll ever learn to speak it fluently.
9. It's a pity that burning coal contributes to acid rain, we have an almost inexhaustible supply of coal in Canada.
10. Our country's culture, attitudes, and even politics are strongly influenced by television, that is why the CRTC insists on a high level of Canadian content in television broadcasting.

3

1. Hitting a golf ball may look easy, but it's not.
2. She spent most of the term playing pinball in the lounge, it's not surprising she failed.
3. Please close the door gently, don't slam it, one hinge is loose.
4. You should always speak the truth, but speak it tactfully, not cruelly.
5. If you find it hard at first to recognize run-ons, don't give up in despair, read the explanation again, then do the exercises slowly and carefully.
6. Frances thought her interview had gone very well, however she wasn't offered the job.
7. General education courses may be broadening and even interesting, on the other hand they don't have any relevance to the job I'm training for.
8. Keep working on your daily exercise program, you'll get over the stiffness in a week or so.
9. If you really want to stay healthy, quit smoking and drinking, cut out junk food and eat a balanced diet, exercise at least three times each week, finally get the brakes on your car fixed.
10. Americans like to tell jokes about Canada's climate, for example here's an old favourite: a Miami businessman, returning to Florida after a prolonged stay in Toronto, was asked, "What was the summer like in Canada?" He replied, "I've no idea, I was there only eleven months."

4

1. A Canadian who speaks three languages is called multilingual, one who speaks two languages is called bilingual, one who speaks only one language is called an English Canadian.
2. I'm sure the job couldn't have been as bad as he claims, maybe he just didn't try hard enough.
3. Meetings such as this are fine for small groups, large groups have to be handled in a different way.
4. I'll be glad to help you out, when you need me just call, I'll be here all day.

5. In Canada, winter is more than a season, it's a bad joke.
6. Perfection is probably impossible to achieve, but that doesn't mean you should stop trying.
7. It may seem foolish, especially after all the wrangling over our new constitution, but I still believe in a unified Canada, I believe in one nation extending from sea to sea. The Fathers of Confederation were right, a federation of provinces can work.
8. Sales of video cassette recorders have really taken off in the last few months, about 150,000 were sold in Canada in 1987.
9. They're expensive, the average selling price is $1200 to $1500 a unit.
10. VCRs can be preset to tape television programs, they can play prerecorded tapes of movies, moreover they can also record through a video camera.

5

1. Career opportunities appear very good for students in a wide range of technical programs, however most employers are looking for people with experience as well as training.
2. The demand for technicians and technologists is highest in resource fields, industries based on oil, petrochemicals, mining, and pulp and paper cannot find enough experienced people to fill available jobs.
3. Job prospects should be bright for those in energy-related industries, moreover if the proposed offshore drilling projects get underway, demand for trained technologists will far exceed supply.
4. There will probably be good employment opportunities in the manufacture of computer parts and peripherals, of telephone and defence equipment, and of avionic equipment.
5. Job prospects in the aviation industry are hard to predict accurately, though, for they depend on export sales which, in turn, depend on the health of the international economy.
6. People with high-technology skills are urgently required in several fields, plastics processing, mouldmaking, and tool- and die-making are three examples.
7. The Ontario government has made millions of dollars available for the establishment of CAD/CAM centres at community colleges, these are centres for instruction in computer-aided design and computer-aided manufacture.
8. Even small manufacturers are showing an interest in robotics and other sophisticated computer-controlled systems, hence an increasing number of engineers, technologists, and designers are going back to school to find out what CAD/CAM can do for them.
9. For community college students in technology programs, then, the future looks bright, however a diploma does not necessarily guarantee job security.
10. As a group, technicians and technologists are less likely than engineers to find their skills obsolete, nevertheless electronics and aeronautics are changing rapidly, people must expect to retrain every few years.

6

Here's a final test of your ability to spot and correct comma splices. Try to use all three ways of fixing comma splices as you correct the errors in this paragraph. No answers have been given for this exercise.

Movies are very important to me, I see at least two shows every week. The old movies that appear on television occupy me at least one night a week, Humphrey Bogart, W.C. Fields, The Marx Brothers, and Alfred Hitchcock classics are among my favourites from the era of black and white film. In the remaining four nights a week, I often rent films to run on my VCR, or review one of the movies I have bought for my permanent collection. This doesn't leave much time for other activities, the time isn't wasted, though, in my opinion. I learn a great deal from watching films, history, psychology, literature, as well as pure entertainment are available to the interested viewer. In addition, I guess you could say that I'm training for my future profession since I want to be a writer or director someday. I don't think that it's possible to see too many films, I'll quit when I look in a mirror and see that my eyes have begun to get square!

The Run-On Sentence

In the true **run-on sentence,** too many ideas are crowded into one sentence. In general, a sentence should convey no more than two ideas. There is no hard and fast rule about how many clauses you may have in a sentence, but more than two independent clauses can result in a sentence that's hard to read and even harder to understand.

> There were still twelve people at the party, but after Janice went home we decided it was time to leave, so we collected our coats and said good-bye to the others, and, after a careful drive home at 50 km/h, we drank coffee and stayed up until three the following morning discussing the evening's events.

It's obvious that the storyteller who created this monster got carried away with enthusiasm for the tale and just scribbled everything down without much thought. Take your time and keep your reader in mind, and you probably won't make this sort of error. If you do find run-on sentences in your writing, however, follow this rule:

> Fix sentences that are too long by breaking them up into shorter sentences.

There were still twelve people at the party, but after Janice went home we decided it was time to leave. So we collected our coats and said good-bye to the others. After a careful drive home at 50 km/h, we drank coffee and stayed up until three the following morning discussing the evening's events.

Exercises

7

Using the four types of corrections you've learned in this chapter, make these sentences easier to read. There is more than one right way of fixing them; just be sure your corrected sentences are easy to read and make sense. The answers we've provided are only suggestions.

1. Beagles, which are a kind of small hound, make excellent pets because of their cheerful, affectionate nature and I know because I have one.

2. In the past fifteen years, we have seen a remarkable increase in the health consciousness of the average North American, and the result has been a huge and growing industry that attempts to make fitness painless or even fun, from health clubs and aerobics classes to weight lifting and diet plans, we have an almost limitless choice of ways to spend our money on our bodies.

3. Since you are interested in both careers, you should probably play hockey now and take up teaching in the future, usually the legs give out before the mind does.

4. I look back with real nostalgia on winter in the small Manitoba town where I grew up with the softly falling snow, the excitement of the year's first snowball fight, and the crunch of snow beneath my boots on those *really* cold prairie mornings, this is all proof that the mind remembers the pleasant and blots out the painful as one gets older.

5. As farm animals, pigs leave a great deal to be desired, as pets, however, they are very clean, intelligent, obedient, and even cute, or so I am told I suspect I shall never personally discover if there is any truth to this notion.

6. Joan is a complete hypocrite now that she is wealthy, insisting with every other breath that she hasn't changed a bit, she drives a Rolls, flaunts her furs, and wears diamonds in bunches.

7. When I woke up this morning, I had a hard time getting out of bed because I knew I ought to eat some breakfast, but I didn't have time, and then I realized I had to finish an essay for a nine o'clock class, but I thought my car probably wouldn't start because of the cold, and I wouldn't be able to get to school anyway and so I just stayed in bed.

8. The hockey season now extends well into the baseball season, which, in turn, encroaches on the football season, and football, being a fall and winter sport, extends halfway into the hockey schedule, and so it goes, with basketball overlapping the other three.

9. Nothing is so relaxing as a whirlpool after a hard day at work, it soothes sore muscles and eases the accumulated aches and pains of the day, while at the same time providing the emotional therapy of a hot bath.

10. Following the high speed chase and subsequent arrest of the car's driver, the police learned that the vehicle had been stolen and they added a charge of theft to the reckless driving charge, and the young man spent the night in jail, there he came to realize the seriousness of his predicament, and he asked for permission to make a telephone call so he could get in touch with his parents' lawyer.

8

Correct the following sentences by rewriting them to eliminate all sentence faults: fragments, comma splices, and run-ons. Your answers may differ somewhat from ours, which are on p. 260.

1. Foster Hewitt, the original voice of hockey, who died in 1985.

2. He scores!

3. Learning to ride horseback without instruction must be difficult, I have a friend who taught himself to ride by watching Clint Eastwood movies.

4. Casting for salmon in the running water just above the dam on the Kennisis River, which is only one-half mile from my home.

5. Her friends say she has a heart of gold, however, her children claim she has ruined their lives.

6. Hoping that Jon and Lynne would be able to join us, I bought extra bottles of wine.

7. Margaret expressed her wish to see them visit Canada, they will probably come despite the difficulties that air travel from New Zealand poses.

8. Where the campers are given recipes and supplies for the meals that they must cook themselves and are made responsible for maintaining their own cabins and establishing their daily routine.

9. To err is human and to forgive, divine.

10. Given his excellent reputation in civil engineering in his own country, his rise through the ranks of the company since his arrival in Canada, and the fact that he now makes more than $100,000 a year.

9

Correct the following sentences where necessary. Your answers may differ somewhat from ours.

Fourteen people live in Punkeydoodle's Corner, Ontario. A town famous for its funny name. Twenty-five kilometres west of Kitchener, Punkeydoodle's Corner was a stagecoach stop on the Huron Trail during the nineteenth century, when it was a bustling town of more than one hundred people, but as stagecoaches gave way to trains, which, in turn, gave way to automobiles, the little town dwindled and shrank until only three families were left to call it home.

Several different stories account for the origin of the town's name, the hero of one of these stories was a man called John Zurbrigg. Who was a Swiss settler and pumpkin farmer. According to the tale, Zurbrigg was a rather lazy man, preferring to "doodle" his time away rather than tend to his pumpkins. One of his neighbours, furious at Zurbrigg's idleness, is said to have labelled him "punkey doodle" during an argument, history does not record Zurbrigg's response.

Another story claims the town got its name from John Zurbuchen. The chubby, genial host of the old hotel in the town who had been born in Germany, then moved to Ontario in the 1860s with his family. Apparently, Zurbuchen never quite mastered English pronunciation, he loved to sing, though, and frequently entertained his beer-drinking customers with his version of "Yankee Doodle." Which he mispronounced "Punkey Doodle." Both of these stories seem a bit farfetched, if you ask me.

Its unusual name attracts hundreds of visitors to Punkeydoodle's Corner every year, however being a tourist attraction has one disadvantage, according to the townspeople. Every time they put up a sign to identify their village. The sign is stolen within a few weeks. Even when it is firmly embedded in concrete.

10

This paragraph contains several kinds of sentence error, all of which can be corrected by changing the punctuation of the passage. Make the necessary corrections; then turn to the answer section to compare your corrections with ours.

Until I moved to the country, I could never see the attraction of bird-watching as a pastime, my parents had enjoyed bird-watching as a hobby for years. Frequently boring me numb with their enthusiastic tales of warblers heard or kingfishers sighted. While I lived in the city I saw birds so infrequently that I was completely indifferent to my parents' enthusiasm, those birds I did see were always pigeons, sparrows, or starlings, anyway. Within a week of moving out of the city to take a new job. I began to take notice of my feathered neighbours, I was awakened three mornings in a row by squawking blue jays. Three days later a convention of crows descended on my property. Sending everyone indoors for two days. My bird-watching really became an obsession when I was dive-bombed repeatedly by an irate woodpecker. Which I had offended in some mysterious way. Now, protected by a surplus army helmet and armed with binoculars. I go on excursions with the most dedicated birders, however where they creep silently through the underbrush, and meticulously record each sighting in a log book, I crash about, threatening and cursing any birds I encounter and now everyone regards me with pity or contempt and more than one former friend has suggested that I've gone ''cuckoo.''

II

As a final test of your ability to identify and correct sentence errors, supply the appropriate sentence breaks to make this garble into a grammatically correct paragraph. No answers are provided.

Gordon is convinced that he is a great musician all that he needs is to discover the instrument on which his genius can flower in the course of trying to make this discovery, he has tried the alto recorder, the B flat clarinet, the Spanish guitar, and the five string banjo each of these instruments was taken up with enthusiasm and devotion, but each was cast aside within a few months as it revealed that it could not bring forth Gordon's hidden musical talents several suggestions were made at about this time in his musical career, the most memorable by his parents who had to endure the loud learning process on each instrument, but Gordon was certain of success and deaf to any hint that his lack of musicianship was due to anything but his bad luck in not being able to discover his proper medium his parents gave up his friends deserted him but still he persisted his refusal to quit was finally rewarded and now he may be heard recorded on several albums and live with his group at many music festivals after about twelve frustrating years of experimentation Gordon discovered the instrument that best expresses his talent: the kazzoo.

12

Write a letter to an out-of-town friend who has accepted a summer job in your home town. Describe what your friend should expect to find when he or she moves to your town and provide any advice you think will be useful in helping your friend get through the summer. Check your letter carefully to eliminate spelling and apostrophe errors and to make sure your sentences are correctly constructed. Watch especially for fragments and run-ons.

The thieves were caught before much of the loot could be disposed of <u>by the police</u>.

<u>Stamping her feet and switching her tail to brush away flies</u>. Susan led the mare out of the barn.

<u>At the age of five</u>, the barber cut Jamie's hair, <u>which curled to his shoulders</u> <u>nearly</u> <u>for the first time</u>.

These sentences show what can happen to your writing if you aren't sure how to use modifiers. **A modifier** is a word or group of words that adds information about another word in a sentence. In the examples above, the underlined words are modifiers. Used correctly, modifiers describe or explain or limit another word, making its meaning more precise. Used carelessly, however, modifiers can cause confusion or, even worse, amusement. There's nothing more embarrassing than being laughed at when you didn't mean to be funny.

You need to be able to recognize and solve two kinds of modifier problems: misplaced modifiers and dangling modifiers.

Misplaced Modifiers

Modifiers must be as close as possible to the words they apply to. Usually a reader will assume that a modifier modifies whatever it's next to. It's important to remember this, because, as the following examples show, changing the position of a modifier can change the meaning of your sentence.

I told Mr. Jones (only) what I had done. (I didn't tell him anything else.)

I told (only) Mr. Jones what I had done. (I didn't tell anybody else.)

(Only) I told Mr. Jones what I had done. (Nobody else told Mr. Jones.)

I told Mr. Jones what (only) I had done. (No one else did it.)

> To make sure a modifier is in the right place, ask yourself, "What does it apply to?" and put it beside that word.

When a modifier is not close enough to the word it refers to, it is said to be misplaced. A **misplaced modifier** can be **a single word in the wrong place:**

The supervisor told me they needed someone who could type badly.

Is some company really hiring people to do poor work? Or does the company urgently need a typist? Obviously, the modifier *badly* belongs next to *needed:*

The supervisor told me they badly needed someone who could type.

> Be especially careful with these words: *almost, nearly, just, only, even, hardly, merely, scarcely.* Put them right before the words they modify.

Misplaced: I almost ate the whole thing.
Correctly placed: I ate almost the whole thing.

Misplaced: When he played goal in the NHL, Glenn Hall nearly threw up before every game.
Correctly placed: When he played goal in the NHL, Glenn Hall threw up before nearly every game.

A **misplaced modifier** can also be **a group of words in the wrong place:**

Scratching each other playfully, we watched the monkeys.

The modifier, *scratching each other playfully,* is too far away from the word it is supposed to modify, *monkeys.* In fact, it seems to modify *we,* making the sentence ridiculous. We need to rewrite the sentence:

We watched the monkeys scratching each other playfully.

Look at this one:

I worked for my father, who owns a sawmill during the summer.

During the summer applies to *worked* and should be closer to it:

During the summer, I worked for my father, who owns a sawmill.

Notice that a modifier need not always go right next to what it modifies; it should, however, be as close as possible to it.

Occasionally, as in the examples above, the modifier is obviously out of place. The writer's intention is clear, and the sentences are easy to correct. But sometimes modifiers are misplaced in such a way that the meaning is not clear, as in this example:

Lucy said on her way out she would give the memo to John.

Did Lucy *say* it on her way out? Or is she going to *deliver the memo* on her way out? To avoid confusion, we must move the modifier and, depending on which meaning we want, write either

[On her way out,] Lucy said she would give the memo to John.

or

Lucy said she would give the memo to John [on her way out.]

Exercises

Some of the sentences in these exercises contain misplaced modifiers. Rewrite the sentences as necessary, positioning the modifiers correctly. Check your answers to each set of ten before going on. (Answers begin on p. 261.) If you get the first two sets entirely correct, skip ahead to exercise 4.

I

1. There is a library on the third floor that has a washroom.

2. He told us on the first day no one works hard.

3. It is usually only once in a lifetime that a golfer gets a hole-in-one.

4. Why did you give the fruit to the customer in that flimsy bag?

5. We almost applied for every job that was posted.

6. He played the piano all the time I was there beautifully.

7. There just are enough pieces to go around.

8. They couldn't remember which house Sean was living in when they drove down his street.

9. Unless they're French or German, these language teachers have no use for dictionaries.

10. By working night and day, he almost managed to pay for all the damage for which his brother had been charged.

2

1. The waitress who normally serves us only was on duty.

2. Brian Linehan, the CITY-TV interviewer, doesn't get his guests to open up easily as they do.

3. The dogs were healthy looking, lively, and well-behaved in that kennel.

4. My supervisor told me in May I would get a raise.

5. One finds the best Chinese cuisine in those restaurants frequented by Chinese people usually.

6. He caught sight of a killdeer and several finches using his new binoculars.

7. He had played ball professionally before coming to the Blue Jays for several major American teams.

8. Increasing numbers of Canadians find that they are unable to feed, clothe, and shelter their children properly.

9. The football practices have been organized for players who are not with a team in the summertime as a keep-fit measure.

10. In a dark corner behind the automatic washer huddled a small cat in a large laundry basket gripping a kitten in its mouth.

3

1. Vancouver is a wonderful city for anyone who likes rain and fog to live in.

2. Analyzing what's going on inside your own head can be a worthwhile learning experience, an education that isn't possible in the classroom.

3. Some games are less demanding in terms of time and equipment, such as tiddlywinks.

4. The Human Rights Code prohibits discrimination against anyone who is applying for a job on the basis of race, age, or sex.

5. I was able to loosen the clamp that held the broken cable in place with a screwdriver.

6. The piece of chalk hit me on the head that my English teacher threw at me.

7. Mile after mile, town by town, Terry Fox fought his battle against time, space, and pain uncomplainingly.

8. They waited breathlessly under the trees for the return of their dog that had been sprayed by a skunk with an open can of tomato juice.

9. As a professional athlete who realizes the seriousness of joint injury, you certainly should take up a style of jogging that will minimize that risk.

10. Tonight Dr. Brothers will lead a panel discussion on relaxation, including how to tone and stretch muscles, how to relieve tension, and even how to sleep through sex.

4

Make up three sentences containing misplaced modifiers; then correct them.

Dangling Modifiers

A **dangling modifier** occurs when there is **no appropriate word in the sentence for the modifier to apply to**. With no appropriate word to modify, the modifier *seems* to apply to wahtever it's next to, often with ridiculous results:

[After four semesters of hard work,] my parents rewarded me with a car.

(This sentence seems to say that the parents are going to school.)

[Jogging along the sidewalk,] a truck swerved and nearly hit me.

(The *truck* was jogging along the sidewalk?)

Dangling modifiers are trickier to fix than misplaced ones; you can't simply move danglers to another spot in the sentence. There are, however, two ways in which you can fix them. One way requires that you remember this rule:

> When a modifier comes at the beginning of a sentence, it modifies the subject of the sentence. [1]

---

[1] *Adverbial modifiers are exceptions to this rule, but they won't give you any trouble. Example:* (Quickly) *she did as she was told.*

This means that you can avoid dangling modifiers by choosing the subjects of your sentences carefully. All you have to do is make sure the subject is an appropriate one for the modifier to apply to. Using this method, we can rewrite our two examples by changing the subjects:

After four semesters of hard work, I got my reward. My parents bought me a car.

Jogging along the sidewalk, I was nearly hit by a swerving truck.

Another way to correct a dangling modifier is by changing it into a dependent clause:

After I had completed four semesters of hard work, my parents rewarded me with a car.

As I was jogging along the sidewalk, a truck swerved and nearly hit me.

Sometimes a dangling modifier comes at the end of a sentence:

McDonald's would be a good place to go, not having much money.

Can you correct this sentence? Try it; then look at footnote 2, below.

Here is a summary of the steps to follow in solving modifier problems:

> 1. Ask "What does the modifier apply to?"
> 2. Be sure there is a word *in the sentence* for the modifier to apply to.
> 3. Put the modifier as close as possible to the word it applies to.

Exercises

Most of the sentences in exercises 5 and 6 contain dangling modifiers. Make corrections by changing the subject of the sentence to one the modifier can apporpriately apply to. There is no one, "right" way to correct each sentence; our answers are only suggestions.

5

1. Cutting the wire for the cable, the pliers broke.

2. The floors should be vacuumed before polishing the furniture.

3. We felt that, being small-town people, Torontonians might not accept us.

4. Leaving the building, it had gotten dark.

---

[2] *Here are two suggestions:* 1. *Add a subject: Not having much money, I thought McDonald's would be a good place to go.*
2. *Change the dangler to a dependent clause: McDonald's would be a good place to go since I don't have much money.*

5. Although adults now, finding time to play is still important.

6. Recognizing it as the ring of the telephone, the noise didn't bother me.

7. After criticizing both my work and my attitude, I was fired.

8. Trying to bunt, the ball went over the fence at centre field for a home run.

9. Trying to focus his binoculars, the eclipse was obscured by clouds.

10. As a jogger, well-fitting shoes are important to me.

6

1. Considering Michael's charm and good manners, his good looks are unimportant.

2. My supervisor gave me a lecture about punctuality after being late twice in one week.

3. After spending all my money, the flowers were delivered to the wrong house.

4. After supplying them with seeds all winter, the wild birds wouldn't forage for insects in the summer.

5. When looking over their résumés, Carol and George have completely different backgrounds, but both could do the job.

6. Rated tops in his field, Stuart will run the first heats in the two sprint relays and the last heat in the marathon relay.

7. Not realizing the implications of the weather reports, they set sail for the distant island.

8. Fifteen minutes after setting sail for the island, the storm struck.

9. After struggling desperately for almost two hours with high winds and torrential rains, it stopped as suddenly as it had begun.

10. Even in hot weather, the legs and feet should be warmed and stretched before doing any serious jogging.

7

Correct the dangling modifiers in exercise 5 by changing them into dependent clauses.

8

Correct the dangling modifiers in exercise 6 by changing them into dependent clauses.

9

Correct the misplaced and dangling modifiers in exercises 9 through 11 in any way you choose. Our answers are only suggestions.

1. As a college student constantly faced with new assignments, the pressure is sometimes intolerable.

2. Being horribly hung over, the only problem with a free bar is knowing when to quit.

3. As a dog allowed to run free, there is great danger their pet will be run over.

4. H. Salt's best dish is giant shrimp deep-fried in their special seafood sauce.

5. Rotting slowly over the years, the villagers no longer drive cars or ride bicycles over the bridge.

6. Burrowing into the wood shavings in the cage that night, Stephen could tell that his gerbil already felt at ease in its new home.

7. The driver who hit my car whose license had been suspended left the scene of the accident.

8. The Canadian Brass receives enthusiastic acclaim for its witty presentation, its wide repertoire, and its clarity of tone from Vancouver to Halifax.

9. Possessing a natural instinct for rhythm and a good musical ear, it is easy for a classical pianist to switch over to jazz.

10. Obviously having drunk too much, I drove Sean to his apartment, made him a pot of coffee, and phoned his AA friend.

10

1. Carrying two shopping bags full of old clothes and several other bags, our hearts were wrung by the frail, unkempt little woman.

2. One passenger said that she saw the engine catch fire and begin spewing smoke from her window seat.

3. The organ had all the power of a full-size symphony orchestra when it had all the stops pulled out.

4. I learned that the provincial premiers will meet in July in the *Toronto Star*.

5. They recognized each other at Jon's Hallowe'en party in the crowd and the confusion although costumed and masked.

6. After looking at the gorgeous dress all week, they sold it before I got there on payday.

7. On the day I was demonstrating how to make a Caesar salad, I left the Parmesan cheese in my locker which was my favourite ingredient.

8. Barry will serve a Japanese sukiyaki dinner for his guests cooked in a wok and served with steamed rice.

9. The person who has lived for a long time in most cases has lived a simple life.

10. Thirteen couples are participating in Dr. Gemini's research program on families of twins who have newborn twins.

II

1. A worm-eating warbler was spotted by Hazel Miller while walking along the branch of a tree and singing.

2. When trying for your Red Cross bronze medal, your examiner will consider speed, endurance, and resuscitation techniques.

3. The University of Toronto's research in heart disease this month will be summarized in a special issue of the *Canadian Medical Journal.*

4. Trapped under a delicate crystal wine glass on the elegantly set table, his guests observed that most despised of uninvited dinner guests, a cockroach.

5. Not being reliable about arriving on time, I can't hire her to supervise others who *are* punctual.

6. The parks superintendent explained that reforestation was urgent in Ontario's northernmost provincial parks on Friday at the Toronto conference.

7. He maintains the tack, grooms the horses, and shovels manure just like his father.

8. At the age of five, his mother took Scott to the movie theatre that had been in the neighbourhood for many years for the first time.

9. We always pay our respects to our friends and relatives when they have passed on in a funeral parlour.

10. "This bus has a seating capacity of 56 passengers with a maximum height of 14 feet, 6 inches." (Sign on a double-decker bus in Charlottetown, P.E.I.)

chapter 9

The Parallelism Principle

When writing about items in a series, you must be sure all the items are **parallel;** that is, they must be written in the same grammatical form.

I like camping, fishing, and to hike.

The items in this list are not parallel. Two end in *ing,* but the third *(to hike)* is the infinitive form of the verb. To correct the sentence, you must make all the items in the list take the same grammatical form — either

I like to camp, to fish, and to hike.

or

I like camping, fishing, and hiking.

> Correct faulty parallelism by giving the items in a series the same grammatical form.

One way to tell whether all the items in a list are parallel is to picture (or actually write) the items in list form, one below the other. That way, you can make sure that all the elements are the same — that they are all words, or phrases, or clauses.

Not Parallel	**Parallel**
Sharon is kind, considerate, and likes to help.	Sharon is kind, considerate, and helpful.
I support myself by tending bar, piano, and shooting pool.	I support myself by tending bar, playing piano, and shooting pool.
Her upbringing made her neat, polite, and an obnoxious person.	Her upbringing made her neat, polite, and obnoxious.

Gordon tries to do what is right,
      different things, and
      make a profit.

Gordon tries to do what is right,
      what is different, and
      what is profitable.

With his sharp mind,
by having the boss as his uncle, and
few enemies,
  he'll go far.

With his sharp mind,
  the boss as his uncle, and
  few enemies,
    he'll go far.

or

Having a sharp mind,
  the boss as his uncle, and
  few enemies,
    he'll go far.

As you can see, achieving parallelism is partly a matter of developing an ear for the sound of a correct list. Practice, and the exercises in this chapter, will help. Once you have mastered parallelism in your sentences, you will be ready to develop ideas and arguments in parallel sequence and thus to write well organized and clear paragraphs, letters, and essays. All this will be discussed in a later unit ("Organizing Your Writing"); we mention it now only to show you that parallelism, far from being a "frill," is a fundamental part of good writing.

Exercises

Correct the following sentences where necessary. As you work through these exercises, try to spot faulty parallelism and correct it from the sound of the sentences, before you examine them closely for mistakes. Check your answers to each set of ten before going on. Answers begin on p. 265.

I

1. Food and a roof over your head are the minimum requirements for survival.

2. My name is difficult to pronounce and you can't spell it easily, either.

3. Snoopy knows what he can do and what he can't do.

4. Slowly, haltingly, and with tears in her eyes, she told them what had happened.

5. This year I intend to go to the Stratford Festival, the Shaw Festival, and I plan to attend the Mariposa Folk Festival also.

6. Make sure that the people you hire are intelligent, articulate, and that they will work hard.

7. My wife told me to stay home and that I should paint the basement.

8. I had a hard time deciding whether to continue my education in a college or university, or plunging right into a job.

9. Lots of swimming, tennis, and seeing all the sights I can are what I plan to do in Bermuda.

10. Turn right at the first stop sign, left at the first traffic light, and then make a right turn at the doughnut shop.

2

1. I'm looking for a babysitter who is intelligent, patient, and who is basically a kind person.

2. Make sure your report is comprehensive, readable, and above all that it records everything accurately.

3. Those in community-service fields must be loving, patient, objective, and they must also be able to understand people's problems.

4. The location, staff, and the way it looked made that hospital a more pleasant place to stay than most.

5. We were told to study the report carefully and that we should make our recommendations in writing.

6. Their chances for a lasting relationship aren't good, considering their goals are extremely different, their temperamental differences, and their cultural differences.

7. Her small build, quick temper, and the fact that she has a criminal record will disqualify her from becoming a corrections officer.

8. Barry is everything a girl could want: handsome, intelligent, successful, and he's even kind to his mother.

9. The space-age kitchen, the pool and sauna, and a security system that was burglar proof were what sold us on the apartment.

10. Mr. Redfern explained how the tape recorder worked, the microphone and camera, and how to use the video cassette recorder.

3

1. Body-building has made me what I am today: physically perfect, very prosperous financially, and practically friendless.

2. If there is no heaven, then hell can't exist either.

3. In my tiny home town, two significantly related crimes prevail: vandalism, and there is a lot of drug-trafficking.

4. I'd like to help, but I'm too tired, I'm too poor, and my time is already taken up with other things.

5. I wanted either a Mother's pizza or I wanted a Big Mac from McDonald's.

6. Every hour each guard counts the prisoners in his care, and the prisoners answer the guard's roll call twice a day.

7. My sister, who's trying to teach me to play tennis, says that my forehand and serve are all right, but to work on strengthening my backhand.

8. The two factors thought to be most important in a long-lasting marriage are how committed each partner is to the marriage and the willingness to compromise.

9. Barry claimed that, through constant repetition and being firm, he had trained his guppy to be obedient, quiet, and show loyalty.

10. The new budget must deal with several major problems, two of them being the devalued Canadian dollar and the fact that the inflation rate rose so high.

4

1. Feeling discouraged and without hope, Sarah and Peter went to the employment office to see if any new jobs had been posted.

2. Here we are, stranded in the middle of the jungle, without food or water. We're sure to die of exposure, or we'll starve, or perish from thirst.

3. We become old too soon and smart too late.

4. In tournament play, good golfers require patience, stamina, and they have to have nerves of steel.

5. Lawn-mowing, painting, and being able to do carpentry and bake cookies are some of the many odd jobs George is doing this summer.

6. Like many politicians, he is fully aware of his capabilities but not of the limits of his talents.

7. Times have changed: we work fewer hours than our parents did and leisure activities are being enjoyed more.

8. Get the ball either to your right forward or in the direction of a guard.

9. In order to guarantee a painless annual visit to your dentist, you should clean your teeth with a brush and dental floss after every meal, and cutting down significantly on sugar consumption.

10. An experiment that removed the TV sets from 100 homes for a month proved to

be a good test of human creativity and ingenuity. One-third of the families in the experiment read books, played games, and talked with other family members; twice as many movies, sports events, and other entertainments were attended by another third; and one-third went to the homes of friends or to pubs and watched even more television at home than they had before the survey period.

5

Make the following lists parallel. In each case there's more than one way to do it, because you can make your items parallel with any item in the list. Therefore, your answers may differ from ours. Here's an example:

wrong: stick handling   score a goal
right: stick handling   goal scoring
or
right: handle the stick   score a goal

1. wrong: wine   women   singing
   right:

2. wrong: privately   in public
   right:

3. wrong: employers   those working for the employer
   right:

4. wrong: lying about all morning   to do whatever I please
   right:

5. wrong: individually   as a group
   right:

6. wrong: happy   healthy   wisdom
   right:

7. wrong: doing your best   don't give up
   right:

8. wrong: information   education   entertaining
   right:

9. wrong: insufficient time   too little money   not enough staff
   right:

10. wrong: French is the lan-   English is the best   Profanity is best in
          guage of love   language for business   German
   right:

6

Create a sentence for each of the parallel lists you developed in exercise 5. Example:
His stick handling was adequate, but his goal scoring was dreadful.

7

As a test of your mastery of parallelism, try these sentences. No answers are
provided for this exercise.

1. Working with children is stimulating, challenging, and has its rewards.
2. Not being able to speak the language causes confusion, is frustrating, and it's
   embarrassing.
3. To prevent crime, attending to victims of accidents and crimes, and how to
   safely apprehend those suspected of crime are a police officer's responsibilities.
4. Being sound of mind and physically strong, the elderly man was able to live
   quite happily by himself.
5. Three of the issues the committee will have to deal with right away are camp
   maintenance, how to get staff for the camp, and promoting the camp.
6. His doctor advised him to eat less, exercise more, and no smoking at all.
7. For many people, attending AA meetings is first embarrassing, possibly even
   humiliating, then helpful, and finally it is a success.
8. A high level of motivation, experience in problem-solving, and not worrying
   about your decisions are necessary if you hope to run a successful business.
9. Influential factors in any nation's economic regression are bad management of
   natural resources, policies regarding national debt might be unwise, and the
   unions' inflationary demands.
10. Although the first applicant seemed scared and showed shyness, the second was
    a composed person and outgoing.

8

Correct the faulty parallelism in this paragraph. No answers are given for this
exercise.

The dictionary can be both a useful resource and an educational entertainment.

Everyone knows that its three chief functions are to check spelling, for finding out

the meanings of words, and what the correct pronunciation is. Few people, however,

use the dictionary for discovery and learning. There are several methods of using the dictionary as an aid to discovery. One is randomly looking at words, another is to read a page or two thoroughly, and still another is by skimming through words until you find an unfamiliar one. It is by this latter method that I discovered the word "steatopygous," a term I now try to use at least once a day. You can increase your vocabulary significantly by using the dictionary, and of course a large and varied vocabulary can be used to baffle your colleagues, employers will be impressed, and your English teacher will be surprised.

9

Write a short paper on a topic you choose or on a topic assigned by your teacher. When you have completed your work, read it over carefully. Check your spelling. Check your sentence structure by reading your work aloud, from last sentence to first. Be sure to correct any unclear modifiers and errors in parallelism before handing in your paper.

You might like to try one of these topics:

1. The ideal job

2. How to annoy others

3. How to make a decision

4. What makes me unique and indispensable

5. What are the two most important things (objects, people, or principles) in your life?

unit

grammar

3

chapter  10

Subject-Verb Agreement

Errors in grammar are like flies in soup: they don't usually affect meaning any more than flies in soup affect flavour. But, like the flies, grammar errors are distracting and irritating. They must be eliminated if you want your reader to pay attention to what you say rather than how you say it.

One of the most common grammatical problems is failure to make the subject and verb in a sentence agree with each other. Here is the rule for subject-verb agreement:

> Singular subjects take singular verbs.
> Plural subjects take plural verbs.

Remember that *singular* words concern one person or thing . . .

The <u>clock</u> <u>ticks</u>.   <u>George</u> <u>works</u>.

. . . and *plural* words concern more than one person or thing:

The <u>clocks</u> <u>tick</u>.   <u>George and his brother</u> <u>work</u>.

The rule for subject-verb agreement will cause you no problem at all as long as you make sure that the word the verb agrees with is really the subject. To see how a problem can arise, look at this example:

One of the boys write graffiti.

The writer forgot that the subject of a sentence is never in a prepositional phrase. The verb needs to be changed to agree with *one:*

One of the boys writes graffiti.

If you're careful about identifying the subject of your sentence, you'll have no trouble with subject-verb agreement. To sharpen up your subject-finding ability, review chapter 4, "Cracking the Sentence Code." Then do the following exercises.

Exercises

1

Identify the subject in each sentence. Answers begin on p. 267.

1. In the dugout are two of my favourite Blue Jays, Lloyd Moseby and Jesse Barfield.
2. Does anyone know how to carve this turkey?
3. There are few tasks more tedious than stuffing envelopes.
4. Toronto's most popular summer attraction, the Canadian National Exhibition, no longer draws huge crowds.
5. Where are the printouts he is looking for?
6. Regrettably, many kinds of job will become obsolete in the next ten years.
7. In order to communicate effectively, a writer must always consider the audience and the purpose.
8. Has anyone in your family ever won a Loto Canada draw?
9. One of Canada's most prominent businessmen was kidnapped recently.
10. Drugs, alcohol, and video games have been banned by the parents' association at the neighbourhood junior high.

2

Rewrite each of the following sentences, following the procedure shown in the example.

Example: She wants to learn about data processing.
　　　　They want to learn about data processing.

1. He sells used essays to other students.
   They
2. They often spend the weekend on their sailboat.
   He
3. The woman maintains that her boss has been ogling her.
   The women
4. Her flight has been delayed because of the storm.
   Their flights
5. That new computer affects the entire office procedure.
   Those
6. She likes to work with children, so she is looking for a job in a day-care centre.
   They
7. Everyone who shops at Pimrock's receives a free can of tuna.
   All those
8. That girl's father is looking for a rich husband for her.
   Those
9. The civil servant with an indexed pension stands to gain from future inflation.
   Civil servants
10. Each of her sons is successful in his own way.
    Both

3

Rewrite each sentence, following the procedure shown in the example.
Example: <u>Chocolate milkshakes</u> <u><u>are</u></u> my weakness.

   My <u>weakness</u> <u><u>is</u></u> chocolate milkshakes.

1. Vince's first love in life is Atari games.

   Atari games

2. What Marcia spends most of her time on is movies.

   Movies

3. Hostess Twinkies are the only junk food Tim eats.

4. Frequent nights of debauchery were the cause of his downfall.

5. What the team needs now is a good pitcher and outfielder.

6. The source of Superman's strength is clean living and Lois Lane.

7. Frequently, absences from class and failed exams are the cause of failure.

8. Brown rice and tofu are what I least like to eat.

9. Something that I didn't understand was accounting procedures.

10. Your stunning good looks are the reason for your success in the aluminum-

    siding business.

So far, so good. You can find the subject, even when it's hiding on the far side of the verb or nearly buried under a load of prepositional phrases. You can match up singular subjects with singular verbs, and plural subjects with plural verbs. Now let's take a look at a few of the complications that make subject-verb agreement into such a disagreeable problem.

Six Special Cases

Some subjects are tricky: they look singular but are actually plural, or they look plural when they're really singular. There are six different kinds of these slippery subjects, all of them common, and all of them likely to trip up the unwary writer.

1. Multiple subjects joined by *or, either ... or, neither ... nor, not ...* *but.* All the multiple subjects we've dealt with so far have been joined by *and*

and have required plural verbs, so agreement hasn't been a problem. But watch out when the two or more elements of a multiple subject are joined by *or, either . . . or, neither . . . nor,* or *not . . . but.* In these cases, *the verb agrees in number with the nearest subject.* That is, if the subject closest to the verb is singular, the verb will be singular; if the subject closest to the verb is plural, the verb must be plural, too.

Neither the <u>prime minister</u> nor the <u>cabinet ministers are</u> responsible.

Neither the <u>cabinet ministers</u> nor the <u>prime minister is</u> responsible.

Exercise

4

Circle the correct verb. For questions 9 and 10, make up two sentences of your own.

1. Not the spooky old mansion but the numerous bats (was were) what scared me.
2. Homes, cars, or travel (is are) available to the person who wins the contest.
3. Either he or you (is are) likely to be awarded the contract.
4. Neither the man nor his previous wives (know knows) who buried the treasure in the orchard.
5. Not high interest rates but high unemployment (is are) our first concern as Canadians right now.
6. The college has decided that neither final marks nor a diploma (is are) to be issued to students owing library fines.
7. Either your job performance or your school assignments (is are) going to suffer if you continue your frantic lifestyle.
8. According to my guidebook entitled *Sightseeing in Transylvania,* not sharp stakes but garlic cloves (repel repels) the dreaded vampires.

9. Neither _____ nor _____.

10. Not _____ but _____ .

2. Subjects that look multiple but really aren't. Don't be fooled by phrases beginning with such words as *with, like, as well as, together with, in addition to, including.* These phrases are NOT part of the subject of the sentence. Cross them out mentally; they do not affect the verb.

My typing teacher, ~~as well as my counsellor~~, has advised me to switch programs.

Obviously, two people were involved in the advising; nevertheless, the subject (<u>teacher</u>) is singular, and so the verb must be singular, too (<u>has advised</u>).

All my courses, ~~including chemistry~~, are easier this term.

If you mentally cross out the phrase "including chemistry," you can easily see that the verb (<u>are</u>) must be plural to agree with the plural subject (<u>courses</u>).

Exercise

5

Circle the correct verb. Then make up two sentences of your own.

1. Prime Minister Mulroney, along with his cabinet ministers, (is are) held responsible for our economic woes by many Canadians.
2. Wayne Gretzky, like Bobby Orr and Gordie Howe, (has have) become a hockey legend.
3. My English teacher, in addition to my math and data processing instructors, (inflict inflicts) a considerable amount of pain on me.
4. Do you think that the turkey, with all the side dishes, (is are) enough food for this crowd?
5. Regardless of the complexity of the mystery, Sherlock Holmes, together with his sidekick Dr. Watson, (unravel unravels) all the clues.
6. Andrew Davis, as well as the Toronto Symphony Orchestra, (is are) appearing at Ontario Place tonight.
7. The company Tim keeps, not to mention the places he frequents, (is are) highly suspect.
8. His parole officer, in addition to the police, (keep keeps) a close eye on him.

9. _____, with _____, _____ .

10. _____, including _____, _____ .

3. Words ending in *one*, *thing*, or *body*. When used as subjects, the following words are always singular, requiring the singular form of the verb:

everyone	everything	everybody
anyone	anything	anybody
someone	something	somebody
no one	nothing	nobody

The last part of the word is the tip-off here: every*one*, any*thing*, no*body*. If you focus on this last part, you'll remember to use a singular verb with these subjects. Usually these words are troublesome only when modifiers crop up between them and their verbs. For example, no one would write "Everyone are here." The trouble starts when you sandwich a group of words between the subject and the verb. You might, if you weren't on your toes, write this: "Everyone involved in implementing the company's new policies and procedures are here." Obviously, the meaning is plural: several people are present. But the subject (every*one*) is singular in form, so the verb must be *is*.

Exercise

6

Circle the right verb. Then make up two sentences of your own.

1. Everybody in the first and second years of this program (is are) affected by the cutbacks.
2. Anyone who has seen the Rolling Stones perform (love loves) them.
3. No one who had anything to do with these projects (was were) talking about them.
4. Everything I enjoy doing on weekends (is are) either illegal, immoral, or fattening.
5. Despite the legislation of the provincial government, not everyone attending Blue Jay games (want wants) to have beer in the ball park.
6. Nothing you can offer me, including your collection of Argonaut autographs, (is are) likely to induce me to change my mind.
7. Anything we said to the players on the losing team (was were) taken as an insult.
8. Before the show, one of the roadies (is are) supposed to set up the amplifiers.

9. Everyone _____ .

10. Something _____ .

---

4. Each, either (of), neither (of). Used as subjects, these take singular verbs.

<u>Either</u> <u>was</u> suitable for the job.

<u>Each</u> <u>wants</u> desperately to win.

<u>Neither</u> of the stores <u>is</u> open after six o'clock. (Remember, the subject is never in a prepositional phrase.)

Exercise
7

Circle the right verb. Then make up two sentences of your own.

1. Each (is are) open this morning.
2. Neither of the schools (was were) accepting students last fall.
3. Either of the televisions (work works) well.
4. Each of the children (like likes) to spend time at the cottage.
5. Unless we hear from the coach, neither of those team members (is are) playing this evening.
6. Either of those courses (involve involves) field placement.
7. You will be pleased to hear that neither (has have) the measles.
8. Each of the women (want wants) to win the Ms. Oshawa competition.

9. Neither _____ .

10. Either of _____ .

5. Collective nouns. A collective noun is a word naming a group. Some examples are *company, class, committee, team, crowd, group, family, audience, public,* and *majority*. When you are referring to the group acting as a *unit*, use a *singular* verb. When you are referring to the *members* of the group acting *individually*, use a *plural* verb.

> The team is sure to win tomorrow's game. (Here *team* refers to the group acting as a whole.)
> The team are getting into their uniforms now. (The separate members of the team are acting individually.)

Exercise

8

Circle the correct verb. Then make up two sentences of your own.

1. The whole class (is are) attending the weekend seminar.
2. The Canadian public (prefer prefers) hockey to opera.
3. Right after breakfast, the family (leaves leave) for various schools and jobs.
4. An exaltation of larks (is are) what you call a whole bunch of them.
5. (Was Were) the company showing a profit before the fraud was discovered?
6. After a performance by Teenage Head, the audience often (brawl brawls) among themselves for hours.
7. The committee (was were) unanimous in its selection of a spokesman.
8. A gaggle of geese (fly flies) south in a close V-formation.

9. The team _____ .

10. The crowd _____ .

6. Units of money, time, mass, length, and distance. These require singular verbs.

> Four dollars is too much to pay for a hamburger.
> Three hours is a long time to wait, and five kilometres is too far to walk.
> Seventy kilograms is the mass of an average man.

Exercises

9

Circle the correct verb. Then write two sentences of your own.

1. Four hours (is are) too long to wait, even for playoff tickets.
2. No wonder you are suspicious if seventy dollars (was were) what you paid for last night's pizza.
3. Roscoe claims that eighty kilopascals (is are) the weight of an average man.

4. Tim told his girlfriend that nine years (seem seems) like a long time to wait.
5. Forty hours of classes (is are) too much in one week.
6. Though it was light and tasty yesterday, 500 grams (seem seems) like the weight of this day-old bagel.
7. When you are anxiously awaiting the next gas station, thirty kilometres (is are) a long distance.
8. Seventy-five cents (seems seem) a fair price for a slightly tattered Kelly Gruber card.

9. Sixteen years _____ .

10. Eleven metres _____ .

In exercises 10 through 12, correct the errors in subject-verb agreement. Check your answers to each exercise before going on.

10

1. Do you know everyone who come to this pub?

2. The whole team were anxious to see Harold Ballard find a pleasant retirement home on another continent.

3. The largest breed of domestic rabbits are the British giant, with a weight of 8-10 kilograms.

4. Tim hope he never meet a bunny that big.

5. Gordon Lightfoot, along with Burton Cummings and Anne Murray, is a Canadian performer who has achieved success in the States.

6. Neither Roger nor I is prepared to confront the instructor over the issue.

7. The rust problem, not the broken water pump or the faulty brakes, were what made me decide to sell the car.

8. Everyone attending this series of meetings have heard a most informative presentation.

9. The money and status accorded to the medical doctor are often envied by the dental practitioner.

10. When there is no pictures, I don't like to read the book.

11

1. My sense of the schools are that none of them are any good.

2. Neither of them remember who ran against Art Eggleton for mayor of Toronto.

3. Every one of the SUNshine Boys appeal to my sense of the sublime.

4. My whole family, with the exception of Fido, dislike anchovy pizza.

5. Popular belief notwithstanding, quicksand do not suck you under or pull you down.

6. It is the suction created by the victims that are responsible for the pulling effect.

7. Neither age nor illness prevents Uncle Alf from pinching the nurses.

8. Eight hundred dollars per term, all students agree, are too much to pay for their education.

9. The birth of quintuplets were too much for the mother to cope with.

10. Everything that we agreed to last night seem silly this morning.

12

Quebec City, along with Montreal, Toronto, and Vancouver, are among Canada's great gourmet centres. While Toronto is a relative latecomer to this list, neither Quebec City nor Montreal are strangers to those who seeks fine dining. Indeed, travel and food magazines have long affirmed that the inclusion of these two cities in a Quebec vacation are a "must." While Montreal is perhaps more international in its offerings, Quebec City provides exquisite proof that French Canadian cuisine and hospitality is second to none in the world. Amid the old-world charm of the lower city is to be found some of the quaintest and most enjoyable traditional restaurants, while the newer sections of town boasts equally fine dining in more contemporary surroundings. The combination of the wonderful food and the city's fascinating charms are sure to make any visitor return frequently. Either the summer, when the city blooms and outdoor cafes abound, or the winter, when Carnaval turns the streets into hundreds of connecting parties, are wonderful times to visit one of Canada's oldest and most interesting cities.

Complete the sentences in exercises 13 and 14 using present-tense verbs. After doing the exercises, check in the answer section to see whether your verbs should be singular or plural.

13

1. Everyone with children

2. Neither her mother nor her friends

3. A school of fish

4. Four hundred dollars

5. The general, as well as the colonels,

6. Either swimming or strenuous exercises

7. Everybody at the steambath

8. Neither of the students

9. Psychology, together with English and history,

10. The Canadian public

14

1. The cost, including meals and accommodation,

2. Seventeen days in a lifeboat

3. Neither radiation nor toxic chemicals

4. Each and every one of us

5. The crowd

6. Each of the stores

7. Anyone knowing their whereabouts

8. Not TV but movies

9. Stories, plays, or poetry

10. One of the weirdest people

15

Write your own sentences, choosing your subjects as indicated and using present-tense verbs.

1. Use *everyone* as your subject.

2. Use a collective noun as a subject.

3. Use *either* as your subject.

4. Use a compound subject.

5. Use *no one* as your subject.

6. Use *not . . . but*.

7. Use a collective noun as a singular subject.

8. Use a compound subject joined by *or*.

9. Use *neither . . . nor*.

10. Use your own weight as a subject.

16

Correct the following passage.

The interest in wrestlers and their managers, fans, and friends are fascinating proof that our society needs cheap thrills. The concept of good and evil fighting it out in epic battles are an enduring one. In simpler times, everyone who felt the need to witness such struggles were able to watch westerns on TV and see the Bad Guy (wearing the black hat) gunned down at high noon by the reluctant Good Guy (wearing the white hat). The complexity of our society, where good and evil is constantly redefined, mean that we seldom get a clear decision in the battles we see each day on the news, let alone witness the triumph of good over evil. Into this frustrating world comes Rowdy Roddy Piper, Hulk Hogan, The Junk Yard Dog, and King Kong Bundy. The variety of names, personalities, and "show biz" tricks are bewildering. Though the staging of the various moves and even the outcomes of the matches are obvious, the immense popularity of the matches, both on television and in the arenas, are undeniable. Like Rambo and Dirty Harry, the professional wrestler cuts through frustrating complexity and represents good or evil in its simplest, most dramatic form. To a great many people, wrestling — not to mention wrestlers — are irresistible.

17

Correct the following sentences.

1. Cloud seeding to enhance rainfall and prevent snowstorms are expected to be a breakthrough in weather control

2. The bizarre lives of many rock stars captivates the attention of young fans.

3. Everybody we see at the wrestling matches root for the Sheik.

4. Many cities in Russia has a "kremlin" because the word simply signify a fortress or citadel.

5. The rate of business bankruptcies are rising monthly.

6. All of us at the college feel that cheating and plagiarism is a serious offence.

7. Either French dressing or mayonnaise go well with that salad.

8. By the time we reached the Festival Theatre at Stratford, there was left only one seat in the balcony and two behind posts.

9. In Canada today, everyone who wants a good education can get it.

10. The variety of Richard's money-making activities are amazing: he plays cards, bets on horses, and sells socks.

11. One can't help noticing that the orchestra are playing better now that the conductor is sober.

12. At lunchtime our cafeteria, with its dreary salad bar, greasy chips, and soggy burgers, take away my appetite.

13. Both of Canada's native groups, the Indian and the Inuit, is thought to have come from Asia via the Bering Sea several thousand years before Europeans arrived in North America.

14. Neither subject-verb agreement nor run-on sentences presents any problem for me now.

18

As a final check of your mastery of subject-verb agreement, correct the following sentences. There are no answers provided for this exercise.

1. Either the woman or her children is going back to claim their belongings.

2. Seven hundred dollars, even for return trips, are too much to pay for Vancouver–Toronto tickets.

3. The reason for Canada's success in the downhill races were many years of hard work on the part of our skiers.

4. My boss, as well as my supervisors and all my co-workers, have encouraged me to pursue another line of work.

5. She insist that headcheese is made by standing a can of milk upside down.

6. Why on earth are that group of girls heading for Ronnie Hawkins's dressing room?

7. Arguments over money and sex causes many marital difficulties.

8. Anyone alleged to have had dealings with the previous rulers were watched carefully by the new regime.

9. Igloos and hockey is the image most Americans have of Canada.

10. Each of the mothers want only the best for her children.

chapter 11

Pronoun-Antecedent Agreement

The title of this chapter may be formidable, but the idea is really very simple. **Pronouns** are words that substitute for or refer to the name of a person or thing. The word that a pronoun substitutes for or refers to is called the **antecedent.**

Bob has his own way of doing things.
antecedent   pronoun

This game is as close as it can be.
antecedent   pronoun

The basic rule to remember is this:

> A pronoun must agree with its antecedent.

You probably follow this rule most of the time, without even realizing that you know it. For example, you would never write

Bob has *its* own way of doing things.
or
This game is as close as *he* can be.

because you know that these pronouns don't agree with their antecedents.

There are three aspects of pronoun usage, however, that you need to be careful about. The first is how to use the relative pronouns — *which, that, who,* and *whom:*

> *Who* and *whom* are always used to refer to people.
> *That* and *which* refer to everything else.

The man *who* was hurt had to quit climbing.
The women *who* were present voted unanimously.
The moose *that* I met looked hostile.
Her car, *which* is imported, is smaller than cars *that* are built here.
The man *whom* the committee had decided to hire refused the job.

By the way, if you aren't sure whether to use *who* or *whom*, rewrite the sentence so you don't need either one: "The man the committee had decided to hire refused the job."

Exercise

I

Correct the following sentences where necessary. Answers begin on p. 270.

1. Yesterday's lecture was given by the English teacher that has a large wart on her nose.

2. Curling's most durable player is a man named Howard "Pappy" Wood, which competed in sixty-five consecutive annual bonspiels between 1908 and 1972.

3. Is this the car that was stolen by the man that escaped last night?

4. We are often attracted to people which are completely opposite to ourselves.

5. When I entered the locker room, I knew the team who had lost had been there before me.

6. Liona Boyd is the musician that is scheduled to perform tonight.

7. The lasagna, which had been cooking all day, was hardly fit for the guests who were late.

8. Rudolf's grandmother always told him that people that couldn't fly as well as eagles should stay out of airplanes.

9. He remembered that sage advice the stormy night when the DC-9 in whom he was flying went into a sickening tailspin over Great Slave Lake.

10. The math problem which we worked out last night would have stymied anyone that hadn't attended class regularly.

The second tricky aspect of pronoun-antecedent agreement concerns words and phrases that you learned about in chapter 10 — words and phrases ending in *one, body,* and *thing:*

everyone	everybody	everything
anyone	anybody	anything
someone	somebody	something
no one	nobody	nothing
none		
each (one)		
every one		

In chapter 10 you learned that when these words are used as subjects they are singular and take singular verbs. So it makes sense that the pronouns that stand for or refer to them must be singular.

> Antecedents ending in *one, body,* and *thing* are singular and must be referred to by singular pronouns: *he, she, it, his, her, its.*

Everyone is expected to do *his* duty.
Each of the students must supply *his* or *her* own lunch.
Every mother deserves a break from *her* routine.
No one can truly say in *his* heart that *he* believes otherwise.

The his/her question deserves mention. It is generally accepted that *his* and *he* stand for both sexes in sentences like the first and fourth above. If you find this usage upsetting, rewrite the sentences to avoid the problem.

We are all expected to do our duty.
No one can honestly believe otherwise.

It is wrong to write

Everyone is expected to do their duty.
No one can truly say in their heart that they believe otherwise.

Another problem involves sentences that are grammatically correct but sound awkward:

If anyone is at the door, he'll have to knock louder.
Everyone arrives on time, but he leaves early.

It is wrong to write

If anyone is at the door, they'll have to knock louder.
Everyone arrives on time, but they leave early.

So, in order to make the sentences sound better, you need to rewrite them. Here is one way:

Anyone who is at the door will have to knock louder.
Everyone arrives on time but leaves early.

In speech it has become acceptable to use plural pronouns with *one, body,* and *thing* antecedents. Although these antecedents are singular and take singular verbs, often they are plural in meaning, and in conversation we find ourselves saying,

> Everyone clapped *their* hands with glee.
> No one has to stay if *they* don't want to.

This rule bending is also used to avoid the *his/her* problem.

> Someone lost *their* coat.

This usage may be acceptable in conversation; *it is not acceptable in written Standard English.*

Exercise

2

Choose the correct word from the pair in brackets. Check your answers before continuing.

1. Everyone in my crowd brings (his their) lunch to school.
2. Each of them would rather prepare it (himself themselves) than eat cafeteria food.
3. No one wants to be a failure in (her their) college career.
4. Unless we finish this job, no one will get (his their) pay cheque this week.
5. All of the people involved in the accident tried to extricate (his their) cars from the pile-up.
6. A child will often show fear or frustration in ways designed to get (his its their) parents' attention.
7. None of the films we saw could be considered offensive by (itself themselves), but the smutty jokes became tedious after a while.
8. Someone punched Tim in order to protect (her their) husband.
9. Accounting and finance were interesting in (its their) way even though (it they) took up a great deal of study time.
10. Everyone must look closely at (himself themselves) to determine whether (he they) is making use of all the potential (he they) has.

Avoiding the third difficulty with pronoun-antecedent agreement depends on your common sense and your ability to think of your reader. If you try to look at your writing from your reader's point of view, it is unlikely that you will break this rule:

> A pronoun must *clearly* refer to the correct antecedent.

The mistake that occurs when you fail to follow this rule is called **vague reference**:

> Sam pointed to his brother and said that he had saved his life.

Who saved whom? Here's another:

> Jackie felt that Helen should have been more careful with her car when she lent it to her because she was a good friend of her husband.

Who owns the car? Who has the husband?

In these sentences you can only guess about the meaning, because you don't know who is being referred to by the pronouns. You can make these sentences less confusing by using proper names more often and changing the sentences around. Try this technique on the two confusing examples above.

Another type of vague reference occurs when a pronoun doesn't have an antecedent at all.

> He loves watching fast cars and would like to do it himself someday. (Do what?)
> Bicycling is her favourite pastime, but she still doesn't own one. (One what?)

How would you revise these sentences?

Be sure that pronouns have clear antecedents and that they agree with their antecedents in number. Both must be singular, or both must be plural. That, in a nutshell (see "Clichés, Jargon, and Slang," p. 220), is the rule of thumb for pronoun-antecedent agreement.

Exercises
3

Correct the following sentences where necessary.

1. Everyone who works in this car wash should pick up their cheque on Monday.

2. Women are treated as equals when she works in the fields.

3. A good manager must have an understanding of every employee and what makes them tick.

4. Do you know whether anyone in this neighbourhood wants to have their windows washed?

5. Men and women, whatever age they may be, are invited to take part in an experiment that will test their ability to enjoy themselves.

6. Virginia claims that every one of her male friends has a room of their own.

7. It is now time to listen to the voice of your conscience and what they have to say.

8. No one living in Canada today believes their country is thriving economically.

9. Bob and Doug bring his own brand of zany humour to "The Great White North."

10. Whenever they appear on the screen, one or the other is holding a bottle of beer in their hand.

4

Correct the following sentences where necessary. In some cases, a perfectly correct answer of yours will differ from the answer we've given. That's because the reference was so vague that the sentence could be understood in more than one way.

1. The gorilla was mean and thirsty because he had finished it all in the morning.

2. If your pet rat won't eat its food, feed it to the kitty.

3. Hockey is his favourite game, and he badly needs new ones.

4. Tim told Rocco his teeth were falling out.

5. Whenever Dennis and Bob played poker, he stacked the deck.

6. Every time Rudolf sat on the frog he croaked.

7. You know that smoking is very bad for your health, but you won't throw them away.

8. Daphne backed her car into a garbage truck and dented it.

9. Lefty was suspicious of handgun control because he thought everyone should have one for late-night subway rides.

10. If Pierre and Joe begin to argue, he'll tell him that he's never had any use for him and that he ought to keep his crazy ideas to himself.

5

Correct the following sentences where necessary. Remember that your answer may differ from the one we've provided and still be correct.

1. I would like to apply for the advertised clerk/typist position, male or female, because I have experience as both.

2. Watching television requires little mental or physical effort, and we need more of this.

3. The only used motorcycles we found had been driven by young punks which were all scratched up.

4. She told her mother she would soon win some money.

5. In this comment, it says that I use too many pronouns.

6. At the Nifty Burger, they play old Beach Boys albums in the evening.

7. They remind me of my California surfing days, but it's a long way from Mississauga.

8. In the first chapter of Pierre Berton's book, he talks about life in the Klondike.

9. Tim sat down next to Chuck and ate his lunch.

10. My boss said that if any shoplifting were detected the store would press charges against them, even if they were cabinet ministers.

6

Correct the following sentences where necessary. Check your answers before continuing.

1. Anyone that has completed introductory sociology should know what a "peer group" is.

2. The team took its positions on the baseball diamond and outfield.

3. Each employee must arrive early if they want to find parking places.

4. All of our students leave their switchblades in their lockers during classes.

5. Everyone we saw was running as though something had terrified them.

6. When the collection agency called they told them to "Take off, eh."

7. Someone that saw the crime had been lying to protect themselves.

8. Everyone knows Gordie Howe is the man that played twenty-five years in the NHL, but do they know he also collected 500 stitches on his face?

9. Unscrupulous preachers try to convince everyone that they can't go to heaven without paying them money.

10. We fed popcorn to the elephant which we had been munching on all afternoon.

7

Correct the errors in this passage. All three kinds of pronoun-antecedent agreement errors are represented in this exercise.

Reading the newspaper the other day, I found the following advertisement intriguing: "Wanted to rent by young couple: modern apartment with view of the river." I wondered why the couple that had placed the ad had wanted it known that they were young. Perhaps they thought they would be more likely to rent to people that did not have teenage children. Everyone that has their choice would like a view of the river, but it is expensive. My friends Conrad and Barry have one. It's on the eighth floor, but Barry won't even look out of the windows they are paying so much for. Conrad advised him to get his finances in order so he could afford a good psychiatrist that could help him with his phobia. But he refuses to believe that not everyone with an apartment above ground-floor level suffers from a fear of heights.

8

Correct the following sentences. No answers are provided for this exercise.

1. Each of her suitors had their own faults, but Drusilla decided to choose the one that had the most money.

2. Embezzling is what he does best, but he hasn't been able to pull one off lately.

3. Everyone may pick up their exams after Tuesday.

4. Our instructor said that passing grades would be given to those that completed the field placement.

5. None of the people in Tuktoyaktuk feels safe without their mukluks.

6. Betty said to Liz that she had no idea how she felt when Alan broke up with her.

7. Everyone but me said that they would like to work for the company who gave me the job.

8. All of the girls are looked on as a sister here at Camp Kitsch-i-koo-mee.

9. Charles and Diana are a couple that don't have to worry where its next dollar is coming from.

10. Danny's boss always gave him directions, but sometimes he wasn't familiar enough with the procedure.

chapter 12

Tense Agreement

Verbs are time markers. The different tenses are used to express differences in time:

I (was fired) two weeks ago; I (hope) I (will find) a new job soon.
     past   present   future

Sometimes, as in the sentence above, it is necessary to use several different tenses in a single sentence to get the meaning across. But usually, whether you're writing a sentence, a paragraph, an essay, or a report, you will use *one tense throughout.* Normally you will choose either the past or the present tense. Here is the rule to follow:

> Don't change tense unless meaning requires it.

Readers like and expect consistency. If you begin a sentence with "I kicked and screamed and protested," the reader will tune in to the past-tense verbs and expect any other verbs in the sentence to be in the past tense too. Therefore, if you finish the sentence with ". . . but he looks at me with those big blue eyes and gets me to take him to the dance," the reader will be abruptly jolted out of one time frame and into another. This sort of jolting is uncomfortable, and readers don't like it.

Shifting tenses is like shifting gears: it should be done smoothly and when necessary — never abruptly, out of carelessness, or on a whim. Avoid causing verbal whiplash: keep your tenses consistent.

Wrong: He kicked a stone from his path as he rambles up the winding driveway.

Right: He kicked a stone from his path as he rambled up the winding driveway.

Also right: He kicks a stone from his path as he rambles up the winding driveway.

Wrong: She hesitated but then began to climb the steps. Suddenly she hears a low groan.

Right: She hesitated but then began to climb the steps. Suddenly she heard a low groan.

Also right: She hesitates but then begins to climb the steps. Suddenly she hears a low groan.

Exercises

Most of the following sentences contain unnecessary tense shifts. Use the first verb in each sentence as your time marker, and change the tense(s) of the other verb(s) in the sentence to agree with it. If you get exercise I entirely correct, skip ahead to exercise 4. Answers begin on p. 272.

I

1. Rolly goes home and kicked his cat.

2. Hank Aaron broke Babe Ruth's record of 714 home runs in a lifetime when he hits number 715 in 1974.

3. Children are quite perceptive and will know when you are lying to them.

4. We had just finished painting the floor when the dog runs through.

5. When Knowlton Nash walked into the room, the ladies go crazy.

6. You ought not to venture into that place until the police arrive.

7. Tim walked into the room, took one look at Lefty, and smashes him right through the wall.

8. First you will greet your guests; then you show them to their rooms.

9. The largest cheese ever produced took 43 hours to make, and it weighs a whopping 15 723 kilograms.

10. He watches television all evening until he finally went to sleep.

2

1. The goons in hockey kept ruining the sport for those who want to play it the way it is intended to be played.

2. Whenever he skipped his chemistry class, it seems old Mr. Bunsen was lurking in the halls to apprehend him.

3. If you will lend me $300, I double your money in Atlantic City.

4. First, the gorilla looks me over; then he turned his back and walks away.

5. Our friends in the country had a prize bull that costs a fortune.

6. Many people think that drowning persons rise three times before they sink, but this will not be true all the time; how many times they surface will depend only on how much they struggle.

7. Because Tim assaulted an officer, he would get a jail sentence.

8. Candy
   Is dandy
   But liquor
   Was quicker.[1]

9. The little boy looked so innocent while he sleeps.

10. While the Argonauts lost game after game, the loyal fans keep coming.

3

1. Murphy's Law states that everything which can go wrong will.

2. I tried to warn him about her evil ways, and what thanks do I get?

3. The embarrassed girl didn't say anything. She just blushes and runs from the room.

4. Before Roger noticed the snowstorm, he's already up and dressed.

5. They agreed to our living here after we pay them a substantial bribe.

6. In the interests of good community relations and to prevent them from blowing up our house, I vote that we will pay what they asked for.

7. Drusilla looks like a sweet young thing; when she spoke, however, the toughest truck drivers blush.

8. Lefty had wanted to have quit drinking many years earlier.

---

[1] *With apologies to Ogden Nash, "Reflections on Ice-Breaking."*

9. It is surprising to learn that the High Arctic is like a desert in terms of precipitation; much more snow fell in Northern Ontario than on Baffin Island.

10. We attempted to change Rudolf's mind all day, but we didn't know he's already voted.

4

1. Are you going to see *The Blob*? It was a great movie!

2. *Prince of Space* and *The Blob* are the best movies I had ever seen.

3. The film begins with a clever sequence in which a girl met a boy and his dog.

4. Little do we realize what kind of dreadful creature our young lovers will encounter, or that it terrifies the whole town!

5. The Blob originates in a test tube as a tiny bit of green ooze that then grew to enormous proportions.

6. The slimy, pulsating mass gathers both speed and size as it moved toward our young lovers necking in a pick-up truck.

7. They repel the fearsome Blob with the defrost button and realized the monster couldn't stand heat, so they rush off to save the town.

8. The Blob is devouring patrons at a local bowling alley, and its increasing girth indicated that it enjoyed every morsel. What gruesome sights did this movie have in store for us next?

9. Much to our relief, our hero arrives and built a huge bonfire out of five-pins; the Blob withered and shrank away before our very eyes. The town was saved!

10. Is it any wonder why this movie was my favourite? I only wish we can see it with 3-D glasses.

5

Correct the faulty tense shifts in the following paragraph. Use the italicized verb as your time marker.

Ken *tried* his best to understand the reasons for the constant unrest in Candeloro, but he finally comes to the conclusion that he doesn't have enough reliable information. The reports in the newspapers give him the impression that most of the problems were caused by external forces. In some papers, communist rebels supported by Cuba are blamed for the trouble; in other papers, the United States' support of the corrupt regime in power was being seen as the cause. Ken decides, after much consideration and discussion, to visit Candeloro and find out for himself what creates the tragic situation. His friends were trying to dissuade him from going to such a dangerous place, but the need to know is too strong in Ken. "It was more dangerous to stay here without knowing," he says, "than to go and find the truth."

6

Correct the faulty tense shifts in this passage.

Having done everything he had ever wanted to do by the time he is 23 years old, Jeffrey *tried* to find new goals in life. At age 7, he predicts to anyone who would listen that he would be a millionaire by the time he is old enough to vote. When he is 11, he predicts that he starred in a major motion picture by the time he could legally drive. At 14, he has prophesied that he would have been elected mayor before his 23rd birthday. Incredibly, his predictions came to pass, one after the other. At 16, he becomes the youngest person ever to play James Bond in a movie; this role leads to other pictures and a salary well into six figures. Careful investing makes him a millionaire within two years. With all that money behind him, there will be no stopping Jeffrey's campaign to have become, at 22, the youngest mayor

in Moose Factory's history. However, his amazing early successes are not repeated

and Jeffrey becomes a has-been by the time he turns 25.

7
Correct the faulty tense shifts in the following passage.

Once he has invested in a telescope and star map, the novice astronomer *is* ready

to begin exploring the wonders of the night sky. It will have been necessary first to

have found a place to set up the telescope where light did not interfere. For the best

viewing, one will need to find a spot well out in the countryside, away from street

lights and the diffuse light of the town. Adequate sightings are possible, however,

in large city parks or on college campuses. The most interesting heavenly bodies to

study will be the moon and the planets, of course. Seen through a telescope, the

moon revealed craters, mountains, and valleys invisible to the unaided eye. The

planets would usually be easy to find since, except for the moon, they would be the

brightest objects in the sky. A fairly small telescope would be able to reveal the

rings of Saturn and at least four of Jupiter's moons. Amateur astronomy will be an

educational and enjoyable pastime if one invests enough patience and study in it.

8
Test your mastery of verb-tense agreement by correcting the following sentences.
There are no answers provided for this exercise.

1. We knew that he would fail math; he keeps skipping class.

2. Eric was quite the outdoor lover; he comes from Flin Flon, you know.

3. Tim likes to watch the dryer spin at the laundromat; he spent many happy hours

   there.

4. The teacher continues to talk, heedless of the uproar that was occurring in the classroom.

5. First they'll appeal to our finer instincts; then they whine and beg.

6. When the umpire asked for respect, we give it to him.

7. Toxemia is a dangerous illness during pregnancy and will be difficult to treat.

8. It was not until the Constitution Act of 1981 that Canada becomes fully responsible for its own destiny.

9. The city of Kitchener, Ontario, was known as Berlin until World War II begins.

10. Jonathan Swift wrote a famous statement on corporal punishment: "Last week I saw a woman flayed, and you would hardly believe how much it alters her person for the worse." (from *A Tale of a Tub*)

chapter 13

Person Agreement

There are three categories of "person" that you can use when you write or speak:

> **first person**: I, we
> **second person**: you (singular and plural)
> **third person**: he, she, one, someone, they

Here is the rule for person agreement:

> Do not mix "persons" unless meaning requires it.

In other words, you must be consistent: if you begin a discussion in second person, you must use second person all the way through. Look at this sentence:

> If *you* wish to succeed, *one* must work hard.

This is the most common error — mixing second-person *you* with third-person *one*. Here's another example:

> *One* can live happily in Winnipeg if *you* have a very warm coat.

We can correct this error by using the second person throughout:

> *You* can live happily in Winnipeg if *you* have a very warm coat.

or by using the third person throughout:

> *One* can live happily in Winnipeg if *one* has a very warm coat.
>
> or
>
> *One* can live happily in Winnipeg if *he* has a very warm coat.

These last three sentences raise two points of style that you should be aware of:

1. Although these three versions are equally correct, they sound somewhat different from one another. The second sentence, with its two *one*'s, sounds the most formal — even a little stilted. Don't overuse *one*. The sentence in the second person sounds the most informal and natural — like something you would say. The third sentence is between the other two in formality and is the one you'd be most likely to use in writing for school or business.

2. As we noted in chapter 11, the pronoun *he* is generally used to represent both sexes. If this usage bothers you, you can substitute *he or she:*

A person can live happily in Winnipeg if he or she has a very warm coat.

But if *he or she* occurs too frequently the sentence becomes very awkward:

A student can easily pass this course if he or she applies himself or herself to his or her studies.

You can fix sentences like these by switching the *whole sentence* to the plural:

Students can easily pass this course if they apply themselves to their studies.

Exercises

I

Choose the correct word from the brackets for each of the following sentences. Check your answers on p. 275 before continuing.

1. One who learns only from experience will find that (you they he) may be learning the hard way.
2. If you want to make good egg rolls, I advise (them her you) to buy the ready-made wrappings.
3. If you win tonight's lottery, will (one he you) tell (one's his your) friends?
4. When one is sure of understanding course materials, (you they he) will be more confident in an exam.
5. Even young children can learn to swim if (one they she) have a good instructor and apply (oneself themselves herself).
6. Every person working in this office should know that (they she) helped finish an important project.
7. One can participate in fitness activities if (you they he) can pass a routine physical exam.
8. Regardless of which side of the bed Tim gets up on, (it he) is always grouchy in the morning.
9. When we toured the House of Commons, (you we he one) didn't see a single senator.
10. Some experts maintain that the later one begins to learn a second language the more difficulty (they you she) will encounter in (their your her) study.

Correct the following sentences where necessary. Check your answers to each set of ten before going on.

2

1. When one has completed all the sentences in one exercise, you should check your answers in the back of the book.

2. Everyone graduating this spring should order your cap and gown now.

3. You should always wear garlic around the neck if one fears vampires.

4. Any girl who does so won't have to worry about men bugging them, either.

5. In fact, everyone wearing a garlic necklace may find themselves suddenly alone.

6. Until she manages to find her money, I think I will avoid her.

7. If one attends enough Blue Jay games, you're bound to see a loss eventually.

8. We were so hungry when we got to Peterborough that even leftovers looked good.

9. If you don't come to class regularly, one runs the risk of failing the course.

10. One shouldn't always look for a scapegoat when you make a mistake.

3

1. After the unfortunate brawl, Tim learned that if a person stomps on policemen, they can expect to end up in jail.

2. Everyone can expect to experience the horrors of nuclear war unless they raise their voices against nuclear proliferation.

3. If one leaves garbage at one's campsite, you may well have bears as midnight callers.

4. I knew she wasn't the girl for me when she asked me if Wayne Gretzky were the leader of Solidarity.

5. One will always think about the opportunities he's missed, even if you're happy with what you have.

6. Canadians who worry about street violence should keep in mind that in comparison to New York, you are safe in downtown Toronto after dark.

7. You know that a young kangaroo is called a joey, but does one realize that a baby eel is called an elver?

8. When one is travelling in a foreign country, he will usually look for somebody who can speak his language.

9. Can one really know another person if you have never been to their home?

10. A sure way to lose one's friends is to eat all the Baskin-Robbins ice cream yourself.

4

Correct the errors in person agreement in the following passage. Use the second-person pronoun (you) wherever possible.

Anyone can enjoy classical music if you are willing to give it a chance and really listen. If we listen closely, you will find relaxation and enjoyment quite different from that which one might experience when listening to "pop," rock, country and western, or any of the other varieties of music. Of course, not all classical music appeals to everyone, but then, everyone doesn't find all rock music to your taste, either. Nevertheless, there are some classical selections we are sure to enjoy. Go to the public library and borrow one or two of the following records and put them on your turntable. If one then relaxes, puts one's feet up and really listens, you will be guaranteed an enjoyable experience. For your introduction to classical music, one might try Beethoven's Sixth Symphony *(Pastoral)*, Grieg's *Peer Gynt Suite*, and Tchaikovsky's *Romeo and Juliet*. These pieces appeal to almost everyone and are ideal selections with which to begin our exploration of a new musical world.

5

This exercise will test and reinforce your understanding of both tense and person agreement. Correct the following sentences where necessary.

1. If you're ready to learn how to operate a motorcycle, one should involve oneself in lessons, especially if you were interested in safety.

2. We often go to wrestling matches at the Gardens, and you're always sure of having a stimulating evening as one watches the Sheik make mincemeat of the Masked Marvel.

3. I don't know whether I can complete the program on time because it always seems either you had to wait for a terminal or the machines were down.

4. Until last week Marcia had us all believing her unlikely story; then we realize that she was lying.

5. You know that Cindy Nicholas holds the record for completing a double crossing of the English Channel, but were you aware that she has swum it a total of six times?

6. You know Orville was a troublemaker when you see his sneaky little face.

7. When one considered the issue carefully, you think better of the more expensive proposal. After all, quality workmanship was what we're looking for.

8. When summer arrives, our patio is where you will find one, relaxing and enjoying our leisure hours.

9. Many women think that the only way you can succeed in the business world is by wearing conservative three-piece suits similar to those men wore.

10. Actually, while you should dress appropriately, one needn't spend undue amounts of time and money trying to ape "the executive look." Competence and ability always had more impact than appearance.

6

Choose the right word from those in brackets, keeping the person and number of the pronouns in agreement with the italicized word in the first sentence.

When *people* see dreadful occurrences like wars, earthquakes, or mass starvation on television, it does not always affect (you one them). It is one thing for people to see the ravages of war (yourself oneself themselves) and another thing to see a three-minute newsclip of the same battle, neatly edited by the CBC. Even the horrible effects of natural catastrophes that wipe out whole populations are some-how minimized or trivialized when (we people you) see them on TV. And while people may be shocked and horrified by the gaunt faces of starving children on the screen, (you one they) can easily escape into (our your their) familiar world of Egg McMuffins, Shake 'n Bake, and Sara Lee Cheesecakes that is portrayed in commer-cial messages.

Thus, the impact of television on *us* is a mixed one. It is true that (you we they) are shown events, tragic and otherwise, which (you we they) could not possibly have seen before television. In this way (our their your) world is drawn together more closely. However, the risk in creating this immediacy, and perhaps the most tragic consequence of all, is that (we people you) may become desensitized and cease to feel or care about (your our their) fellow human beings.

7

Rewrite the paragraphs above, only this time match your nouns or pronouns to the italicized words below.

1. When *you* see dreadful occurrences like wars, earthquakes, or mass

   starvation...

2. Thus, the impact of television on *people* is a mixed one.

8

As a final check of your mastery of person agreement, correct the following sentences. There are no answers provided for this exercise.

1. When we finally reached the crest of the hill, you could see for miles.

2. Because one's parents think that a daughter should get married and have

   children, I think so, too.

3. One is not likely to part with one's most treasured possession, even if you are

   offered more money than it's worth.

4. You will find the reason for Torontonians' love affair with "cottage country" if one stays in the hot, muggy city for a summer.

5. A man who expects his wife to do all the cooking and cleaning should have their head examined.

6. Anyone who goes to Honest Ed's for the "Door Crasher Specials" is going to get what they came for.

7. Rudolf often claims he can't feel safe knowing that aliens from space could snatch you any time and whisk you off to another planet.

8. A good way to develop one's writing ability is to make yourself keep a journal.

9. Everyone who wants to see Karen Kain dance can get your tickets at the O'Keefe Centre.

10. When you're dieting, one must avoid Bagel World.

9

Think of an important personal experience you've had. (If you don't like important, try embarrassing or frightening.) Write an account of this experience, telling your story in the third person (that is, instead of using *I*, use *he* or *she*). When you've completed your work, reread it carefully. Check your spelling. Check your sentence structure. Check carefully subject-verb, pronoun-antecedent, tense, and person agreement.

unit

punctuation

chapter 14

Question and Exclamation Marks

Everyone knows that a question mark follows an interrogative, or asking, sentence, but we all sometimes forget that it does. Let this chapter simply serve as a reminder not to forget!

> The question mark is the end punctuation for all interrogative sentences.

The question mark gives the reader an important clue to the meaning of your sentence.

There's more?

is vastly different in meaning from

There's more!

and that difference is communicated to the reader by the punctuation alone.

The only time you don't end a question with a question mark is when the question is part of a statement.

Are you going?   (question)
I asked whether you are going.   (statement)
Do you know them?   (question)
I wonder whether you know them.   (statement)

Exercises

I

Put a check next to the sentences that have correct end punctuation. Turn to p. 277 to check your answers before going on.

1. _____ When will my ship come in.
2. _____ I am always asking when my ship will come in.
3. _____ Do you think you'll pass the exam?
4. _____ Everyone wants to know whether he or she has learned enough to pass the exam?

5. _____ Can you teach an old dog new tricks.
6. _____ You often stop in at this video arcade, don't you.
7. _____ If your Pacman scores are so good, why can't you beat me at Space Invaders?
8. _____ There are many questions as to whether the woman is guilty of murder?
9. _____ This is the first nice day we've had in a long time, isn't it?
10. _____ How can you just stand there when a man is being beaten in the subway.

2

Put a check next to the sentences that have correct end punctuation. Turn to p. 277 to check your answers before going on.

1. _____ Who's afraid of Virginia Woolf?
2. _____ No, I asked whether you were afraid of the Big Bad Wolf?
3. _____ Haven't you eaten enough of these egg rolls for one day.
4. _____ I wonder whether you understand the seriousness of the plagiarism offense.
5. _____ The other kids can stay out all night, so why can't we.
6. _____ If ever we needed a strong leader in Parliament, it's now?
7. _____ How in the world did you get that ship into the bottle?
8. _____ Rudolf wondered whether he would ever be free of the extra-terrestrial creatures who plagued him?
9. _____ Both of those young men are handsome, kind, and intelligent, so how could I possibly choose between them.
10. _____ If you had seen what happened before the opening performance, you would have questioned our ability to stage the show?

3

Supply the correct end punctuation for these sentences. Then check your answers.

1. Did you ever think that the Canadian dollar would drop below the U.S. seventy-cents mark
2. Our trip to the States this summer is going to be very expensive, isn't it
3. The Blue Jays will never be a pennant contender unless they get some good relief pitchers
4. If you let me show you how to hold the club properly, your putting will improve
5. Little Lamb, who made thee
   Dost thou know who made thee
      (William Blake)
6. If we can't finish the project on time, I wonder if we will lose the contract
7. Finish your quiche, children, or you won't get any dessert
8. It's difficult to meet eligible bachelors in their 80s, isn't it

9. I don't know whether you've ever thought about it, but we have no answer to the question as to whether we could live happily in Frobisher Bay
10. Did you know that Harpo Marx was just as capable of talking as his brothers Groucho, Chico, Gummo, and Zeppo

---

The Exclamation Mark

The exclamation mark can be a most valuable piece of punctuation for conveying your tone of voice to the reader. There is a distinct difference in tone between these two sentences:

> There's a man behind you.

> There's a man behind you!

In the first case, a piece of information is being supplied, possibly about the line-up at a grocery-store check-out counter. The second sentence might be a shouted warning about a mugger in the back seat of a car.

> Use an exclamation mark as end punctuation in sentences requiring extreme emphasis or dramatic effect.

The only way that the exclamation mark can have any punch or drama is if you use it sparingly. If you use an exclamation mark after every third sentence, how will your reader know when you really mean to indicate excitement? The overuse of the exclamation mark is a result of too much comic-book reading. The writers of comics use the exclamation mark after every sentence to try to heighten the impact of their characters' words. Instead, they've robbed their exclamation marks of all meaning.

Practically any sentence may have an exclamation mark after it, but remember that the punctuation changes the meaning of the sentence. Read the following sentences with and without an exclamation mark, and picture the situation that would call for each reading.

He's gone	Don't touch that button
The room was empty	There she goes again

Exercises

4

Supply the correct end punctuation for these sentences. In many cases, the punctuation you use will depend on how you want the sentence to be read. Notice the extent to which different punctuation can change the meaning of a sentence.

1. There's a vampire in my attic

2. Perhaps it's merely a bat in your belfry
3. Come here and say that
4. I can't believe how badly the Maple Leafs play hockey
5. Oh no   You've done it again
6. Why do you always run over the cord with the lawn mower
7. Congratulations   You've finally graduated
8. When E.F. Hutton talks, people listen
9. Rudolf wasn't kidding when he said his backyard had been invaded by aliens
10. Look at all those tiny, two-headed creatures

5

Provide each of these sentences with appropriate punctuation — an exclamation mark, question mark, or period.

1. Help   There's no way I can pay this bill
2. Workers of the world, unite   (Karl Marx)
3. Can that guy ever run
4. Watch out   The pie is falling
5. Do you want to come out with your hands up or get carried out
6. Come and get me, copper
7. Oh no   We're late for the last ferry to the mainland
8. Don't touch that dial
9. How Desmond manages to get by on $28.50 a week, I can't imagine
10. Abandon all hope, you who enter here   (Dante's inscription at the entrance to Hell)

6

Add the correct punctuation to these sentences. Choose a period, a question mark, or an exclamation mark.

1. We aren't sure if we're getting paid this week or not
2. Reginald wanted his broker to tell him whether pork bellies would be a good investment
3. Where in the world are you going with your hair dyed green and that safety pin in your nose
4. Arthur asked Catherine where she was going
5. Would you believe that the heaviest world champion boxer, Primo Carnera, weighed in at 123 kg in a 1933 fight
6. That's one king-size heavyweight
7. Do you mean to tell me that your lovely necklace is made of shellacked moose droppings
8. You must be kidding
9. Dr and Mr Widget arrived at the reception in their new Rolls Royce
10. Hooray   This exercise is finished

7

Correct the punctuation in the following sentences.

1. The question was whether we would spend the night in Cornwall or push on for Montreal?
2. "Help," he screamed "The piranha has my finger"
3. Just think!! We have two glorious weeks free of English class!!!
4. Tim thought he looked lovely(?) in his new sharkskin suit!
5. If you think you're confused, just imagine how I must feel?
6. If I ever hear him tell that joke again, I'll box his ears!
7. Catherine asked Arthur if he would like to stay over?
8. Her Ph D didn't seem to impress her co-workers at the doughnut shop
9. Despite the fact that he was busy with his weightlifting, jogging, swimming, tumbling, etc., Jacques always had time for a little drinking?
10. We studied the poems of Irving Layton, who was born in Romania, I think(?)

8

Supply the punctuation in this passage.

Gordon and I have often questioned the meaning of life as it relates to fishing are there fish why are there fish what do fish think about why do people try to catch fish our last fishing expedition was no less successful than most but it got us thinking about these great philosophical questions more intensely than usual with my brand-new and very expensive fishing gear I caught a clam Gordon was only slightly more successful, catching three small bass he later confessed however, that he had sat for an hour with one of those fish on his line because he was embarrassed to be catching fish with his bamboo pole while I thrashed about unsuccessfully with my high-tech rod and reel there is no justice

The cry of "Fish on" fills me with loathing for the successful fisherman "Why him" I cry "What an idiot look at the lure he was using no one can catch a fish at this time of year using one of those" But the fact remains the fish has selected his offering and not mine by my calculations the few fish that have managed to impale themselves on my hooks have made it to the table at an average cost of some $137.67

per kilo I'd be better off dining on lobster every night what a ridiculous sport

---

9

Here is a toughie: a passage from *Macbeth*. Try to supply the end punctuation and then compare your version with the original as provided in the answer section.

Lady Macbeth (sleepwalking); Out, damned spot — Out — I say — One: two: why, then 'tis time to do 't — Hell is murky — Fie, my lord, fie — A soldier and afeard — What need we fear who knows it, when none can call our pow'r to account — Yet who would have thought the old man to have had so much blood in him —
Doctor: Do you mark that —
Lady Macbeth: The thane of Fife had a wife; where is she now — What, will these hands ne'er be clean —

10

Supply correct end punctuation for these sentences. There are no answers for this exercise.

1. She would like to take part in the preparations, but can she cook as well as her father
2. Who's been sleeping in my bed
3. Imagine our surprise when Mortimer appeared outside the window of our fourteenth-floor apartment
4. The students question whether this exam is fair
5. There has to be a better way, doesn't there
6. Are the Argos likely to win the Grey Cup   Absolutely not
7. The angry parents descended on the board of education with cries of "Save Our School "
8. After seeing your test results, I wonder if you read the textbook at all
9. When will you be finished with that job so that we can begin our vacation
10. Congratulations   You've just mastered end punctuation marks

chapter 15

Quotation Marks

Quotation marks (" ") are used to set off direct speech (dialogue), quoted material, and some titles. Quotation marks come in pairs; there has to be a set to show where the dialogue or quotation begins and a set to show where it ends. You must be absolutely sure that whatever you put between them is *exactly* the way it is stated in the source you are using. The only other thing you need to know about quotation marks is how to punctuate what comes between them.

Dialogue

When you quote direct speech, include normal sentence punctuation. If the speaker's name is also included in your own sentence, set it off with commas. The comma or the end punctuation mark comes *inside* the final set of quotation marks.

"Did you," Tim asked in a rage, "drink all of my Brador?"

"No, there are a couple of swigs left," I said.

Be careful that you put quotation marks only around direct speech (someone's exact words). Don't use quotation marks with indirect speech:

Tim, in a rage, asked me if I had drunk all his Brador. (These are not Tim's exact words, nor is the sentence a question.)

Quoted Material

When you quote a *short* written passage (three lines of print or less), you can work it into your own sentence. Again, include normal sentence punctuation within the quotation marks.

"Marriage," wrote Dr. Johnson, "has many pains, but celibacy has no pleasures."

"The medium is the message," Marshall McLuhan points out in his book *Understanding Media.*

If your own introductory words form a complete sentence, use a colon:

Dr. Johnson made an interesting statement on wedded life: "Marriage has many pains, but celibacy has no pleasures."

Marshall McLuhan captured the imagination of a generation brought up on television: "The medium is the message."

A *long* written passage (more than three lines of print) should be indented from both margins on your page so that the quotation stands apart from your own text. An indented quotation is not enclosed in quotation marks.

Titles

Titles of whole books or volumes are *underlined*; titles of parts of those books or volumes are placed in quotation marks. Thus, books, names of magazines, pamphlets, newspapers, plays, and films are underlined. Titles of single articles, essays, stories, or poems should be placed in quotation marks.

"The Bear on the Delhi Road," by Earle Birney, in <u>Fifteen Canadian Poets</u>

"I Am Jane's Pancreas," in <u>Reader's Digest</u>

Exercises

I

Place the quotation marks correctly and insert the necessary punctuation in these sentences. The answers for this chapter begin on p. 279.

1. Pardon me, boys, is this the Transylvania Station? asked the man in the black cape.
2. Every day Rudolf asked the same question When do you think E.T. will arrive?
3. The child asked when his mother would return.
4. This film exclaimed Granny is more explicit than *National Geographic*!
5. As the *Globe and Mail* put it The Canadian dollar went on a roller coaster ride yesterday.
6. It was the philosopher Ludwig Feuerbach who first said Man is what he eats, and we here at Big Boy restaurants certainly agree with that.
7. Roger claimed that he was deathly afraid of airplanes.
8. Your every whim will be catered to stated the Sybaritic Spas brochure.
9. I wondered whether they would peel grapes for me and find slaves to perform lomi-lomi on my aching muscles.
10. If not I asked my friend why should we spend $800 for a weekend in Collingwood?

2

Insert quotation marks and appropriate punctuation where necessary in these sentences.

1. Oswaldo has flown the coop again they told her.

2. They told her that Oswaldo had flown the coop again.
3. Unless you pay us by Friday the letter threatened you'd better start wearing knee pads.
4. Each of the students made the same comment about the instructor He'd be a good teacher if he'd show up for class once in a while.
5. Is it Daffy Duck or Porky Pig who says Tha-tha-that's all, folks at the end of the cartoon?
6. Merriweather said she thought it was Tweetie Bird.
7. Anyone with any brains at all sniffed Bugs knows it's Foghorn Leghorn.
8. At the gates of the Sunny Buff Nudist Colony, we were greeted by a huge sign that read Have a Good Time . . . Or Else!
9. We asked each other whether this was a welcome or a threat.
10. Griselda persuaded us to proceed Well, we've been looking for the perfect tan she said Let's try it.

3

Place the quotation marks and punctuation correctly in these sentences. Be sure to check your answers in the back before going on to the next exercise.

1. The *Guinness Book of World Records* claims that the oldest living thing is the California bristlecone pine tree which is almost 5,000 years old.
2. Did you see the strange look on his face asked Roderick.
3. Frank asked Rita if she would like to play bridge.
4. Of course she answered, usually willing to oblige.
5. Have you read my new essay, Dreaming Your Way to an Energized Future Dr. Piffle asked his numbed audience. It's in my next book entitled Upscale Networking in a Self-Actualized Cosmos.
6. The fellow to my left hissed I'd sooner be horsewhipped; where do they find these guys?
7. I forget whether it was John Paul Jones or George Chuvalo who said I have not yet begun to fight.
8. The vice-president had bad news for the staff Due to lack of funds and excessive vandalism at the parking gates, you're all terminated.
9. The book claims that someday we will get injections of our own white blood cells taken during our youth; these injections will ward off infections and aging.
10. Wow I said that's amazing!

4

Insert the necessary quotation marks and punctuation into this passage of dialogue.[1]

Kezia stood on the bench and pulled down three bearskins, marred with bulletholes. A rank and musty smell arose in the cold. She considered the find gravely.

[1]*From "The Wedding Gift," by Thomas Raddall. Reprinted by permission of the Canadian Publisher, McClelland and Stewart Limited, Toronto.*

You take them Mr. Mears said gallantly. I shall be quite all right.

You'll be dead by morning, and so shall I she answered vigorously if you don't do what I say. We've got to roll up in these.

Together? he cried in horror.

Of course! To keep each other warm. It's the only way.

She spread the skins on the floor, hair uppermost, one overlapping another, and dragged the flustered young man down beside her, clutched him in her arms, and rolled with him, over, and over again, so that they became a single shapeless heap in the corner farthest from the draft between door and chimney.

Put your arms around me commanded the new Kezia, and he obeyed.

Now she said you can pray. God helps those that help themselves.

5

Now test your understanding of quotation marks and the punctuation that goes with them. There aren't any answers provided for this exercise.

1. Look out he shouted. There's a dump truck behind you!
2. Cinderella had a few choice words for her fairy godmother How am I supposed to walk on glass slippers anyway?
3. Would you rather the fairy asked go to the ball in Adidas sneakers?
4. Many of the fans said they'd pay top dollar to see Wayne Gretzky.
5. Joseph Conrad makes a chilling comparison in his novel *The Secret Agent* The terrorist and the policeman are startlingly similar in character.
6. Pierre Trudeau once told Canadians that the state had no business in the nation's bedrooms.
7. Tim said That's sure a relief; I wouldn't want him to see what I've got growing on my windowsill.
8. You'll be glad to hear that we are planning to bring the whole family down from Moosonee for a month wrote Uncle Morty.
9. Good grief! said my wife. The last time they did that Aunt Madeline had to be bailed out of the Don Jail, and I ended up in a rest home she added nervously.
10. The teacher said that she was pleased we all understood the mysteries of quotation marks so thoroughly.

chapter 16

The Colon

The colon functions as an "introducer." When a statement is followed by a list or by one or more examples, the colon between the statement and what follows alerts the reader to what is coming.

We have only two choices: for and against.

There are three things I can't stand: brussels sprouts, cats, and Robert Redford's films.

One person prevented her rise to wealth and fame: herself.

The statement that precedes the colon must be a complete sentence (independent clause). Therefore, a colon can never come after *is* or *are*. For example, the use of the colon in the sentence

Two things I cannot stand are: cats and brussels sprouts.

is incorrect because the statement before the colon is not a complete sentence.

The colon, then, follows a complete statement and introduces a list or example that defines or amplifies something in the statement. The information after the colon very often answers the question "what?" or "who?"

There is a new danger to consider: (what?) inflation.

He peered into the clear water to see his favourite friend: (who?) himself.

The colon is also used after a complete sentence introducing a quotation.

Irving Layton is not fond of academic critics: "There hasn't been a writer of power and originality during the past century who hasn't had to fight his way to acceptance agains the educated pipsqueaks hibernating in universities." (Layton, in a letter to the *Montreal Star*)

The uses of the colon can be summed up as follows:

> The colon follows an independent clause and introduces one of three things: examples, a list, or a quotation.

Exercises

I

Put a check next to the sentences that are correctly punctuated. Check your answers on p. 280 before going on.

1. _____ The three people having trouble with their nursing techniques course are: Tanya, Eddy, and Rufus.
2. _____ There are three people having trouble with their nursing techniques course, Tanya, Eddy, and Rufus.
3. _____ We lacked only one thing: money.
4. _____ The only thing we lacked was: money.
5. _____ Our friends are certain to remain loyal if we treat them with: courtesy, kindness, and honesty.
6. _____ There are three characteristics of a good paragraph: unity, coherence, and clarity.
7. _____ Two places I wouldn't want to visit are: Tuscaloosa and Saskatoon.
8. _____ I'll give you an example: Brian Peckford.
9. _____ I often attend the film festival: but this year I'm broke.
10. _____ Two very good CFL quarterbacks were Russ Jackson and Ron Lancaster.

2

Put a check next to the sentences that are correctly punctuated. Check your answers before going on to exercise 3.

1. _____ Four of my favourite TV characters are: Fred, Wilma, Barney, and Betty.
2. _____ Whom do you trust: no one at all.
3. _____ There is one subject that will arouse heated debate: capital punishment.
4. _____ Everyone wants to hire her for her: looks and brains.
5. _____ It's too bad she's only interested in one thing: power.
6. _____ We're having some visitors this weekend: Barb, Bob, David, and Aaron.
7. _____ The economy was battered by: crushing interest rates, sagging production, and continued inflation.
8. _____ Tim picked up a new skill in Kingston Penitentiary; terrorizing weaker inmates.
9. _____ The warden presented him with an ultimatum: "Smarten up or it's solitary for you!"
10. _____ Roderick's needs in life were: sex, drugs, and rock 'n roll.

3

Insert colons in the following sentences where necessary, and then check your answers. If you find you've made any mistakes, review the explanation, and be sure you understand why your answers were wrong.

1. We'll finish the repairs by tomorrow only if we work all night or call a plumber.

2. Unless you work consistently throughout the term and prepare thoroughly for your final exam, you will achieve only one result failure.
3. There are several troublesome implications of biological engineering, but one in particular is frightening to most people, the cloning of human beings.
4. Their credit consultant asked them an important question after their bankruptcy "Why don't you cut up your credit cards?"
5. Only one thing prevents me from pulverizing you the Masked Marvel, who is standing behind you.
6. Canada has attained international literary acclaim with novelists of the stature of Richler, Atwood, and Laurence.
7. The bulk of Canada's population is worn out and exhausted at the end of a long, hard winter, but most people console themselves with one thought, spring will arrive sometime in May or June.
8. There are a number of activities that will improve physical fitness; swimming, tennis, jogging, even brisk walking.
9. Melanie is trying very hard to accomplish two things a significant weight loss and success as a restaurant critic.
10. Several of the animals on the endangered species list are native to Canada the wood bison, the Northern kit fox, and the whooping crane.

4

Correct the incorrectly punctuated sentences in exercise 1.

5

Correct the incorrectly punctuated sentences in exercise 2.

6

As a test of your knowledge of colons, put a check before the sentences that are correctly punctuated. There are no answers given for this exercise.

1. _____ Several people missed yesterday's exciting meeting: Carol, Jack, George, and Bonita.
2. _____ There are several families that are considerably richer than the Rockefellers, the du Ponts, the Mellons, and the Gettys.
3. _____ Three qualities of a good computer programmer are: intelligence, accuracy, and patience.
4. _____ The TV is always asking me challenging questions "It's 11:05. Do you know where your children are?"
5. _____ He won a prize in spite of his ineptitude the slow-but-steady-progress award.
6. _____ He wants to talk to you: but he won't.
7. _____ You have all the qualities of a dog except one: loyalty.
8. _____ Three things that always make me mad are: "The Gong Show," Glen Campbell, and beer commercials.

9. _____ In the paper are two career opportunities that Dudley may find intriguing undertaking and sky-diving.
10. _____ The desert is: hot in the day and cool at night.

7

Now correct the incorrectly punctuated sentences in exercise 6.

---

chapter 17

The Comma

The comma is the most frequently used and the most frequently misused punctuation mark. The omission of a necessary comma can distort the meaning of a sentence. Unnecessary commas ("comma-itis") can distract the reader and give the sentence a jerky quality. Perhaps nothing is so sure a sign of a competent writer as the correct use of commas, so it is very important that you master them. This chapter presents four rules that will give you a good indication of when you should use a comma. If the sentence you are writing is not covered by one of the four rules remember this:

> When in doubt, leave the comma out!

Four Comma Rules

In this section we will present the four most helpful rules for using the comma. Here's the first rule:

> Use commas to separate items in a series of three or more.

Required subjects are math, English, bookkeeping, and business law.
Walk up the hill, turn left, go two blocks, and you'll be there.
Henry went to the show, Joan went home in tears, Norah and Phil talked until dawn, and I went upstairs to bed.

The comma before the *and* at the end of the list is optional; use it or leave it out, but be consistent.

Exercise

Insert commas where necessary in the following sentences. Check your answers on p. 282.

1. Be sure to pick up gin tonic limes and ice.
2. Women and children are traditionally the first people into the lifeboats.
3. Labatt's Molson's and O'Keefe are major breweries and patrons of sport and culture.
4. I am going to hire a cleaning man to clean floors dust furniture scour the oven and wash clothes.
5. We're tired of watching pretty faces belonging to people who can't act: Burt Reynolds Tom Selleck Warren Beatty and Woody Allen.
6. Americans and Canadians share a continent and a similar cultural heritage.
7. We are going to see *The Tempest Julius Caesar* or *The Merry Wives of Windsor* this weekend.
8. How can anyone choose between John Turner and Brian Mulroney?
9. Tim stomped into the room threw himself into a chair drained a six-pack of Budweiser and crushed the cans against his forehead.
10. Three things that can hinder your relaxation at a cottage are rainy weather black flies and unwanted guests.

Here is the second rule:

> Use comma(s) to separate from the rest of the sentence any word or expression that is not *essential* to the sentence's meaning or that means the same as something else in the sentence.

Writing business letters isn't difficult, if you're careful.

The phrase "if you're careful" is not essential to the meaning of the sentence, so it's separated from the rest of the sentence by a comma.

Stephen Leacock, one of the world's great humorists, was a professor of economics at McGill.

The phrase "one of the world's great humorists" means the same as "Stephen Leacock." The two expressions refer to the same person, so the second is set off by commas. When a nonessential word or phrase occurs in the middle of a sentence, rather than at the beginning or the end, be sure to put commas *both* before and after it.

If it were up to me, Judy, I'd hire you right now.

The word "Judy," the name of the person spoken to, is unnecessary to the meaning of the sentence, so it's set off by commas.

Exercise

2

Insert commas where necessary in the following sentences. Check your answers before going on.

1. What's it all about Alfie?
2. The cheetah is of course the fastest animal on earth.
3. Everyone who sees the movie will be shocked.
4. Malcolm Lowry an alcoholic British expatriate wrote *Under the Volcano* perhaps the finest novel ever written in Canada.
5. When everyone joins in cleaning up isn't difficult it seems.
6. Do you know class what is the largest city in Canada in terms of area?
7. It is believe it or not Whitehorse with 162 square miles.
8. Many children in this school it seems are coming in the morning without having had an adequate breakfast.
9. Phil Esposito who played for the Boston Bruins scored 100 points or more in six different seasons.
10. The lead singer in a bid for notoriety bit the head off a bat during the performance.

The third rule is as follows:

> Place a comma between independent clauses when they are joined by these transition words:
>
> | and | nor | for |
> |-----|-----|-----|
> | or | but | yet |
> | so | | |

It was a good party, but last year's was better.
I'm not speaking to her, so you'll have to tell her.
I can't make it to class, yet I feel I should go.
Ross is a good student, for he studies hard.

Be sure that the sentence contains two independent clauses rather than a single subject and a multiple verb (see p. 43 for a further explanation of this).

We ate very well in Paris and gained 3 kilograms each. (Here We is the subject, and there are two verbs: ate and gained. No comma is needed between two verbs with a single subject.)

We ate very well in Paris, and each of us gained 3 kilograms. (This sentence has two independent clauses — we ate and each gained — joined by an *and*. The comma is required here.)

Exercise

3

Insert commas where necessary in the following sentences. Then check your answers.

1. I refuse to wear that turkey costume to the party nor will I go as a horse's rear end.
2. Yesterday he broke up with her but today he is begging for forgiveness.
3. The whole class knows what the teacher is up to so we are going to surprise him by studying for the final exam.
4. We loved the book but hated the movie.
5. The boss told him to stop leering at the ladies or she would fire him.
6. Felix searched and searched for the perfect accessories for he has sophisticated taste.
7. The day was clear and warm so we spent the afternoon on our sailboat.
8. Susan and Sarah have left for Prince Albert and David is going to Rainy River.
9. Waving a red flag in front of a bull is supposed to enrage it yet experiments have shown that bulls are colour blind.
10. She bit into the taco and burst into tears for the jalapeña peppers were far too hot for her gringo taste buds.

Finally, here is the fourth comma rule:

> Put a comma after any word or group of words that comes before an independent clause.

Charley, you aren't paying attention. (The second rule applies here, too.)
Though tattered and torn, the book was worth a fortune.
Wherever you go, remember me.
If that's all there is, we'd better buy more.
Until he got his promotion, he was quite friendly.

Exercise

Write out the four comma rules on a sheet of paper. Then do the exercise.

4

Insert commas where necessary in the following sentences. Check your answers when you're done.

1. Esmeralda please leave those plants on the table.
2. Third insert your finger into the electrical socket.
3. Overwhelmed by the generous offer we spent the evening watching Paul's home movies.

4. On her way into the Governor General's awards ceremony Ruth was stopped by security guards.
5. By the way young man your account is overdue.
6. With the water running the plumber will be unable to repair the faucet.
7. For your convenience deposit your clothes with the attendant.
8. If you work for an airline company policy states you are entitled to one free trip a year.
9. In addition your next of kin is entitled to reduced fares.
10. Unless you learn to use commas properly your writing will lack sophistication and polish.

One final note about the comma, before you try your hand at the review exercises: never place a *single* comma between a subject and its verb:

> right: Adam and Liz are going into business.
> never: Adam and Liz, are going into business.

Two commas between a subject and its verb are all right, however, *if* they are setting off nonessential material:

> Adam and Liz, both recent graduates, are going into business.

Exercises

Insert commas where necessary in the following exercises. Check your answers to each set of ten and make sure you understand any mistakes before you go on to the next exercise.

5

1. Caffeine which is present in coffee tea and cola stimulates the heart and raises blood pressure.
2. If a thing is worth doing it is worth doing badly. (G.K. Chesterton)
3. The agency interviewed tested investigated and rejected thirty applicants.
4. That man is in my opinion guilty and should be convicted of murder.
5. Roger checked his parachute carefully before take off but he forgot to pull his rip cord after he jumped out of the plane.
6. Fortunately he landed in a tree and later that afternoon was found dangling helplessly.
7. Unfortunately he had some very nasty contusions and developed an entirely justifiable fear of flying.
8. However you choose to write your resignation is up to you.
9. Having left my wallet at home I am unable to buy lunch.
10. Having no money is embarrassing.

6

1. We are pleased with your résumé and we are offering you an interview this week.
2. We are pleased with your résumé and are offering you an interview this week.
3. As a receptionist your duties are to greet clients type reports file correspondence and answer the phone.
4. The Maple Leafs acknowledging inferiority and lack of determination gave up on or about December 1.
5. Computing the interest is his job but collecting the debts is hers.
6. Marijuana has been called a killer drug by some people and a healthy tension reliever by others.
7. Oswald would have nothing more to do with his wife or her mother or her lawyers.
8. I have striven not to laugh at human actions nor to weep at them nor to hate them but to understand them. (Baruch Spinoza)
9. Although Tim begged his girlfriend refused to wear a tattooed heart with his name in the middle.
10. Whomever you name as your guest will be invited to the opening performance.

7

1. Fascinating challenging high-paying jobs are available to the people who transfer to our exciting Beirut branch office.
2. Oswald your lawyers agreed to work with you not against you didn't they?
3. Our guard dog a Doberman pinscher caught an intruder and maimed him for life.
4. Unfortunately my Uncle Ladislaw was the intruder and he intends to sue us for every penny we have.
5. The year 1945 marked the end of World War II and the beginning of assistance to war-torn nations.
6. All warm-blooded animals that give live birth and suckle their young are classified as mammals but no one knows how to classify the warm-blooded egg-laying chick-nursing platypus.
7. It is as absurd to argue men as it is to torture them into believing. (Cardinal Newman)
8. The top executives and board members have large oak desks with swivel chairs.
9. While he was eating his dog stood beside him.
10. Igor asked "May I show you to your quarters or would you prefer to spend the night in the dungeon?"

8

For the past ten years oil-consuming nations have been struggling with the ''energy crisis'' or more specifically the ''oil crisis.'' Everyone is familiar with the problems the crisis has created: ever-increasing prices higher taxes and political conflict to name only a few. Many solutions ranging from the practical to the fantastic have been proposed. Almost every magazine or newspaper we read contains at least one article on the exciting possibilities of solar power tidal power biomass or wind power. Despite the optimism of the writers however most readers do not find such articles very reassuring. All the solutions proposed are realizable in the future; the problem confronts us here now today.

What is needed immediately is not new sources of electric power: we have time to develop those. What is needed immediately is a new source of fuel. The ideal fuel would be first one that could be manufactured from an inexhaustible Canadian resource. Second the ideal fuel would be one that could be used to power existing cars trucks buses planes and other transit vehicles without major mechanical alterations. Third the ideal fuel must be safe powerful and nonpolluting. One possible fuel that meets these requirements is hydrogen the most abundant element in the universe. According to Roger Billings who is the leading expert on hydrogen-powered automobiles almost any internal-combustion engine that runs on gasoline can be converted to run on hydrogen.

9

''The world is changing'' my friends in data processing courses told me. They maintained that I a harmless English teacher would be unable to cope without the skills necessary to run a microcomputer. They assured me that ominous blinking machines with deceptively cute names like Amiga and Apple would relieve me of the repetitive tasks of teaching commas colons semicolons and spelling to reluctant students. I would be free my friends maintained to teach the things that really mattered. In the cybernetic world of the future people would come up with the ideas and the machines would handle the mechanics. By looking at other enthusiastic descriptions of the microcomputer revolution I learned that silicon chips would in the near future do my cooking balance my chequebook and go shopping for me yet could they ever I wondered dreamily be programmed to change the cat litter?

Nevertheless commas colons cooking and chequebooks were enough for me and so despite my lifelong distrust of blinking machines I enrolled in a course called "Your Friendly Computer." I must admit the little demon seemed friendly quickly establishing itself on a first name basis with me but the bewildering array of disks data bases inputs outputs bugs bytes backups and buffers soon left me in a microdaze. My friendly computer attempting to beguile me with fun and games allowed me to pick off Pacmans blast Rasters and incinerate Invaders; dots gobblers and rocket ships appeared on my screen with annoying rapidity. Ever cheerful the affable machine consoled me for my pitiful scores: "Nice try" it blinked but my hand-eye co-ordination was obviously unequal to the demands of video games. Feeling somewhat more comfortable in the slower world of punctuation I tried a program on commas and semicolons. Now I thought happily I'm really hands-on online and programmed. Alas my machine friendly no more flashed "BDOS ERROR. REBOOT." It had found me out detecting my fear and loathing of all things electronic. Defeated I left the glowering machine behind me and went home to change the cat litter.

10

I sometimes wonder what our ancestors, were they able to observe us now would think of some of the activities we take for granted. I'm sure that breakdancing would seem peculiar to them as would surfing water-skiing and hang-gliding. However I suspect that our forebears would find even those strange activities understandable perhaps even enjoyable compared to jogging. The sight of otherwise perfectly reasonable people decked out in various types of colourful underwear doggedly puffing and sweating along every pathway road and trail would I am convinced put The Fear into Great Grandad and send him scurrying back whence he had come.

All kinds of people jog: there are short joggers tall joggers fat joggers thin joggers; serious joggers light-hearted joggers fashionable joggers and practical joggers; joggers with outfits of every hue from black to white and every shade in between. In fact there may be more people who jog than don't!

I gave up on jogging some years ago with the excuse that although I adored distance running an old basketball injury prevented me from measuring up to my own expectations. This pitiful story together with a wistful sigh for lost youth usually gets me off the hook. While my friends claim to be fit and keen I take satisfaction in quoting Satchel Paige the famous baseball player who at age 60 pitched three scoreless innings in the major leagues. In his ''Six Rules for a Long Life,'' Satch warns ''On no account run.'' This is sound advice and I intend to live by this sensible and energy-efficient rule.

II

To test your mastery of commas, provide the necessary commas for these sentences. There are no answers for this exercise.

1. His face turned purple when he saw the exam results but he said nothing.
2. Clarity conciseness and courtesy are important in both personal and business communication.
3. The Blue Jays in case you haven't noticed have been playing better ball this season.
4. Unless you come with us now you won't be able to get to the island tonight.
5. Samuel de Champlain Jacques Cartier and Etienne Brûlé were among the first Europeans to explore what is now Canada.
6. In spite of its reputation the Spadina Hotel is you know a good place to have a drink.
7. Adam and Eve are supposed to have been the first people on earth but they apparently ran into some trouble with their supervisor.
8. Cedric why are you wearing those nose plugs?
9. Running jumping and shouting loudly the children ran across the yard and into the house.
10. Unless I am sadly mistaken you now have a firm grasp of the intricacies of comma use.

chapter  18

The Semicolon

The colon and semicolon are often confused and used as if they were inter-changeable. They serve very different functions, however, and their correct use can dramatically improve a reader's understanding of your writing. Here is one function of the semicolon:

> The semicolon can replace the period; in other words, it can appear between two independent clauses.

You should use the semicolon when the two clauses (sentences) you are joining are closely connected in meaning or when there is a cause-and-effect relationship between them.

I'm too tired; I can't stay awake any longer.

There's a good movie on tonight; it's a Canadian film called *Decline of the American Empire*.

A period could have been used instead of the semicolon in either of these sentences, but the close connection between the clauses prompted the writer to use a semicolon.

Certain connecting or transition words are sometimes put between independent clauses to show cause and effect or continuation of an idea. Words used in this way must be preceded by a semicolon and followed by a comma.[1]

> Put a semicolon in front of these words and a comma after:
>
> | ; consequently, | ; besides, | ; furthermore, |
> | ; however, | ; for example, | ; in fact, |
> | ; therefore, | ; nevertheless, | ; thus, |
> | ; moreover, | | |

[1]*Sometimes the words listed in the box are used in sentences as nonessential expressions rather than as connecting words. They are then separated from the rest of the sentence by commas. See chapter 17, p. 155.*

We had hiked for two hours; consequently, we were glad for the rest.
There are only two of us; however, we're both pretty big.
The sun was very hot; therefore, we stopped at an ice-cream store.

Note that the semicolon and transition word *together* are used to connect the two independent clauses.

Sometimes semicolons should be used in a list instead of commas:

> To make a lengthy, complex list easier to read and understand, put semicolons between the items instead of commas.

Here's an example:

A few items are necessary: matches to start a fire; an axe or hatchet to cut wood; cooking utensils and eating implements; and, of course, the food itself.

Exercises

I

Put a check next to the sentences that are correctly punctuated. Check your answers on p. 286 before continuing.

1. _____ We checked into the price of flying to Montreal; the train is much cheaper.

2. _____ I'd like to meet your friend; so bring him to the party tonight.

3. _____ We've eaten all the goodies, it's time to go home.

4. _____ There's a storm on the way, let's head for shelter.

5. _____ We're seeing a wave of 60s nostalgia, for example, miniskirts have made a comeback.

6. _____ Many doctors claim weather affects our health; in fact, barometric pressure has a direct effect on arthritis.

7. _____ The Argos are my favourite team, I always buy season tickets.

8. _____ Your instructor would like to pass you, however, there may be a small fee involved.

9. _____ Florence is going to Hollywood, she wants to appear on "Let's Make A Deal."

10. _____ We knew that the party was a huge success: Uncle Morty tap-danced across the top of the piano Aunt Madeline did her Big Bird imitation and Tim ignited two of his cousins.

2

Put a check next to the sentences that are correctly punctuated. Then check your answers.

1. _____ Many people dislike hockey; because some of the players act like goons rather than athletes.

2. _____ Orville tried and tried; but he couldn't get the teacher's attention.

3. _____ So he dangled one of his classmates from a window; that caught the teacher's eye immediately.

4. _____ I'd like to take a southern vacation this year, however, I don't think I can afford it.

5. _____ The car sped quickly past the spectators for a moment the driver could see their faces.

6. _____ I don't believe, however, that you would do that to me.

7. _____ First we'll have a cool drink then we'll see if we can find a way to start this car.

8. _____ Dudley left his clothes by the pool; so it's no wonder people in the lounge are looking at him strangely.

9. _____ Electrical plugs come in both male and female versions; so you can raise your own.

10. _____ Uranus is Rudolf's favourite planet, therefore, he is making preparations to live there someday.

3
Correct the faulty punctuation in exercise 1.

4
Correct the faulty punctuation in exercise 2.

5
Correct the faulty punctuation.

1. Mrs. Reagan had a message for the unemployed: "There is no hunger in America, let them eat Kraft Dinner."

2. Lionel hates country music, therefore he brought his earplugs to the Dolly Parton concert.

3. Unless everyone here is lying; UFOs are flying.

4. Most computer languages have been developed for a specific purpose, for example, COBOL is used in business while FORTRAN is used for mathematics, science, and engineering.

5. Some sociobiologists believe that human beings have evolved socially because female humanoids learned to barter sex for food and protection, however, this theory is controversial in academic circles.

6. Native land claims are a very complex issue nevertheless many of the Indian and Inuit groups are in the process of negotiating these claims with federal and local governments.

7. Andy, Pat, Annah, and Maggie are four of my favourite people; who can always have fun with the rest of us.

8. Louis Riel led a Métis rebellion in Manitoba in 1885; but he was defeated, tried, and executed the same year, his death caused a deep rift between English and French Canada.

9. The house was ridden with termites sagging from age littered with garbage and bereft of charm; yet the owner was asking $260,000 because of its location.
10. Go left at the next fork in the road, or you will end up at a nuclear-waste disposal site and come out all aglow.

6

Insert commas and semicolons where necessary in these sentences. Then check your answers carefully.

1. The entire town is in an uproar it seems Rudolf has been missing since yesterday.
2. Of course everyone knows Rudolf is a bit wacky he's been very strange since his close encounter of the fourth kind.
3. He claims that a hamburger-shaped chrome-coloured smoke-belching UFO pinned him under its wheels and its inhabitants kept him prisoner for several hours.
4. The creatures spoke to him through little slits however Rudolf says he got a good look at them.
5. According to him the aliens looked like a cross between Bonzo the Chimp and Sylvester Stallone.
6. The creatures told Rudolf many secrets one thing they told him was that they had searched the universe for a perfect specimen like him.
7. He considered this a friendly gesture and immediately felt more kindly toward the aliens.
8. In fact Rudolf later told us he is under the aliens' control perhaps this explains why he talks like Donald Duck.
9. But now everyone is beginning to worry there's an unexplained burned spot in Rudolf's yard and he's been gone since yesterday.
10. Do you think they've whisked him away for a tour of the galaxy?

7

Insert commas and semicolons where necessary in these sentences. Then check your answers carefully.

1. One dark windy stormy night I settled myself into bed and almost immediately fell into a deep sleep suddenly a dreadful noise jolted me awake.
2. My door swung open and a hideous howling beast leapt into my room and ran over to my bed.
3. Frozen with panic I could hear it snarling and snorting beside me it was huge doglike and fierce.
4. There was no weapon in the room except a sturdy baseball bat near the window.
5. As I made a lunge for the bat the beast leapt on my back then it inflicted a dozen or so savage bites.

6. Screaming in pain I thought I was going to die but just then my trusty Great Dane Hrothgar ran into the room.
7. Hrothgar went straight for the beast's jugular and gnawed him mercilessly until it was dead.
8. My attacker was finished I was able to attend to my wounds.
9. If it hadn't been for Hrothgar the bloody pulp on the floor would have been me instead of the vicious beast that had stalked me.
10. I patted the Great Dane gratefully "Hrothgar my friend" I said "I owe you several juicy steak bones above and beyond your daily ration of Burger Bits."

8

Provide the necessary punctuation in these paragraphs.

Two young women we'll call Linda and Meredith began college in September, both were nineteen, high school graduates, and eager to succeed in their educational careers. By December and the end of the first term Linda had enjoyed her courses and passed with A's and B's, however Meredith had fallen badly behind, failed four of five courses, and decided to leave college permanently. What caused this difference between two people's college experience? Some of the reasons may originate in the subtle but important distinctions between high school and college.

Both Linda and Meredith were exhilarated by what they saw as the freedom of college studies, no one forced them into classes, checked up on them, or phoned parents to verify absences. Linda appreciated this but made sure that she attended classes regularly. Meredith took this freedom as a licence to skip numerous classes or to come late. Teaching methods were different, instructors never hounded students for assignments and often did not provide the lecture notes as high school teachers had. Linda made sure she turned in all assignments promptly and took care to prepare her own notes, however Meredith was slack about assignments and rarely took notes in class. By the end of November the workload had increased to a level unprecedented in high school. Linda felt pressured but she was able to cope and do well because she was on top of her work. Meredith was hopelessly behind and unable to complete her work despite frantic, last-minute efforts. Understanding the nature of college studies is crucial to success, high school work does not always provide this understanding. Consistent effort discipline and responsibility for oneself are absolutely essential if a person is going to make the most of a college education.

9

Correct the punctuation in these sentences[1] by changing commas to semicolons or colons where necessary.

---

[1] *Adapted from "Notes on Punctuation," in* The Medusa and the Snail, *by Lewis Thomas, New York: The Viking Press, 1979, pp. 126-7.*

1. I have grown fond of semicolons in recent years. The semicolon tells you that there is still some question about the preceding full sentence, something needs to be added.
2. It is almost always a greater pleasure to come across a semicolon than a period. The period tells you that that is that, if you didn't get all the meaning you wanted or expected, you got all the writer intended to parcel out and now you have to move along.
3. But with a semicolon there, you get a pleasant little feeling of expectancy, there is more to come, read on, it will get clearer.
4. Colons are a lot less attractive, for several reasons, firstly, they give you the feeling of being rather ordered around, or at least having your nose pointed in a direction you might not be inclined to take if left to yourself, and, secondly, you suspect you're in for one of those sentences that will be labelling the points to be made, firstly, secondly, and so forth, with the implication that you haven't enough sense to keep track of a sequence of notions without having them numbered.
5. Also, many writers use this system loosely and incompletely, starting out with number one and number two as though counting off on their fingers but then going on and on without the succession of labels you've been led to expect, leaving you floundering about searching for the ninethly or seventeenthly that ought to be there but isn't.

10

There aren't any answers for these sentences, so test your mastery of the semicolon.

1. Acid rain is a serious problem however the U.S. seems unwilling to deal with it.
2. The lawn needs to be cut, get going on it right away.
3. The team lost seven games in a row consequently the coach was fired.
4. Lester Pearson won the Nobel Peace Prize in 1957, he was the only Canadian to do so.
5. Dragonflies have a fearsome appearance, nonetheless they are harmless insects.
6. I have a quick cure for insomnia, try to stay awake through a Sunday night episode of "The Nation's Business."
7. We've spent all our money, therefore we won't be dining out tonight.
8. The furniture looks like North York Provincial to me all the chairs are covered with plastic.
9. The abacus is an ancient computational device in skilful hands it can calculate sums as quickly as most modern gadgets.
10. The semicolon is an often misunderstood piece of punctuation now that you have mastered it your writing will be enhanced by its use.

chapter 19

Capital Letters

Capital letters should be used in a few specific places and nowhere else. Some people seem to have "capitalitis": they put capital letters on words randomly, regardless of whether the words are nouns, adjectives, or verbs. Like "exclamatosis," "capitalitis" is a disease communicated by comic books, which capitalize every word.

Not very many people have this problem; if you are in the majority who generally use capitals properly, skip this chapter and go on to something else. If you are puzzled about capital letters, though, or have readers who are puzzled by your use of them, read on.

Capitalize the first letters of the following words:

1. the first word of a sentence:

> Put out the garbage.

2. the names of specific persons:

> Anne Murray   Mordecai Richler

the names of specific places:

> Alberta   Elm St.
> Mars   Morocco
> Oz   Regina

and the names of specific things:

> St. Lawrence River
> British North America Act
> Hilltop Towers

3. the days of the week and the months of the year (but not the seasons):

> Monday   July
> Friday   summer
> October   winter

4. the titles of specific people (but not the names of their positions), books, films, and courses (but not subject names, unless they're languages):

Governor General Jeanne Sauvé   *but*   the position of governor general

Pope John Paul II   *but*   the position of pope

Mr. and Ms. O'Connor

The Bare Essentials

Star Wars

Mathematics 101   *but*   the subject of mathematics

English 101; the English language

5. the names of specific companies, businesses, organizations, and departments:

Chateau Gai   Conservative Party
Arc Industries   Personnel Department
Winnipeg Rotary Club

Exercises

I

Correct the capitalization in these sentences. Answers are on p. 289.

1. joanna is a regular Princess.

2. why on Earth would you buy a toyota?

3. We need to get rid of some of our High School habits when we start College.

4. The depression is a period that has been on everyone's mind during the present Hard Times.

5. have you read dr. Ernie 1. Piffle's new book, *I'm OK—You're Fat: A Self-Help guide to fitness fascism?*

6. The english language has its roots in northern european germanic tongues.

7. Montague will be staying at the harbour castle Hilton this Summer.

8. The loyalists were considered Patriots to inhabitants of upper Canada but Traitors to people in the united states.

9. The Upper Classes often resent Economic schemes that attempt to redistribute Wealth.

10. Garth Drabinsky has produced numerous Canadian Horror Films; *Shivers* is one of his most famous.

2

1. I didn't do very well in my Fluid Power Course; maybe I'd better switch to Culinary Arts.

2. When I grow up, I'd like to be a Duchess or at least a Movie Star.

3. well, look who's here; it's mr. olympics.

4. Take a right at Yonge Street, a left at lawrence avenue, and a right at Avenue road.

5. My english teacher also teaches french to Asian Immigrants.

6. Marcia's Father, being Conservative in his tastes, disapproved of Ronald's leather jacket and harley-davidson 750.

7. Neither was he amused when marcia ran off with Ron's Rock Group, the stoned angels.

8. The french were very much a part of canada for more than a Century before the english became its Rulers.

9. My guess is that this artifact dates back to the bronze age.

10. Can you tell me whether the roughriders are from ottawa and the rough riders from saskatchewan, or is it the other way around?

3

1. Several Psychiatrists in california are developing Computer Programs to treat patients with mild forms of Depression or Neurosis.

2. They envision Computer Therapy Programs within the next fifteen years that will diagnose the Patient's problem (To be confirmed by a Psychiatrist) and select a Treatment Program.

3. The Computer would interact with the Patient and switch to various Sub-programs to analyse his mental problems.

4. A tv camera could view the Patient to see if he exhibits signs of Stress, Nervousness, or Lying.

5. Thus, a computer with a sophisticated psychiatric program could appear to understand and empathize with a troubled patient.

6. Most psychiatrists are against such Unorthodox Treatment Methods, but proponents of Computer Therapy argue that it has many advantages.

7. These advantages include low cost and convenience: the Computer would function as a cheap Psychiatrist, available on Weekends and Holidays, Summer or Winter.

8. Other advantages are the long-term total Memory of the Computer and its appearance of honesty and objectivity.

9. Personally, I am surprised that anyone in the Medical Profession takes such a proposal seriously; treatment of complex Human Problems by machine seems perverse to me.

10. Taking my own personal depressions, fears, and phobias to a vdt would be likely to trigger a massive Anxiety Attack.

4[1]

By this time I was in High School. I resisted my Mother's plan to send me to a Private Girls' School, where the pupils wore kilts and little plaid ties. Ever since brownies I'd been wary of any group composed entirely of women, especially women in uniforms. So instead I went to the nearest High School, which was second-best in my Mother's opinion but not as bad as it might have been, since by now we were living in a respectable neighbourhood. The catch was that the children of the families my Mother viewed as her peers and models were sent to the kind of Private School she wanted to send me to, so the High School got mostly the leftovers from the smaller houses around the fringes of the area, the brash new apartment buildings which had been opposed by the Established Residents, and even worse, the flats above the stores on the commercial Streets. Some of my classmates were not at all what she had in mind, though I didn't tell her this as I didn't want to be forced into Uniform.

5

Correct the capitalization in these sentences. There are no answers provided for this exercise.

1. The way to a man's Heart is through his Stomach.

2. Being a Born-Again Christian, Dudley believes the world will end one second after Midnight, december 31, 1999 a.d.

3. Dominion day is on july 1, but firecracker day is another name for queen Victoria's birthday in May.

4. The progressive conservative party seems to be a contradiction in terms.

[1]*Adapted from* Lady Oracle *by Margaret Atwood. Reprinted by permission of the Canadian Publisher, McClelland and Stewart, Toronto.*

5. May I introduce professor Eli Green?

6. Dr. Green teaches french, spanish, italian, and Comparative Literature.

7. In the misfortunes of our Best Friends, we always find something which is not displeasing to us. (la Rochefoucauld)

8. If you want cheap curtains, come to crazy joe's next sunday for their big Sale.

9. This semester your Schedule will include Data Processing, Accounting, Math, philosophy, and english.

10. It's part of our Human Rights to be able to tell the Instructor what's bugging us on a daily basis.

The next four exercises will test your mastery of all punctuation studied in Unit Four. Go through them carefully, and check the answers as you go along (except for number 9, for which no answers are provided). If you make a mistake, locate the rule and review the use of that particular punctuation mark.

6

1. What kind of fool am I.
2. Mary Wollstonecraft makes an interesting comparison in *A Vindication of the Rights of Woman* (1792), The divine right of husbands, like the divine right of kings, may, it is hoped, in this enlightened age, be contested without danger.
3. There are three kinds of body type; ectomorph mesomorph and endomorph.
4. I wonder whether I'll remain an Endomorph forever?
5. Unless everyone donates some money we won't have enough for the trip and the children will be disappointed.
6. The bible the torah the koran and the upanishads are all Sacred Texts.
7. Jacob said You Roderick are my very best friend.
8. I understand that the regulations do not allow us to increase salaries more than 8 percent however the fact remains that inflation is running at 11 percent.
9. The english course you take in College is sure to be different from the english courses you took in High School.
10. The necessary steps for a successful building are to plan and design carefully to purchase and order carefully and to build and construct wisely.

7 [1]

Coureurs de bois are frenchmen who were either born in canada or who came to settle there they are always young men in the prime of life for older men cannot endure the hardships of this way of life. Some are of good social standing others are merely farmers or sons of farmers others still have no occupation

Since all of Canada is a vast and trackless forest it is impossible for them to travel by land they travel by lake and river in canoes usually occupied by three men

Since little time is required to carry out this trade the life of the *coureur de bois* is spent in idleness and dissolute living they sleep smoke drink brandy and no matter what the cost gambling drinking and women often consume all their money and the profits of their voyages they live in complete independence and account to no one for their actions.

8

Many studies have been done on the changing sex roles in western society in the late Twentieth Century; yet no one is quite sure what these changes mean. What are the implications of women pursuing careers, having smaller families, and of men assuming more responsibility for childrearing. Some people say that these changes will free both men and women from hidebound restrictive inflexible traditions. Women they say will become more independent and productive, moreover men will benefit from closer ties with their offspring. On the other hand some people maintain that there are numerous destructive effects of changing sex roles; broken families neglected children and lonely people. Proponents of this view argue that selfish and aggressive instincts flourish in an unstable society where no one is sure what is expected of him or her and pursues only self-gratification. The arguments will continue; for the answers are as yet unclear. But there is no doubt that the changes will continue, and even accelerate.

9

1. Egad. Did you see the size of that horsefly!
2. Ruth said I think my son daughter-in-law and the children are going to the maritimes this Summer.
3. Since you seem to enjoy tennis why don't you play more often.
4. The woman's attitude is unsuitable for this position and we intend to terminate her employment here.
5. Whistler Banff and Lake Louise are world-class Canadian ski resorts and people from all over the world flock to them.
6. You're always picking on me, it doesn't seem fair.

[1]*Adapted from* Call Us Canadians, *by Martinello & Evans, Toronto, McGraw-Hill Ryerson, 1976, pp. 131-132.*

7. Driven to desperate measures Tess attacked Alec with a carving knife.
8. A palindrome is a word that has the same spelling backward as forward, the longest one in english is redivider.
9. There's only one thing I'm worried about in this whole operation; the police.
10. If I were you Roscoe I wouldn't worry about wearing last year's Tuxedo you look stunning as a matter of fact.

10

Write a *process paper* of about two pages explaining how to do or make something or giving directions on how to get somewhere. Don't forget to check your spelling, sentence structure, and grammar. Pay particular attention to correct punctuation, and try to use an exclamation mark, a semicolon, and a colon at least once in the paper. Here are some topics you might choose from:
1. how to ride a skateboard
2. how to prepare your favourite meal
3. how to be a bore
4. how to find your way home
5. how to win friends and influence people
6. how to program a computer
7. how to play blackjack (poker, backgammon, Monopoly, etc.)
8. how to choose a lover (college, career, apartment, etc.)
9. how to get rich
10. how to be happy

unit

5

organizing your writing

chapter 20

Finding Something to Write About

Everybody knows that "content" is important in writing. Not so many seem to know that organization is just as important. In fact, you can't really separate the two: *what you say is how you say it.* Writing a paper (or an essay, or a report, or a letter, or anything else) is like doing a chemistry experiment: you need the right amount of the right ingredients, put together in the right proportions and in the right order. There are five steps to follow:[1]

1. choose a satisfactory subject;
2. choose the main points of your subject;
3. write a thesis statement
   OR
   write an outline;
4. write the paragraphs; and
5. revise the paper.

If you follow these steps faithfully, in order, we guarantee that you will write clear, organized papers.

Notice that when you get to step 3 you have a choice. You can choose to organize your paper either by means of a thesis statement or by means of an outline. The thesis-statement approach works well for very short papers — those no longer than about 400 words. An outline is necessary for longer papers and is often useful for organizing shorter papers, as well. (Ideally, you should learn to use both methods of organizing your writing; in fact, your teacher may insist that you do.)

Steps 1, 2, and 3 make up the preparation stage of the writing process. Be warned: these three steps will take you as long as — if not longer than — steps 4 and 5, which involve the actual writing. *The longer you spend on the preliminary steps, the less time your writing will take, and the better your paper will be.*

[1] *Some of the ideas presented in this unit are adapted from the approach developed by Sidney P. Moss in* Composition by Logic *(Belmont, Calif.: Wadsworth, 1966).*

Step 1: Choose a Subject

Unless you are assigned a specific subject by a teacher or by a superior at work, choosing your subject can be the most difficult part of writing a paper. Apply the following guidelines carefully, because no amount of instruction can make you write a good paper on something you don't know anything about or on something that is inappropriate for your purpose.

> A satisfactory subject is significant, single, specific, and supportable.

1. Your subject should be **significant.** As we have been suggesting all the way through this book, it is essential that you *keep your reader in mind.* Here, this means that you should write about something that someone would like to read about. Consider your audience and choose a subject that will be significant to that audience. This doesn't mean that you can't ever be humorous, but, unless you're another Stephen Leacock, an essay on "how I deposit money in my bank" will probably be of little significance to your reader. The subject you choose must be worthy of the time and attention you expect your reader to give to your paper.

2. Your subject should be **single.** Don't try to do too much in your paper. A thorough discussion of one topic is much more satisfying to read than a skimpy, superficial treatment of several topics. A subject like "the problems of league expansion in hockey and other sports" includes too much to be dealt with well in one paper. Limit yourself to a single topic, such as "the problems of league expansion in the NHL."

3. Your subject should be **specific.** This requirement is very closely tied to the "single" requirement. Given a choice between a broad, general topic and a narrow, specific one, you should choose the latter. In a short paper, you can't hope to say anything new or significant about a large topic — "employment opportunities in Canada," for example. You can write an interesting, detailed discussion of a more specific topic, such as "summer employment opportunities at the Banff Springs Hotel." You can narrow a broad subject by applying one or more *limiting factors* to it. Try thinking of your subject in terms of a specific *kind,* or *time,* or *place,* or *number,* or *person* associated with it. To come up with the Banff Springs Hotel topic, for example, we limited the subject of employment opportunities in Canada in terms of both place and kind.

4. Your subject must be **supportable.** You must know something about the subject (preferably more than your reader knows about it), or you must be able to find out about it. Your discussion of your subject will be clear and convincing only if you can include examples, facts, quotations, descriptions, anecdotes, and other supporting details. Supporting evidence can be taken from your own experience or from the experience of other people. That is, your topic may or may not require you to do some research.

Exercises

I

Test the following subjects against the guidelines we've given. Can you tell what's wrong with them? Check your answers on p. 292.

1. the history of women
2. alienation
3. my favourite breakfast
4. Canadian heroes
5. childbirth through the ages
6. sports in the twenty-first century
7. how to buy TTC tickets
8. the causes of inflation in Canada and the Third World
9. how humans evolved
10. today's society

2

Consider the following subjects in terms of the "4 S" guidelines. Five of them are hopeless. The other five could be turned into possible subjects. Locate the five possibilities and make each of them into a significant, single, specific, and supportable subject.

1. automation in the car industry and other factories
2. drug abuse and alcoholism
3. in today's society, there are many problems
4. a college education vs. other options
5. computers in 100 years
6. TV evangelists and other hucksters
7. giving myself a pedicure
8. capital punishment
9. TV for kids
10. nowadays, women are getting ahead

3

List five subjects that you might choose to write about. Be sure each subject is significant, single, specific, and supportable.

Step 2: Choose the Main Points of Your Subject

Now that you have an appropriate subject for your paper, give some thought to the approach you're going to take to it. There are many possible ways of thinking and writing about a subject. In a short paper, you can deal effectively with only a few aspects of your topic. How do you decide what is the best approach to take? How do you decide which aspects of your subject to discuss, what **main points** to make and explain? One way is to make a list of everything you can think of that you might want to say about the subject. Some preliminary research may help, too; you may turn up some points about the subject that you hadn't thought of.

Another way — especially useful if you find you're stuck for ideas — is to ask yourself questions about your subject. Run your subject through this list of questions and see which one "fits" it best. (The symbol S stands for your subject.)

---

1. How is S made or done?
2. How does S work?
3. What are the main parts of S?
4. What are the main functions of S?
5. What are the important features or characteristics of S?
6. What are the causes of S?
7. What are the effects or consequences of S?
8. What are the main kinds or types of S?
9. What are the main points of comparison (or contrast) between S and _____?
10. What are the main advantages (or disadvantages) of S?
11. What are the reasons for (or against) S?

These questions suggest some of the various ways of looking at or thinking about a subject. Most subjects will yield answers to more than one of these questions, but the question that produces the answers closest to what you want to say about your subject is the one that you should focus on. The answers to that question are the main points that you will discuss in your paper.

Here's how the procedure works. Assume you've been forced to accept as your subject "writing good business letters." Don't despair. Run down the list of questions until you find the one you can answer best. The process might go something like this:

1. How is a business letter written?
   No answer comes to mind. Scratch that question.
2. How does a business letter work?
   Silly question; it doesn't make sense.
3. What are the main parts of a business letter?
   Well, there are the inside address, the body, the salutation, and the complimentary close, but you don't know enough about these to write on them.
4. What are the main functions of the business letter?
   You can think of three: to request information, to place an order, and to complain about some product or service. This has possibilities, but you're not wildly enthusiastic about these aspects of your subject, so you go on.
5. What are the important characteristics of a good business letter?
   At last! Here's one you can answer satisfactorily. You know that a business letter should be clear, brief and to the point, and courteous. Assuming that you know (or can find out) a fair amount about these characteristics, you

don't need to look any further. *Clarity, conciseness,* and *courtesy* are the main points of your subject that you will discuss in your paper. (Before you go any further, though, it's a good idea to apply the remaining questions in the box to your subject, just to be sure there isn't another question that yields answers you like even better.)

Selecting the main points to write about isn't really a difficult process, but it can be time consuming. Don't rush. Take the necessary time; this is a crucial stage in the writing process.

Here are a few sample subjects, together with some main points that were discovered through this questioning procedure. Study this chart until you're sure you understand how to find suitable main points for any subject.

Subject	Selected Question	Main Points
violent pornography	11. What are my reasons for disapproving of violent pornography?	—it degrades the people who make it —it desensitizes viewers to cruelty against other people —it may encourage people to equate sexuality with violence
the child-care worker	4. What are the main functions of a child-care worker?	—ensuring the child's physical safety —ensuring the child's mental development —ensuring the child's emotional and social development —delivering the necessary therapeutic services
co-education in high school	10. What are the advantages of co-education in high school?	—having an opportunity to work with the opposite sex —having increased social opportunities —having an environment that is more closely related to the larger world
the National Football League	3. What are the main parts of the NFL?	National Conference —Eastern Division —Central Division —Western Division American Conference —Eastern Division —Central Division —Western Division

a successful garden	1. How do you grow a successful garden?	—by planning early —by cultivating the plot —by seeding —by maintaining and fertilizing —by harvesting on time
a good parent	5. What are the important characteristics of a good parent?	—ability to love —kindness —firmness and discipline

As a general rule, you should try to identify *between two and five main ideas* for your subject. If you have only one main idea, you have a subject suitable for a paragraph, not an essay. If you have more than five, you have too much material for a short paper. Choose only the most important aspects of the subject, or else take another look at your subject to see whether it can be narrowed down somewhat.

Exercises

4

In this exercise, select a question from the box on p. 182 and come up with good main points for each subject.

Subject	Selected Question	Main Points
teenage drug abuse		
a part-time job		
teachers		
video games		
living on your own		

5

For each of the five subjects you chose in exercise 3, list two to five main points. If suitable main points do not immediately leap to mind, apply the eleven questions in the box on p. 182 one at a time to your subject, until you find the one that fits best. The answers to that question are your main points.

Now take a close look at the main points you've chosen in exercise 3. It may be necessary to revise some of these before going any further. Are some points really too minor to bother with? Do any of the points overlap in meaning? Are there any points that are not really related to the subject?

To be completely satisfactory, the main points you have chosen must all be **significant** — worth writing a paragraph or more on. You shouldn't have any trivial ideas mixed in with the important ones.

Second, each of the main points you've chosen must be **different** from all the others: there must be no overlap in meaning. Check to be sure you haven't given two different labels to what is really only one aspect of the subject.

Third, the main points you have chosen must all be clearly **related** to the subject. They must all be aspects of *that* subject, not some other subject. For example, if you're writing about the advantages of a subject, cross out any disadvantages that may have appeared on your list.

Exercises

6

Here is a list of subjects, each followed by some possible main points. Circle the unsatisfactory point(s) in each group.

1. reasons for attending college
   —provides career skills
   —improves general knowledge of world
   —intramural sports
   —provides social opportunities

2. kinds of pop music
   —rock 'n roll
   —rhythm 'n blues
   —opera
   —reggae
   —country and western

3. essentials of a good paragraph
   —unity
   —good quality paper
   —coherence
   —topic sentence

4. advantages of living at home while attending college
   —financial saving
   —privacy
   —familiar surroundings
   —freedom
   —emotional support from family

5. genres (or kinds) of literature
—fiction
—poetry
—stories
—drama

6. benefits of a balanced diet
—better health
—better appearance
—more dates
—look better

7. day-care system should be expanded
—more children could be accommodated
—more women could work, knowing children were well cared for
—more jobs for day-care workers
—more spaces for children

8. features of parliamentary government
—representatives are elected
—party system
—Canadian system
—president is elected
—majority party chooses prime minister

7

Circle the unsatisfactory point(s) in each group.

1. disadvantages of early marriage
—lack of money
—lack of career stability
—lack of financial stability
—pregnancy

2. differences between college and university
—college takes less time
—career training
—college provides more practical training
—college is less expensive
—knowledge

3. reasons for studying literature
—to learn about our cultural heritage
—to learn to see people and things through others' eyes
—poetry and drama
—to enjoy it more

4. kinds of Olympic ski events
—Alpine
—downhill
—speed

	—Nordic
	—cross-country
5. how to write a short essay	—choose a satisfactory subject
	—choose a satisfactory topic
	—choose the main points of your subject
	—write a thesis statement
	—write the paragraphs
	—revise the paper
6. the main branches of Christianity	" —Catholicism
	—Reformed
	—Protestantism
	—Judaism
	—Eastern Orthodox
7. detrimental effects of TV on children	—increases vocabulary
	—impedes imagination
	—improves general knowledge
	—inhibits creativity
	—gives a distorted view of life
8. main kinds of parapsychology	—clairvoyance
	—extra-sensory perception
	—depression
	—telepathy

8

Study the main points you chose in exercise 5 (p. 185). Cross out any that aren't significant, different from all the others, or related to the subject. If necessary, add new main points, so that you end up with at least two main points for each subject.

Now that you've decided on a few good main points to discuss, put them in the **order** in which you want them to appear in your paper. There are four main ways to arrange your points; choose the way that is most appropriate for your particular subject.

1. **Chronological order** means in order of time, from first to last. Here's an example:

Subject	**Main Points**
the process of dating	attraction
	meeting
	discovery
	intimacy
	disillusionment

2. **Climactic order** means saving your strongest or most important point for last. Generally, you would present your strongest point last, your second-strongest point first, and the others in between, like this:

Subject	Main Points
disadvantages of cigarette smoking	danger to those around you
	disapproval of others
	expense
	danger to yourself

3. **Logically linked order** means that the main points are connected in such a way that one point must be explained before the next can be understood. Look at this example:

Subject	Main Points
main causes of juvenile delinquency	lack of opportunity for work
	lack of recreational facilities
	boredom

The logical link here is this: it's because of unemployment that recreational facilities are needed, and it's because of both unemployment and inadequate recreational facilities that boredom becomes a problem. The first two points must be explained before the reader can fully understand the third.

4. **Random order** means the points can be explained in any order. A random arrangement of points is possible only if the main points are all equal in significance and not logically linked, as in this case:

Subject	Main Points
the garbage-disposal crisis	disposal sites are hard to find
	costs are high
	new technologies are not yet fully developed

Exercises

9

In this exercise, you are asked to arrange the main points of the subject according to the order proposed. Put the numbers in the blanks before the main points.

Subject	Order	Main Points
1. learning to drive a car	chronological	_____ taking lessons
		_____ taking road test
		_____ obtaining permit
		_____ driving on one's own
		_____ studying manual

2. why free public education through high school is essential	climactic	_____ the education of young people is crucial to a society _____ poor as well as rich children must be educated _____ every child needs an education
3. breaking a bad habit	chronological	_____ substituting other activities _____ recognizing the bad habit _____ eliminating the bad habit completely
4. causes of failure in college	logical	_____ student drops out _____ student misses classes _____ student lacks basic skills _____ student is unable to comprehend course material _____ student fails courses
5. why hockey violence must be curtailed	climactic	_____ violence jeopardizes entire future of the sport _____ individual players may be injured _____ children are encouraged to play hockey at too young an age
6. why economic recessions occur	logical	_____ buying of consumer goods decreases _____ unemployment causes general economic slowdown _____ inflation causes fear and and decreased consumer confidence _____ lowered demand for consumer goods causes widespread unemployment

7. how to change a tire	chronological	_____ loosen nuts completely and remove wheel
		_____ raise the car until tire clears ground
		_____ block the wheels
		_____ lower vehicle and retighten nuts
		_____ park on flat ground
		_____ slightly loosen wheel nuts
		_____ put the jack under the car's frame
		_____ install spare and retighten nuts
8. problems associated with alcoholism	climactic	_____ being socially ostracized
		_____ having poor health
		_____ losing one's job
		_____ making a fool of oneself
		_____ endangering one's own and other people's lives as a drinking driver

In 9 and 10, choose your own main points and order them as you think best.

9. how to buy a _____

10. causes of divorce

10

Using the list of subjects and main points that you came up with in exercise 8, arrange the main points for each subject in the most appropriate order.

In this chapter you've learned how to choose a satisfactory subject and how to select (and order) the main points of that subject — the first two steps in the five-step process we outlined at the beginning of the chapter. Now it's time to decide whether you'll organize your paper by the thesis-statement method or by the outline method. Although we think the former generally works better for short papers and the latter for longer papers, this distinction isn't hard and fast. So, depending on your teacher's instructions, turn now to either chapter 21, "Writing the Thesis Statement," or chapter 22, "Writing the Outline."

chapter 21

Writing the Thesis Statement

Now that you've chosen your topic and selected some main points to discuss (see chapter 20), you're ready for the third step in organizing your writing. Remember that there are two ways of carrying out the third step: by writing a thesis statement and by writing an outline. If you're writing a very short paper (400 words or less), we recommend that you use the method presented in this chapter. If you're writing a longer paper, though, or if your teacher prefers the outline method, turn now to chapter 22, "Writing the Outline."

Step 3: Write a Thesis Statement

The key to clear organization of a very short paper is the **thesis statement** — a statement near the beginning of your paper that announces its subject and scope. The thesis statement is a tremendous help both to you and to your reader. It plans your paper for you, and it tells your reader exactly what he or she is going to read about. In fiction, letting readers know in advance what they're going to find would never do. But, for practical, everyday kinds of writing, this "advance notice" works very well. Term papers, technical reports, research papers, office memoranda, and business letters are no place for suspense or surprises. In these kinds of writing, you're more likely to get and keep your readers' interest if you indicate the subject and scope of your paper at the outset. The thesis statement acts like a table of contents, giving a clear indication of what is to follow. It's a kind of map of the territory covered in your paper; it keeps your reader (and you) on the right track.

Specifically, *a thesis statement is a sentence that clearly and concisely indicates the subject of your paper, the main points you will discuss, and the order in which you will discuss them.*

To write a thesis statement, you join the **subject** to the **main points**, which you have already chosen and arranged in order. To join the two parts of a thesis statement, you use a **link**. Your link can be a word or phrase, such as *are, include, consist of, because, since,* or it can be a colon.[1] Here is the simple formula for constructing a thesis statement:

---

[1] *Remember that a colon can be used only after an independent clause. See chapter 16 if you need a review.*

S	consists of	I, II (III, IV, V)
(subject)	(link)	(main points)

Here's an example:

<pre>
                            S   I
Three characteristics of a good business letter (are) conciseness,

    II   III
clarity, and courtesy.
</pre>

Exercise

I

In each of the following thesis statements, underline the subject with a wavy line, circle the link, and underline the main points with a straight line. Answers are on p. 294.

1. There are four kinds of driver who cause accidents on expressways: road hogs, tailgaters, speed demons, and Sunday drivers.

2. Cigarette smoking is a habit to be avoided at all costs, for it detracts from appearance, diminishes finances, and threatens health.

3. The five steps for reading assigned material efficiently consist of previewing chapter headings, reading the assignment carefully, taking careful notes, looking up unfamiliar terms, and reviewing the material thoroughly.

4. Einstein's General Theory of Relativity fundamentally changed the way we think about the nature of matter, the extent of the cosmos, and the fate of the universe.

5. Because owning and maintaining a home involves considerable amounts of money, time, and work, one should carefully consider the decision to buy a house.

6. The principles of dealing with handicapped children include accepting their limitations, understanding their development, allowing them to take some risks, and encouraging them to develop to their fullest potential.

7. In British aristocracy, the five ranks of peer, or title holder in the peerage, are, in ascending order, barons, viscounts, earls, marquises, and dukes.

8. It is by the goodness of God that in our country we have those three unspeakably precious things: freedom of speech, freedom of conscience, and the prudence never to practice either of them. (Mark Twain)

9. Getting the job you want requires that you prepare a flawless résumé, research the firm you are interested in, respond intelligently at the interview, and follow up the interview in an appropriate manner.

10. The most prevalent types of crime fiction are detective stories, in which particular private eyes take part; "whodunits," in which a criminal is identified; mystery stories, in which supernatural elements may intervene; and puzzle mysteries, in which clues, not characters, are all-important.

When you combine your subject with the main points into a thesis statement, there is one rule to remember:

> The main points should be grammatically parallel.

This rule means that, if main point I is a word, then main points II and III and so on must be words, too. If point I is a phrase, then the rest must be phrases. If I is a dependent clause, then the rest must be dependent clauses. Study the model thesis statements you analysed in exercise 1, noting that in each case the main points are in grammatically parallel form. For each of those thesis statements, decide whether words, phrases, or dependent clauses were used. If you feel your understanding of parallelism is a bit wobbly, review chapter 9 before doing the following exercises.

Exercises

2

Here is an exercise to help you remember the parallelism principle. In each set of words below, one word, phrase, or clause is not parallel to the others. Circle the letter of that item and rewrite it so that it is parallel.

1. He
   a. came
   b. went
   c. stayed
   d. leaves
2. His wife is a woman of
   a. beauty
   b. intelligence
   c. charm
   d. kind
3. You will be unlikely to see her
   a. happy
   b. cheerful
   c. feeling any joy
   d. thrilled

4. Whether you are
   a. in the city
   b. at the beach
   c. driving
   d. by the airport
5. Unless you have been
   a. trying for many months
   b. learned to accept disappointment
   c. contacting everyone in the group
   d. willing to spend more time waiting
6. He found his boss's action
   a. without fairness
   b. underhanded
   c. capricious
   d. discriminatory
7. The whole team acted
   a. stupidly
   b. fatuously
   c. without any wits
   d. vacantly
8. A home with a
   a. lovely family
   b. den that is book-lined
   c. decrepit porch
   d. beautiful yard
9. Too much television will
   a. stifle our imagination
   b. stunt our creativity
   c. desensitize our feelings
   d. cause our intelligence to diminish
10. You will find us
   a. the most efficient restaurant when you want a quick lunch
   b. the most relaxing restaurant when you want a leisurely dinner
   c. the best whenever good food is what you're after

3

Put a check before the sentences that are grammatically parallel.

1. _____ It's important that every college student have enough time to study, sleep, work, and seeing friends.

2. _____ They like to hang-glide, parachute, and diving through the sky.

3. _____ The downtown streets were dirty, noisy, and the weather there was hot and humid.

4. _____ Jude didn't know whether he wanted to attend university or spend his life with Arabella.

5. _____ Lucinda will always be remembered for her insane jealousy, venomous tongue, charmless personality, and being completely crazy.

6. _____ Before every flight he took, Maxwell rewrote his will, said a prayer, and gets really drunk.

7. _____ The movie you recommended was neither timely, interesting, nor informative.

8. _____ Give me the liberty to know, to utter, and to argue freely according to conscience, above all liberties. (John Milton)

9. _____ After a big party like that one, people always help us to clean up the living room, dining room, den, yard, and counting up the empties.

10. _____ That's the last time I go to a croquet tournament, because the fans are inevitably wild, riotious, and act like beasts.

4

Now correct the faulty parallelism in the sentences in exercise 3.

5

Correct the faulty parallelism in the following thesis statements.

1. The chief characteristics of a good parent are kindness, firmness, and you have to be consistent, too.

2. Frequent causes of failure in college are lack of responsibility, lack of discipline, and not knowing basic skills.

3. Organization, expression, and revising are the three keys to good writing.

4. The celebrity fund raiser featured the greats of rock, the elite of sport, film stars, and the giants of television.

5. Being unemployed, broke, and feeling alone all contribute to depression.

6. Moving to a rural environment is attractive to some people, because of the slower pace, cleaner air, and the communities are more closely knit.

7. A first-class baseball team must have a superb pitching staff, a top-notch hitting line-up, and an outfield with speed.

8. There are two important questions about the burgeoning high technology field: will it remain a fast-track industry and Canada's part in it?

9. To be an effective manager, an administrator or executive must ensure that he or she is maintaining open lines of communication, allowing a free exchange of ideas, encouraging input from subordinates, and to give them opportunities for achieving greater responsibility.

10. Though both Canadians and Americans are part of a highly affluent society, Canadians seem to be more obsessed with life insurance, pension plans, and having a high level of savings.

6

Correct the faulty parallelism in the following thesis statements.

1. Children of working parents sometimes suffer from inferior day-care arrangements, insufficient after-school supervision, and not having enough time with their parents.

2. Over the years, boycotts of consumer goods have proved to be effective political tools. Among the goods that people have refrained from buying are lettuce from California, grapes from Chile, and South African wines.

3. Among my favourite works of drama are Shakespeare's plays of the sixteenth century, Sheridan's plays of the eighteenth century, and Eugene O'Neill's drama from fifty years ago.

4. It will be many generations before human beings will even understand, let alone benefit from, quarks, or make use of black holes, or antimatter can be understood.

5. The new charter of rights precludes discrimination on the grounds of sex, age, racism, or where you do or do not worship.

6. Though their elder sisters and brothers may have been interested in changing the world, today's college students seem primarily interested in a secure job and having a good salary.

7. Newcomers to Canada who come from warm climates with no snow often find themselves depressed by the drizzly autumns, freezing winters, and spring that never happens.

8. We are constantly being bombarded with messages in the form of oral communication, written communication, and what we see.

9. When I can afford it, I will choose among a Jaguar for its prestige, a Porsche for its speed, and the reliability of a Mercedes.

10. Writing a clear, coherent paper is guaranteed if you are very careful about finding a subject, writing the thesis statement, writing the paragraphs, and revise the essay.

7

Find the subjects and main points you produced for exercise 10 in chapter 20. Combine each subject with its main points to make a thesis statement. Be sure the main points are in parallel form.

We said at the beginning of this chapter that the thesis statement plans your whole paper for you. Before we turn to the actual writing of the paper, it will be useful for you to have a general idea of what the finished product will look like. In a very short paper each main point can be explained in a single paragraph. The main points of your subject become the **topics** of the paragraphs, as is shown in this model format for a paper with three main points:

Title _____

Paragraph 1:
contains the intro-
duction and the
thesis statement

_____
_____
_____ S consists of I, II, and III.
Topic sentence introducing main point I. _____

Paragraph 2:
contains your
explanation of
main point I

_____
_____
_____
_____
_____
_____ .
Topic sentence introducing main point II. _____

Paragraph 3:
contains your
explanation of
main point II

_____
_____
_____
_____
_____ .
Topic sentence introducing main point III. _____

Paragraph 4:
contains your
explanation of
main point III

_____
_____
_____
_____
_____
_____ .

Paragraph 5:
conclusion

_____
_____
_____ .

Chapter 23 will tell you how to fill in the blanks. But, before you go on to that chapter, notice the proportions of the paragraphs in the model format. Since the main points are approximately equal in significance, the paragraphs of the body of the paper are approximately equal in length. (If your last main point is more important than the other points, however, the paragraph that explains it may be longer than the other paragraphs.)

Notice, too, that the beginning and ending paragraphs are much shorter than the ones that explain the main points. Your introduction should not ramble on, and your conclusion should not trail off. Get to your main points as quickly as you can, and end with a bang, not a whimper.

Exercise

8

A paper that follows the model format exactly is Brian Green's "In Defence of Video Games," which appears in Appendix A. Read it and place the thesis statements and topic sentences into the correct slots on the blueprint on p. 198. Then turn to chapter 23.

chapter 22

Writing the Outline

For longer compositions, business and technical reports, research papers and the like, the outline method often proves more successful than the thesis-statement approach. A good outline maps out your paper from beginning to end. It shows you — *before* you begin to write — what you have to say about each of your main points. Outlining spares you the agony of discovering too late that you have too much information about one point and little or nothing to say about another.

Step 3: Write an Outline

Once you've chosen a satisfactory subject and the main points you wish to discuss, the next step is to expand what you have into a point-form plan for your finished paper. To do this, you may need to do some further thinking or reading, gathering additional information and supporting facts. For ideas about what kinds of information you might use, see "Developing Your Paragraphs," p. 206. After you've assembled all the information you think you'll need, prepare the outline.

First, write down your main points in the order you've decided to discuss them. Leave lots of space under each main point. Using Roman numerals, number your main points I, II, III, etc. Now, under each point, indent and list the examples, facts, ideas, or other information you're going to use to explain it. Again, leave lots of space. Check to be sure these items are arranged in an order that will be clear to your reader.[1] Now label these A, B, C, etc.

If any of these pieces of information needs to be explained or developed, indent again and list the supporting materials, numbering them 1, 2, 3, etc. Minor details, if there are any, are indented under the supporting materials to which they relate and are labelled a, b, c. Add the introduction and conclusion, and you're done. Your outline might look something like this:

```
Intoduction[2]
     Attention-getter
     Thesis statement or statement of subject
I.   First main point
     A.  item that develops first main point
     B.  item that develops first main point
          1.  supporting material that develops subheading B
          2.  supporting material that develops subheading B
```

[1] *The four kinds of order explained in chapter 20 can apply to the arrangement of ideas within a paragraph as well as to the arrangement of main points in a paper.*

[2] *Chapter 23 explains how to construct an introduction and conclusion.*

II. Second main point
    A. item that develops second main point
    B. item that develops second main point
    C. item that develops second main point
III. Third main point
    A. item that develops third main point
        1. supporting material that develops subheading A
            a. detail
            b. detail
        2. supporting material that develops subheading A
    B. item that develops third main point
Conclusion
    Summary
    Memorable statement

You'll probably find that before you can assign a number or a letter to a piece of information, you need to think carefully about where the item belongs in the structure of your paper. Questions about how to arrange your information under each main point and how much time to spend on any one point should be cleared up at the outline stage. If, for example, you find you have nine subheadings under main point I and only one under main point II, you need to do some rethinking to balance your paper. Main points should contain approximately equal amounts of information.

Preparing a satisfactory outline takes time. Be prepared to spend time adding, deleting, and rearranging your ideas and supporting materials until you're completely satisfied both with the arrangement and with the proportion of your outline.

Exercise

I

Below are the main points from a paper on writing good business letters. Beneath these are nine statements that might be used to support and develop these points. Read through the list and complete the outline by arranging the supporting items logically below the appropriate points. Discard any items that are not relevant to the main points. Turn to p. 297 to check your outline against ours.

I.   conciseness

II. clarity

III. courteousness

1. avoid sarcasm and insults
2. don't waste time with irrelevant personal details
3. use an accepted business-letter format
4. include all information your reader might need
5. include specific information such as names, dates, product numbers
6. always type your letter
7. cut out all unnecessary words
8. include file number or other reference number, if possible
9. politely request what action you want the reader to take

With your outline in hand, all you have to do to write your paper is to make the supporting points into sentences and the main points (and the introduction and conclusion) into paragraph divisions. Chapter 23 explains how.

To show you the relationship between an outline and the final product, we've recreated the outline that Martin Luther King might have used in writing "The Dimensions of a Complete Life" (reprinted in Appendix A).

The Dimensions of a Complete Life

Introduction
    Attention-getter: John's vision of the new Jerusalem and its meaning
    Statement of subject: The three dimensions of a complete life: length,
            breadth, and height

I. The length of life
    A. definition: the dimension of life in which one is concerned with self
    B. the need to love oneself properly
        1. Joshua Liebman's explanation in *Peace of Mind*
        2. responsibility of each person to discover his "calling"
            a. example of streetsweeper
            b. Douglas Mallock's verse
    C. the danger of getting "bogged down" in the length of life

II. The breadth of life
    A. definition: the dimension of life in which one is concerned about others
    B. the need to be concerned about all humanity
        1. the parable of the Good Samaritan
        2. the significance of the parable in our time
            a. racial groups often interested only in their own status
            b. nations often concerned only about their own well-being
        3. the interdependence of all individuals and nations
            a. poverty affects all
            b. disease affects all
            c. John Donne, "No man is an island ..."

III. The height of life
    A. the danger of neglecting this dimension
    B. the difficulty of maintaining religious belief in our modern world

    C.   the need to remember that "great things" are invisible
        1.   law of gravitation
        2.   the mind of an architect
        3.   human personality
        4.   God
    D.   the power of belief in God
Conclusion
    Summary: relationship between the three dimensions of life and the
             Commandments
    Memorable statement: prayer that all people may share in John's vision

Once you've mapped out your plan in an outline, writing the paper becomes perhaps not an easy task but certainly not the terrifying, impossible task it often seems to be if you have no plan to follow. Remember, *the more time you spend planning, the less time you spend writing — and the better your writing will be.*

Exercises

2

Read "The Dimensions of a Complete Life" in Appendix A. Find the paragraphs that correspond to the various headings and subheadings in our outline of the piece. Label King's paragraphs to show where you think they fit in the outline: I, A, B, 1, 2, etc. Then turn to the answer section to check your labelling.

3

Read Caroline Gunn's "My Student Career" in Appendix A and write an outline for this essay. To get you started, we've provided the numbers and letters for the first and second main points. After you've filled these in, add the necessary numbers and letters for the third and fourth main points. Then outline the conclusion and turn to p. 298 to compare your outline with ours.

INTRODUCTION
    Attention-getter: I've devoted 14 years to the career of being a student
    Thesis statement: I've become an expert in several fields: I know what makes
                  a good teacher, what makes a good course, how to write an
                  exam or term paper, and how to learn.

I. _____

   A. _____

   B. _____

      1. _____

      2. _____

      3. _____

II. _____

   A. _____

      1. _____

      2. _____

   B. _____

      _____

      _____

   C. _____

      1. _____

      2. _____

      3. _____

4

Turn to the subjects and main points you developed for exercise 10 in chapter 20 and create an outline for a paper on one of those subjects.

chapter 23

Writing the Paragraphs

You are now at step 4 in the writing process. Armed with either your thesis statement or your outline, you are ready to turn your main points into paragraphs. Sounds like a magician's trick? It isn't. The "sleight-of-pen" involved requires only that you know what a paragraph looks like and how to put one together.

A paragraph looks like this:

	A sentence that introduces the **topic** (or main idea) of the paragraph goes here.
Three or more	_____
sentences that	_____
specifically sup-	_____
port or explain	_____
the topic go in	_____
here.	_____
	_____
	_____

Sometimes a main point can be explained satisfactorily in a single paragraph. Sometimes, if it's a complicated main point requiring lots of support, several paragraphs are needed. Nevertheless, whether it is explaining a main point of a paper or an item supporting a main point, every paragraph contains two things: *a statement of the topic* (usually the first sentence in the paragraph) and a *development of the topic*.

As the blueprint above shows you, beginning with a sentence that states clearly your main idea (or *topic*) is a good way to start a paragraph. The next three, four, five, or even more sentences will develop the topic. The key to making the paragraph *unified* (an important quality of English paragraphs) is to make sure that each of your supporting sentences relates directly to the topic introduced in the first sentence.

Exercise

I

Turn to Appendix A and read Caroline Gunn's "My Student Career." Find and underline the statement of topic in the second, third, fifth, and sixth paragraphs. Check your answers on p. 298.

Developing Your Paragraphs

How do you put a paragraph together? First, write your **topic sentence**, telling your reader what point or idea you're going to discuss in the paragraph. Next, develop your point. An adequately developed paragraph gives enough supporting information to make the topic completely clear to the reader. An average paragraph runs between 75 and 150 words (except for introductions and conclusions, which are shorter), so you can see you will need lots of supporting information for each point.

Now, unless you are writing from a very detailed outline and have all the supporting material you need listed in front of you, you need to do a little more thinking at this point. Put yourself in your reader's place. What does the reader need to know in order to understand your point clearly? If you ask yourself the six questions listed below, you'll be able to decide what **kind of development** to use to support a particular topic sentence. The choice of development is up to you. Decide on the basis of your topic and what the reader needs to know about it.

1. Would a *definition* help your reader understand?

A definition paragraph explains and clarifies the meaning of a word or idea that is central to your topic. The definition paragraph is most often used to explain a term that may be unfamiliar to your reader. (Use your own definition; quoting from a dictionary is a very boring way to start a paragraph.) In paragraph 3 of "My Student Career," Caroline Gunn defines the good teacher by describing what such a person is like:

> A teacher is someone who communicates by word, action, or example to effect a desirable change in an audience. A *good* teacher is someone who does all this and at the same time inspires, motivates, and participates in the learning of his or her students. Such a person is always an interesting individual. Scratch a good teacher and you'll find a world traveller, amateur actor, part-time farmer, inventor, writer, baseball player, taxi driver, television hostess, or film-maker. The good teacher relates to students as people, acknowledging and forgiving us our faults, while recognizing and encouraging our strengths. Good teachers are people who enjoy learning. Good teachers are themselves always learning, always receptive to new ideas; they delight in the insights and fledgling creativity of young people. I have been privileged to know five good teachers in my student career.

You should include a definition, too, if you're using a familiar term in an unusual way. Here, Martin Luther King defines what he means by "the length of life":

> Now let us notice first the length of life. I have said that this is the dimension of life in which the individual is concerned with developing his inner powers. It is that dimension of life in which the individual pursues personal ends and ambitions. This is perhaps the selfish dimension of life, and there is such a thing as moral and rational self-interest. If one is not concerned about himself he cannot be totally concerned about other selves.

Exercise

2

Write a definition paragraph of four to six sentences based on the following topic sentence:

Many people are puzzled when they first encounter the word "misogyny."

2. Would *examples* help clarify the point?

Listing a number of examples is probably the most common method of developing an idea. Readers become suspicious when they read unsupported statements of opinion or emotion. One of the best ways of supporting your opinion or feeling is by providing clear, relevant examples. In paragraph 4 of "Look Who's Listening!" Brian Green uses five examples to prove his point:

> Knowledge of your audience will also enable you to devise an effective approach to your topic. A hostile or reluctant reader may have to be presented with a step by step build-up of evidence before being exposed to your main argument; with a sympathetic receiver, you may want to begin with your conclusion and then reveal how it was developed. A business contact will want a concise report in the form of a business letter or memorandum, while a friend or colleague will want to hear all the details together with your opinion and feelings about the same transaction. Even a good joke teller will tailor his approach to an audience to suit what he sees as their tastes and tolerances.

Sometimes a single, detailed example is enough to allow your reader to see clearly what you mean. In this paragraph, King uses a famous story from the Bible as an example of showing proper concern for others:

> You remember one day a man came to Jesus and he raised some significant questions. Finally he got around to the question, "Who is my neighbor?" This could easily have been a very abstract question left in mid-air. But Jesus immediately pulled that question out of mid-air and placed it on a dangerous curve between Jerusalem and Jericho. He talked about a certain man who fell among thieves. Three men passed; two of them on the other side. And finally another man came and helped the injured man on the ground. He is known to us as the good Samaritan. Jesus says in substance that this is a great man. He was great because he could project the "I" into the "thou."

Exercise

3

Write a four- to six-sentence paragraph based on the topic sentence below, using the example method of paragraph development.

My high school English classes prepared (*or* did not prepare) me for the writing demands of college. (Defend one side or the other.)

---

3. Is a *series of steps* or *stages* involved?

Sometimes the best way to develop the main idea of your paragraph is by telling how it is done; that is, by relating the process or series of steps involved in the main idea. Make sure that you break the process down into its component parts and detail the steps logically and precisely. Be particularly careful about including appropriate transition words (see p. 212). Notice how the fifth paragraph of "My Student Career" describes a series of steps that lead to better marks:

> An unavoidable part of any course is evaluation. I have learned many techniques for doing well on tests, exams, and term papers, but there's no substitute for knowing the material thoroughly. This means taking careful notes in class and reading the text closely. Next, you can improve your chances of

getting a good mark if you write well. I recently got back a paper from a teacher on which she had written, "You have misinterpreted or ignored most of the relevant material on this topic." But she gave me a mark of seventy-four per cent! The reason, as I see it, is that while I didn't say very much, I said it very well. A third key to success in essays or class tests is neatness. I suspect that neatness gains me the benefit of the doubt on questionable answers, and means the difference between eighty per cent and one hundred per cent on good answers. Finally, your success in a course can be favourably influenced if you appear interested in and enthusiastic about the course, without becoming a pest. I try once a week to ask a question in each course and often have the question thought out before class to make sure it's interesting and doesn't sound like a challenge to the teacher.

Exercise

4

Write a six- to seven-sentence paragraph developed as a series of steps telling your reader how to make or do something.

4. Would *specific details* be useful?

Providing your reader with concrete, specific, descriptive details can be a very effective way to develop your main idea. In some paragraphs, numerical facts or statistics can be used to make your argument convincing. (Just make sure that your facts are 100 percent correct!) Pick out the details Brian Green uses to develop his point in this paragraph:

> Video games are not the mindless diversion that television is; they demand skill. The hand–eye co-ordination, reflex response, swiftness and precision of action required would do credit to a hockey goaltender or a jet pilot. Most of the skills called upon are inborn, but even the slowest and clumsiest of us could benefit from developing and augmenting what poor skills we have. On my favourite game I have twice achieved a score of 9000; last week in a video arcade across town, I watched a young lady of about fourteen rack up over 200,000 on the same game. I would not hesitate to put my life in her hands in any situation which required manual dexterity, quick reflexes, and steady nerves.

Exercise

5

Write a five- to seven-sentence paragraph describing an interesting-looking person of your acquaintance. Be sure to include a topic sentence at the beginning.

5. Would a *comparison* be meaningful?

A comparison shows similarities between things; it shows how two different things are alike in a particular way. If you have a difficult, abstract topic to explain, try comparing it to something with which your reader is familiar, as King does in this paragraph:

These are the three dimensions of life, and without the three being correlated, working harmoniously together, life is incomplete. Life is something of a great triangle. At one angle stands the individual person, at the other angle stand other persons, and at the top stands the Supreme, Infinite Person, God. These three must meet in every individual life if that life if to be complete.

Exercise

6

Write a five- to seven-sentence paragraph comparing two of your favourite performers. Be sure to include a topic sentence at the beginning.

6. Would a *quotation* or *paraphrase* be appropriate?

Occasionally you will find that someone else — an expert in a particular field, a well-known author, or a respected public figure — has said what you want to say better than you could ever hope to say it. In these cases, quotations — as long as they are kept short and not used too frequently — are useful in developing your topic. Notice how King uses a famous quotation to sum up the point of this paragraph.

As long as there is poverty in the world I can never be rich, even if I have a billion dollars. As long as diseases are rampant and millions of people in this world cannot expect to live more than twenty-eight or thirty years, I can never be totally healthy even if I just got a good check-up at Mayo Clinic. I can never be what I ought to be until you are what you ought to be. This is the way our world is made. No individual or nation can stand out boasting of being independent. We are interdependent. So John Donne placed it in graphic terms when he affirmed, "No man is an island entire of itself. Every man is a piece of the continent, a part of the main." Then he goes on to say, "Any man's death diminishes me because I am involved in mankind, and therefore never send to know for whom the bell tolls; it tolls for thee." When we discover this, we master the second dimension of life.

A paraphrase is a summary — in your own words — of someone else's idea. Don't forget to indicate whose idea it is you are paraphrasing, the way King does:

Some years ago a learned rabbi, the late Joshua Liebman, wrote a book entitled *Peace of Mind*. He has a chapter in the book entitled "Love Thyself Properly." In this chapter he says in substance that it is impossible to love other selves adequately unless you love your own self properly. Many people have been plunged into the abyss of emotional fatalism because they did not love themselves properly. So every individual has a responsibility to be concerned about himself enough to discover what he is made for. After he discovers his calling he should set out to do it with all of the strength and power in his being. . . .

In writing your own paragraphs, you will often find that you need to use more than one method of development to explain your point. The six methods can be used in any combination you choose.

Exercise

7

Name the kinds of development used in the following paragraphs. Then turn to p. 299 to check your answers.

1. ''My Student Career,'' paragraph 3.

2. ''In Defense of Video Games,'' paragraph 3.

3. "The Dimensions of a Complete Life," paragraph 3.

4. "The Dimensions of a Complete Life," paragraph 7.

5. "The Dimensions of a Complete Life," paragraph 16.

6. ''My Student Career,'' paragraph 4.

7. ''Look Who's Listening!'' paragraph 4.

8. "In Defense of Video Games," paragraph 2.

9. "Look Who's Listening!" paragraph 2.

10. "Look Who's Listening!" paragraph 3.

8

Choose one of the following topic sentences or make up one of your own. Write a paragraph of about 100 words, using at least two different methods of development.

1. True education takes place outside the classroom.

2. Money can't buy happiness.

3. Horror movies are popular because . . . .

4. I am convinced I made the right career choice.

5. _____ is the most interesting person I know.

Writing Introductions and Conclusions

Two paragraphs in your paper are *not* developed in the way we've just outlined: the introduction and conclusion. All too often, these paragraphs are dull or clumsy and detract from a paper's effectiveness. But they needn't: here's how to write good ones.

The introduction is worth special attention because that's where your reader either sits up and takes notice of your paper or sighs and pitches it into the wastebasket. Occasionally, for a *very* short paper, you can begin simply with your thesis statement or statement of subject. More usually, though, an **attention-getter** comes before the statement of subject. An attention-getter is a sentence or two designed to get the reader interested in what you have to say.

There are several kinds of attention-getter to choose from:

> 1. interesting incident or anecdote related to your subject (see "The Dimensions of a Complete Life," paragraphs 1 and 2)
> 2. statement of opinion that you intend to challenge (see "In Defense of Video Games," paragraph 1)
> 3. definition (see "My Student Career," paragraph 3)
> 4. quotation
> 5. little-known or striking fact

Add your thesis statement to the attention-getter and your introduction is complete.

The closing paragraph, too, usually has two parts: a summary of the main points of your paper (phrased differently, please — not a word-for-word repetition of your thesis statement or your topic sentences) and a **memorable statement**. Your memorable statement may take several forms:

> 1. show the value or significance of your subject (see "My Student Career," paragraph 6)
> 2. refer back to the content of your opening paragraph (see "Dimensions of a Complete Life," paragraph 20 and "Look Who's Listening!" paragraph 5)
> 3. relevant or thought-provoking quotation
> 4. relevant or thought-provoking question
> 5. suggestion for change
> 6. challenge (see "In Defence of Video Games," paragraph 5)
> 7. solution to the problem discussed in your paper

9

Using as many of the different kinds as you can, write an attention-getter and a memorable statement for each of the following topics. No answers are provided for this exercise.

1. I love (hate) baseball.
2. Canada needs a new immigration policy.
3. The best defence is a good offence.
4. Movies today are better (worse) than ever before.
5. Money is all that matters.
6. Computers are (not) just another fad.
7. Cigarette smoking should (not) be prohibited in the workplace.
8. Ottawa is (not) the best location for the capital of Canada.
9. Post-secondary students should (not) be paid to go to school.
10. A causeway from P.E.I. to the mainland should (not) be built.

Keeping Your Reader With You

As you are writing your paragraphs, keep in mind that you want to make it as easy as possible for your reader to follow you through your paper. Clear **transitions** and an appropriate **tone** can make the difference between a paper that confuses or annoys the reader and one that enlightens and pleases him.

Transitions are those words or phrases that show the relationship between one point and the next, causing a paragraph or a paper to hang together and read smoothly. They are like turn signals on a car: they tell the person following you where you're going. Here are some common transitions that you can use to keep your reader on track:

> 1. *to show a time relation:* first, second, third, next, before, during, after, now, then, finally, last
> 2. *to add an idea or example:* in addition, also, another, furthermore, similarly, for example, for instance
> 3. *to show contrast:* although, but, however, instead, nevertheless, on the other hand, in contrast, on the contrary
> 4. *to show a cause-effect relation:* as a result, consequently, because, since, therefore, thus

Here is a paragraph that has adequate development but no transitions:

> There are many reasons why you should not smoke. Smoking is harmful to your lungs and heart. It is annoying and dangerous to those around you who do not smoke. It is an unattractive and dirty habit. It is difficult to quit smoking. Most worthwhile things in life are hard to achieve.

Not very easy to read, is it? The reader is jerked abruptly from point to point until, battered and bruised, he reaches the end. This kind of writing is unfair to a reader. It makes him do too much of the work. The ideas may all be there, but the reader has to figure out for himself how they fit together. After a couple of paragraphs like this one, even a patient reader can become annoyed.

Now read the same paragraph with the transitions added:

> There are many reasons why you should not smoke; among them, three stand out as the most persuasive. First, smoking is harmful to your lungs and heart. Second, it is both annoying and dangerous to those around you who do not smoke. In addition to these compelling facts, smoking is an unattractive and dirty habit. On the other hand, once you begin, it's awfully difficult to quit; but then, most worthwhile things in life are hard to achieve.

Here the reader is gently guided from one point to the next. By the time he reaches the conclusion, he knows not only what ideas the writer had in mind but also how they fit together. The transitions make the reader's job easy and rewarding.

One final point. As you write the paragraphs of your paper, try to be conscious of your **tone**. *Tone* is a word used to describe a writer's attitude towards the subject and the reader. The words you use, the examples, quotations, and other supporting materials you choose to help explain your main points — all these contribute to your tone. When you are trying to explain something to someone — particularly if it's something you feel strongly about — you may be tempted to be highly emotional in your discussion. If you allow yourself to "get emotional," chances are you won't be convincing. What will be communicated is the strength of your feelings, not the depth of your understanding or the validity of your opinion. To be clear and credible, you need to restrain your enthusiasm (or your anger) and present your points in a calm, reasonable way.

We have two suggestions that may help you find and maintain the right tone. First, never insult your reader, even unintentionally. Avoid phrases like "any idiot can see," "no sane person could believe," and "it is obvious that...." Remember that what is obvious to you isn't necessarily obvious to someone who has a limited understanding of your subject or who disagrees with your opinion. Don't "talk down" to your reader, as though he or she were a child or a simpleton. Don't use sarcasm. And avoid profanity.

Second, don't apologize for your interpretation of your subject. Have confidence in yourself: you've thought long and hard about your subject, you've found good supporting material to help explain it, and you believe in its significance. Present your subject in a *positive* manner. If you hang back, using phrases like "I may be wrong, but ..." or "I tend to feel that ...," your reader won't be inclined to give your points the consideration they deserve. Keep your reader in mind as you write, and your writing will be both clear and convincing.

Exercises

10

Rewrite the following paragraph, adding transitions where necessary and correcting lapses in tone. Turn to p. 299 to compare your revision with ours.

If you like gardening, you're a wimp. It's such a dumb hobby, I don't even know where to begin listing the reasons I hate it. Flowers grow perfectly OK in the wild. Why force them into rows and beds? They claim it's relaxing. I know a guy who got a hernia from lifting manure and another who developed ulcers because his dahlias died. Inside the house, plants are a hazard. They attract insects, aggravate allergies, poison pets, and spread dirt. Gardening is a dangerous activity. Everyone I've met who likes it is a complete twit.

11

Write a reply to this attack on gardening. Remember to keep your tone consistent, and don't forget transitions.

12

Rewrite the following paragraph, adding transitions where necessary and correcting any lapses in tone. Turn to p. 299 for our suggested revision.

I'm no expert — in fact, I really don't know anything about it — but it seems to me that anyone who enjoys baseball is a masochist. I may be wrong (I usually am) but it's a very dull game, don't you think? About every third pitch the batter swings. The fielders do nothing. There are about fifteen hits in a three-hour game. The players actually do something for approximately seven and one half minutes of an entire afternoon. Home runs are dull. One man trots around the bases. The others stand and watch. An awful lot of people seem to like baseball, so I guess there's something wrong with me. People who like baseball are probably boring people.

13

Write a reply to this attack on baseball. Remember to keep your tone consistent, and don't forget transitions.

14

Do either A or B:

A.   Using one of the thesis statements you prepared in chapter 21, exercise 7, write a paper of approximately 300 words.

B.   Using the outline you prepared in chapter 22, exercise 4, write a paper of approximately 500 words.

---

chapter 24

Revising the Paper

At last you've reached the final step in the writing process. By now you're probably tired, fed up, and wishing you'd never even heard of your subject. Revising the paper is a step you'll be strongly tempted to skip. Don't! Until you've looked back (which is what *revised* means), your paper is not ready to be sent out into the world. Ideally, you should revise *several days after writing the paper.* After this "cooling off" period, you'll be able to see your paper more accurately than you could right after you finished writing it. The danger in rereading too soon is that you're likely to "read" what you *think* you've written — what's in your head rather than what you've really got on the paper.

A thorough revision requires at least two "looks back." The first time, read the paper aloud from beginning to end. Check for the overall effectiveness of your paper. Does it do what you hoped it would? Are your points all clearly explained? Has anything been left out? Now read through your paper again, and check carefully for proper transitions and tone.

The second time you read through your paper, do it with the "Revision Guide" (which is on the inside of the back cover) in front of you for easy reference. As you follow the Guide, pay particular attention to the points that tend to give you trouble. (The more of these points there are, of course, the more rereadings will be required.) The last time you reread, do it from end to beginning to check your spelling. Reading from back to front, you're forced to look at each word in isolation, so you're more likely to spot your spelling mistakes. If you find this step too much to bear, ask someone else to read over your paper for you, while you check his or hers.

Exercise

Using the Revision Guide, reread and revise the paper you wrote for exercise 14 in chapter 23.

unit

6

beyond the bare essentials

Introduction

Introduction

We have now covered all the essentials for clear, correct, well organized, and easily understood writing. In this short unit we will go beyond those essentials to some of the pitfalls you may encounter when applying all you've learned up to now. We'll discuss levels of usage; how to avoid clichés, jargon, and slang; the problem of wordiness; and what we call *abusages* — misused phrases and words that creep into writing and reveal ignorance of the language.

Many of the errors we will describe in this unit are not grammatical errors; however, they do interfere with your ability to communicate with your reader. A reader may simply not understand what you're talking about if you use jargon or slang; he or she may think very poorly of you (and your message) if your level of usage is inappropriate or if you use clichés or abusages. Your message will be communicated if your writing is clear and correct (the bare essentials); your message will be more easily and favourably received if your writing is appropriate to the message and to the reader (beyond the bare essentials).

Although these chapters do not concern the essential nuts and bolts of writing, they do contain information that may improve your writing as much as anything else you've learned in this book. Now that you're writing longer papers and having less trouble with the essentials, you are ready to consider the points in this unit in your rereading and revision. The result will be writing that is not only technically correct but also stylistically appropriate.

chapter 25

Levels of Usage

All communication involves three factors: a sender, a message, and a receiver. This book is designed to help the sender — the person who has something to say — to communicate clearly and correctly. What the sender has to say is, of course, the message. Messages should always be adjusted to suit the receiver. This adjustment is the responsibility of the sender. There is no point in sending a message, whether it's a love letter or a spoken instruction, in Spanish if the receiver understands only English. Likewise, there is little to be gained from sending a message in colloquial English (such as you would use when speaking with your close friends) when the receiver is a prospective employer whom you have just met.

There are many **levels of usage** in spoken English. They range from almost unintelligible mutters and groans, through colloquial slang and professional jargon, right up to the formal, correct English used in the law courts, in the Speech from the Throne, and on other formal occasions. The same range is possible in written English: from graffiti up to the formal essay. The subject matter often helps determine the level.

The key to finding the proper level for your message is to consider not only the subject but also the receiver. Sometimes compromises must be made, as when you send one message to a wide variety of receivers. In general, you aim at the higher level of receiver and trust that the others will understand. Thus, wedding invitations, even those to the bridegroom's buddies, are usually stylized and formal.

No one has to tell you what level of language to use when you communicate with your friends at lunch or after school; that level has been clearly established over many years. Sometimes, however, it's not clear what level you should be using, and at such times a careful consideration of the needs and preferences of your receiver is necessary. If your sociology teacher wants you to write papers in a formal style, and you want to get good marks, you will have to write formally. Likewise, because employers in general favour formal letters of application over casual ones, if you want to get a job you will have to write your letter in a formal style. A more relaxed and personal style may be appropriate for a talk given to your class. Letters to friends and conversations with parents are still less formal, although they probably retain a degree of correctness not found in your conversations with your friends (or enemies).

There are no hard and fast divisions of language into levels; nevertheless, to help you choose the style most appropriate to the message and the receiver you are considering, we have outlined the basic characteristics of colloquial, general, and formal language.

	Colloquial	**General**	**Formal**
Vocabulary	casual, everyday; usually concrete; some slang, colloquial expressions, contractions	the language of educated persons; nonspecialized; balance of abstract and concrete; readily understood	often abstract; technical; specialized; no contractions or colloquialisms
Sentence and Paragraph Structure	sentences short, simple; some sentence fragments; paragraphs short	complete sentences of varying length; paragraphs vary, but often short	all sentences complete; sentences usually long, complex; paragraphs fully developed, often at length
Tone	conversational, casual; sounds like ordinary speech	varies to suit message and purpose of writer	impersonal, serious, often instructional
Typical Uses	personal letters, some fiction, some newspapers, much advertising	most of what we read: newspapers, magazines, novels, business correspondence	legal documents, some textbooks, academic writing, scientific reports

No level is "better" than another. Each has its place and function. Your message, your receiver, and your purpose in writing are the factors that determine which level of usage is appropriate.

Exercises

1

Write three paragraphs explaining why you were late for an important meeting — one for an employment interviewer, one for your father, and one for your teammates.

2

In the books, magazines, newspapers, or other materials in your library, try to find a piece of writing that is clearly colloquial, one that is general, and one that is formal. Then list briefly the characteristics of the typical person for whom each piece of writing is intended. What level of education does he or she have? Speculate on the intended reader's interests, beliefs, and lifestyle.

chapter 26

Clichés, Jargon, and Slang

Clichés

A **cliché** is a group of words that was put together, quite creatively, long ago and that has been used and overused ever since. To write in clichés all the time is to write boringly or, even worse, to have your serious meaning found funny.

He was sick as a dog, but we got him to the hospital in the nick of time.

"Sick as a dog" and "nick of time" are clichés. They do have meaning for your reader, but they're tired, worn-out ways of expressing that meaning. It is difficult, if not impossible, to eliminate clichés from your writing, but you can be aware of them and try to use them infrequently. Don't write automatically. Spend some time thinking about what you want to say; then say it in your own words, not someone else's.

Exercise

I

Rewrite these sentences, expressing the ideas in your own words.

1. Jack stopped in his tracks, went pale as a ghost, and fainted dead away.

2. By hook or by crook, even if the going gets rough, we'll stick to our guns and come out on top.

3. The test on clichés is a piece of cake. You'll ace it, as a matter of fact.

4. Far be it from me to destroy your illusions, but Georgia is no marshmallow: she's hard as nails and steady as a rock.

5. Cool as a cucumber, Phyllis slowly but surely gained on the other cyclists, and by pedalling with all her might and main, managed to win the race.

6. Since he'd been up until the wee small hours the night before, Michael felt anything but as fresh as a daisy when he got up at the crack of dawn.

7. Last but not least, I'd like to take the opportunity to introduce my better half, the little woman who has seen me through thick and thin all these years.

8. It goes without saying that, first and foremost, we want employees who are tried and true, who are willing to work like dogs until they know the ropes, and who will be as loyal as the day is long.

9. With her hair as black as coal and face as white as a sheet, Carol is known as "Morticia" to her friends.

10. Children are a pain in the neck: first, they eat you out of house and home, then they leave the nest and never give you the time of day as they concentrate on climbing the ladder of success.

Broadcasting is one of the chief refuges of the cliché. It's a rare newscast that doesn't include the expression "informed sources" or "claimed the life" or "skyrocketing inflation." Listening carefully for such overworked phrases on the radio and TV will make you more aware of them in your own writing and perhaps less likely to use them.

Exercises

2
List ten clichés that you hear every day from teachers, friends, and parents.

3
List ten clichés that you might hear on tonight's news and sports broadcast.

Jargon

Jargon is a special breed of cliché. It is made up of the technical words or phrases used in connection with a particular trade or profession. Often such "trade language" enters the everyday language we use outside our jobs. Like other types of cliché, jargon is a poor substitute for creative, original expression.

The sports world has a highly developed jargon: "third and six," "at the post," "slapshot," "uppercut," "on deck." Many of these expressions find their way into everyday conversation. Other professions have their own jargon. Although jargon may be useful or even necessary in the context of the job, it is clumsy and inappropriate in most writing.

The chief fault in using jargon is that it limits your audience to those who have the same vocabulary as you. To the rest of the world, your writing becomes difficult to understand or even meaningless. You can't expect to communicate in your English essays with sentences like this: "The professor replied with a logical uppercut that caught George right between the eyes and laid him out for the count." This may be a colourful way to describe the winning of an argument, but it will be effective only with readers who are boxing fans.

At its worst, jargon is the imitation of a specialized vocabulary. With its abstract words and long, complicated sentences, such jargon becomes sound without meaning, as the following sentence illustrates.

> Thus the meaningful verbalization of conceptual improvisation at the interpersonal interface is contra-indicated by frustrations arising from idiosyncratic linguistic actualization, vocabulary-wise, so that the verbalized formulations of the initiating consciousness actuate the latent rejection mechanisms of the ....

The cure for this kind of jargon is consideration for your reader. If you really want your reader to understand you, write in a simple, straightforward style.

Exercise

4

Write as many examples of jargon as you can for each of the following professions. If you treat this as a class exercise, you'll quickly see just how many examples there are.

1. filmmaker: pan, wipe, tracking shot ...

2. cardplayer: hit, stay, run, cut ...

3. microcomputer enthusiast: keyboarding, debugging, booting the DOS ...

4. salesperson: territory, distribution strategy, closing ...

5. nurse: hang an IV, push fluids, no code ...

Slang

Slang is street talk, inappropriate for the written language. There are innumerable examples of slang, from *A-OK* to *zowie*, and even dictionaries don't attempt to keep all the terms straight. Unless you're quoting someone who uses slang, avoid it and find words or expressions appropriate to written English. If you're in doubt, check your dictionary. The notation *sl.* or *slang* will appear after the word if it is slang, or after the meaning of the word that is a slang meaning. (Some words, such as *chick* and *neat,* have both a general meaning and a slang meaning.)

Like jargon, slang can limit, or even block, your communication with a reader. Slang is the most quickly dated type of language: what is appropriate now may well be laughed at in a few months. ("Right on, man. What a groovy scene! Far out!") Also, like jargon, slang is understood only by a limited group of people. You may exclude many readers if you use slang familiar only to a small group.

Exercise

5

For one day, keep a list of the slang expressions you hear or read.

chapter 27

Wordiness

Wordiness is a problem that may develop if you try too hard to impress a reader with your use of words. Keep in mind that no reader wants to read "fill" or "padding." All writing should be as concise as it can be and still convey the message clearly. Even authors like Dickens and Michener, who have written huge quantities, choose their language carefully and don't waste their readers' time with unnecessary words.

Here's an example of what can happen when, in trying to impress, you lose sight of the need to communicate. Do you recognize any of your writing in this?

> In my own opinion, I feel very strongly indeed that the government of this Dominion of Canada is basically in need of an additional amount of meaningful input from its electors, the people of this country, at this point in time, frankly speaking. For too long a period of time, the leaders of this nation in Ottawa have, rightly or wrongly, gone heedlessly off on their own particular course of action without the benefit of consultation or dialogue with the people, who, it stands to reason, are most willing and able to provide, clearly and without doubt, a distinct and clear path to follow into the future world of tomorrow.

By eliminating wordiness, make this into a clear statement.

The following are some of the worst offenders we have discovered in student writing. In some cases, many words are used when one or two would do. In other cases, the wording is redundant (says the same thing twice).

Wordy	Acceptable
"absolutely complete"	complete
"absolutely nothing"	nothing
"at that point in time"	then
"basic fundamentals"	fundamentals
"circled around"	circled
"collect together"	collect
"completely free"	free
"continue on"	continue
"dead bodies"	corpses

Wordy	**Acceptable**
"disappear from view"	disappear
"entirely eliminated"	eliminated
"equally as good"	as good
"exactly identical"	identical
"final conclusion"	conclusion
"green in colour"	green
"having the same thing in common"	having in common
"I personally feel"	I feel
"in my opinion, I think"	in my opinion
"in this day and age"	now
"new innovation"	innovation
"personal friend"	friend
"proceed ahead"	proceed
"real, genuine leather"	genuine leather
"repeat again"	repeat
"repeat the same"	repeat
"seven A.M. in the morning"	seven A.M.
"small in size"	small
"such as, for example"	such as
"surround on all sides"	surround
"true fact"	fact
"very (most, quite, rather) unique"	unique

Exercises

Revise these sentences, making them more concise and understandable. Suggested answers are on p. 299.

1. Even at that point in time, dead bodies were treated with respect, just as they are by civilized nations in this day and age.

2. My final conclusion concerning the real, genuine value of Bargain Barry's reduced price sale goods is exactly identical with yours.

3. Small in size as he was, and surrounded on all sides by strange children he didn't know, the quite uniquely courageous seven-year-old challenged the class bully to a fight.

4. The sergeant repeated again to the brand-new recruits, "You will be called at 5:30 A.M. in the morning, and you will have circled around the barracks on the double by 5:45. You will at that point in time be completely free until 6:00, when you will continue on to the barracks mess for breakfast."

5. The new recruits disappeared from view after the 7:00 A.M. breakfast, to discuss what they could do to get even with a sergeant who woke them up one full hour before the necessary time.

6. They personally thought that the sergeant would probably repeat the same obnoxious behaviour again each day, so they decided to proceed ahead with a new, innovative plan as an appropriate response.

7. The basic fundamentals of their plan included getting the sergeant very drunk one evening and putting him to bed at about 4:30 A.M. — not in his own bunkhouse next to theirs, but in one that was next to the officers' quarters.

8. In my opinion, I must admit that I thought their plan was absolutely and completely foolproof, and that it was a great idea.

9. They had entirely eliminated the possibility that the sergeant would know where he was in the morning by bribing their friends in that bunkhouse to leave it empty and by arranging it like the sergeant's own personal barracks.

10. It is a real fact that, at 5:30 A.M., the sergeant, true to his own promise that nothing would prevent his wake-up call, staggered into the bunkhouse next to his and blasted with bugle and voice until he woke all the inhabitants. He never did a 5:30 A.M. morning reveille again.

chapter 28

Abusages

Some words and terms that appear in writing are simply incorrect or used incorrectly. We've named these misspelled, misused, or made-up words **abusages.** The presence of abusages in writing makes the writer appear ignorant in the eyes of anyone who knows anything about the English language. The list of abusages that follows is a partial one but does include some of the worst offenders. You should add to it the abusages that your teacher hates most.

"alot"	There is no such word. Use *many* or *much.*
"anyways"	Also, "anywheres" and "a long ways." There is no *s* on these words.
"could of"	Also, "would of," "might of," "should of," and so on. The helping verb is *have*: "could have."
"didn't do nothing"	This, along with all other double negatives ("couldn't get nowhere," "wouldn't talk to nobody," and so on), is wrong. Write "didn't do anything" or "did nothing."
"irregardless"	There is no such word. Use *regardless.*
"irrevelant"	This is a misspelling. Spell the word *irrelevant.*
"media" used as a singular word	The word *media* is plural. The singular is *medium.* Write "TV is a mass medium. Print and radio are also examples of mass media."
"off of"	Use *off* alone: "I fell off the wagon."
"prejudice" used as an adjective	It is wrong to write "She is prejudice against men." Use *prejudiced.*
"prejudism"	There is no such word. Use *prejudice*: "He should show no prejudice to either side."
"real" used as an adverb	"Real sad," "real swell," and "real nice" are wrong. Use *really* or *very.*

"reason is because"   Use "the reason is that": "The reason is that I don't use a deodorant."

"suppose to"   Also, "use to." Use "supposed to" and "used to."

"themself"   Also, "theirself," "ourselfs," "yourselfs," and "themselfs." The plural of *self* is *selves: themselves, ourselves,* and so on. Don't use "theirselves," though; there's no such word.

"youse"   There is no such word. "You" is used for both singular and plural. When waiting on tables, don't say "May I help youse?" to a group of English instructors, if you want a tip.

Exercise

I

Correct the following sentences where necessary. Answers are on p. 300.

1. Nell should of gone with us to the beach; now she can't go nowheres.

2. Alot of us thought he might be prejudice, but actually he turned out to be a real nice man.

3. I'm suppose to see whether the reason for the delay is because it's raining.

4. They are suppose to get the ball themselfs, irregardless of where it is when they come off of the field.

5. Because I won't lend her my homework, she thinks I'm showing prejudism, but she was suppose to do her own homework anyways.

6. If youse don't do nothing about boarding the windows, you'll have pieces of glass everywheres in the house.

7. It's real sad to see signs of prejudism in young children, who must have been influenced by their parents.

8. It is irrevelant whether she fell off of or was pushed off of her bicycle; she is disqualified anyways.

9. They should of finished the race even though they were behind, since every entrant is suppose to finish unless disqualified or injured.

10. I didn't talk to nobody about seeing one cyclist cheat, since the judges don't

consider a spectator's remarks to be revelant.

A whole category of abusages is created by misuse of pronouns.

> Him and I had a fight.
> Bob and her are the best spellers.
> It came down to a choice between she and me.

(handwritten: C use)

There are two groups of pronouns: those used for subjects and those not used for subjects. In chapter 4 you reviewed how to find the subject of a sentence. When that subject is, or is referred to by, a pronoun, the pronoun should be one of these:

I	we
you	
he, she	they

When the pronoun is *not* the subject of the sentence, you should use one of these:

me	us
you	
him, her	them

He and *I* had a fight. (The pronouns are the subject of the sentence.)

Bob and *she* are the best spellers. (The pronoun is part of the multiple subject "Bob and she.")

It came down to a choice between *her* and *me*. (The pronouns are not the subject of the sentence.)

The girls in the blue uniforms are *they*. (The pronoun stands for the subject of the sentence, *girls*.)

He is more honest than *she*. (The verb *is* is understood at the end of the sentence, and *she* is the subject of that verb.)

Exercise

2

Correct the pronouns in these sentences as necessary.

1. No one except you and me *(handwritten: I)* would go cycling in this rain.

2. Him and I can't push this car any farther than you and her could.

3. Her and me *(handwritten: I)* did a really stupid thing.

4. He is a better cook than her *(handwritten: she)*, and she plays snooker better than him.

5. You and I can use the Caravan passports all week, and you and her can use them on the weekend when I'm not here.

6. As we walked along Bloor Street, we saw Marie and he going into Toby's restaurant.

7. The police stopped he and I at the door of our apartment building.

8. Everyone had to wait outside except them.

9. Us and them are not very good friends anymore.

10. No one is happier than me that youse got the job.

3

Eliminate all of the abusages from this dreadful paragraph.

The 1987 Rendezvous at Thunder Bay would of been the best party him and me ever attended if the weather would of only been better. The Rendezvous is a annual event that brings together alot of folks who come dressed as voyageurs and fur traders. People are suppose to wear canvas and leather and wool. There isn't no polyester or nylon allowed, irregardless of how wet it gets. The reason is because everyone is suppose to dress exactly the way they did in the eighteenth century. But canvas don't hold out water, and the rain couldn't of come down harder. Youse wouldn't of believed how soaked us all got.

Then the people of Thunder Bay come out to Old Fort William with food and drink and throw a party for us in the shelter of a huge barn. We forgot about our sodden clothing real quick as we found ourselfs laughing and dancing with our new friends. The party was a real big success, and the reason was because the people of Thunder Bay showed such alot of generosity and friendship that even the torrential rains couldn't do nothing to spoil our stay.

appendices

Look Who's Listening!

Brian Green

The single most important factor in becoming a good communicator is having a clear idea of who your audience is. This simple principle is the most often overlooked aspect of effective communication. Whether you are speaking to a professional organization, constructing a business report, or writing a love letter, knowledge of your audience is vital to your success. This knowledge will shape the tone, content, and approach of your communication.

Tone and language can contribute greatly to the success of your message, but to do so they must be carefully chosen to appeal to the specific audience you wish to reach. Slang, which is inappropriate in a formal school or business report, may be the most effective way of conveying your message to your teammates or younger brother. Formal language and tone have their specialized uses but would be out of place in many settings: "Wasn't that a handsome execution of a most difficult manoeuvre at second base!" would strike most listeners as sounding distinctly peculiar. It is through consideration of the people who will receive your message that you determine the tone and language that will carry your content most directly and effectively to them.

Content, too, is influenced by your perception of the receivers of your message. For example, it is pointless to explain the plot of a movie to people who have seen it; instead, criticize or comment on the film. Your judgment of the audience's knowledge, experience, or expertise on your topic must be taken into account when you are deciding on the amount of detail and background to include in any message. As any competent public speaker will tell you, nothing will ruin the effect of your communication more quickly than speaking over the heads of an audience or, even worse, talking down to them.

Knowledge of your audience will also enable you to devise an effective approach to your topic. A hostile or reluctant reader or listener may have to be presented with a step-by-step build-up of evidence before being exposed to your main argument; with a sympathetic receiver, you may want to begin with your conclusion and then reveal how it was developed. A business contact will want a concise report in the form of a business letter or memorandum, while a friend or colleague will want to hear all the details, together with your opinions and feelings about the same transaction. Even a good joke teller will tailor his approach to an audience to suit what he sees as their tastes and tolerances.

Communication is only effective — indeed, it only takes place — when your message reaches and is understood by the intended receiver. Before you decide on the tone, content, and approach of your message, look who's listening!

In Defense of Video Games

Brian Green

"Video game backlash" is both a headline in Canadian newspapers and a current trend among legislators, parents, teachers, and miscellaneous other adults. I suspect few of them have ever stepped inside a video game arcade, much less dropped some change into one of the machines and tried to save the world from invading monsters, marauding spacecraft, or chunks of space debris. As an adult (alas!) and a teacher, I wish to register my lone cry of dissent against video hatred. Unlike the lowly billiard parlour and pinball arcade that were its predecessors, the video arcade does have considerable redeeming value: it teaches real skills; it develops concepts that have practical and valuable applications; and it delivers positive social lessons.

Video games are not the mindless diversion that television is. They demand skill. The hand–eye co-ordination, reflex response, swiftness and precision required would do credit to a hockey goaltender or a jet pilot. Most of the skills called upon are inborn, but even the slowest and clumsiest of us could benefit from developing and augmenting what poor skills we have. On my favourite game I have twice achieved a score of 9000; last week in a video arcade across town, I watched a young lady of about fourteen rack up over 200,000 on the same game. I would not hesitate to put my life in her hands in any situation that required manual dexterity, quick reflexes, and steady nerves.

Aside from honing mechanical skills, video games encourage the development of practical concepts and attitudes. No young person who is familiar with the games has any fear of computers, yet computer fear, amounting to paranoia in many, is a very common and debilitating adult ailment. The video game is an enjoyable, educational, and relevant introduction to the workplace of tomorrow. Most computer programmers and "software people" delight in the games that are made possible by the same micro-chips on which their careers depend. In fact, several of the most fanatic players in my local arcade are computer experts in large companies. It is a short step from manipulating rocket ships and anti-aircraft guns on a screen to manipulating bits of information in an automated office.

There are many senses in which video games are socially educational as well. First, a healthy sense of competition is engendered, since one is usually playing against a machine and trying to perform better against it than other players have done. Most games have a facility for storing and displaying the names of the players who have scored highest. A great deal of social interaction and co-operation takes place in video arcades, despite the apparent isolation of individual players. Instructions on video games are often so terse they require explanation. The rules, scoring, hints, and method of play are passed from player to player in an atmosphere of friendly co-operation, the objective of which is to beat the machine. Second, the player is always on the side of "good" against "evil." The goal of most games is to save the world, a city, or oneself from marauding villains of all sinister sorts and shapes. I would like to see someone do a study of the social impact such indoctrination has on young minds. What defensive posture is most often taken? How is the status quo preserved in the face of external threat? Third, there is the cathartic value of video violence. TV violence seems to stimulate aggression: the result, perhaps, of the viewer's passivity. In contrast, anyone who has pushed him or herself to the limit in a video game, scoring a "personal best" in the effort to ward off alien invaders, feels only a sense of achievement and exhaustion; there is nothing left over for a continuation of the carnage in real life.

I challenge any video critic to visit an arcade and watch the computer programmers, teachers, pilots, technicians, inventors, and philosophers of tomorrow in training. You needn't feel out of place: pretend you're a visiting computer whiz checking out the competition — lots of us adults may be found waiting our turn to save the world. But please don't refer to the ideas I've summarized in this essay. We don't want to know that we're being taught skills, concepts, and values: we're having fun!

My Student Career

Caroline Gunn

I have always felt astonished whenever someone tells me that he has held the same job for ten years (or fifteen, or twenty). The prospect of a career that lasts so long terrifies me. Since I'll be graduating in another month, I've been giving a good deal of thought to my career choices. Suddenly it struck me: I'm in my fourteenth year as a student. I've already had a career! I began to understand some of my panicky feelings about graduating. Throw anyone out of a fourteen year career with no promise of secure employment and see if she doesn't sweat a bit!

In reflecting on my career as a student I realize that I have learned a great deal. In fact, I've become an expert in several fields: I know what makes a good teacher and what makes a good course; I know how to write an exam or term paper; and, most important, I know how to learn. These skills are not ones the school system set out to teach me, but they are the ones I have been drilled in, the ones I have practised most intensively. Of course, I have perfected other skills that will be useful in my second career, but it is these four student skills that interest me now.

A teacher is someone who communicates by word, action, or example to effect a desirable change in an audience. A *good* teacher is someone who does all this and at the same time inspires, motivates, and participates in the learning of his or her students. Such a person is always an interesting individual. Scratch a good teacher and you'll find a world traveller, amateur actor, part-time farmer, inventor, writer, baseball player, taxi driver, television hostess, or film-maker. The good teacher relates to students as people, acknowledging and forgiving us our faults, while recognizing and encouraging our strengths. Good teachers are people who enjoy learning. Good teachers are themselves always learning, always receptive to new ideas; they delight in the insights and fledgling creativity of young people. I have been privileged to know five good teachers in my student career.

A good course doesn't require a good teacher (though having one helps); a competent teacher can do wonders with a well prepared program. A good course is not an easy course. There are plenty of "bird" courses — the student underground network is humming with information on which courses are easy credits. Such courses are about as satisfying as junk food: they fill you up but leave you hungry. A good course is one that supplies lots of information but doesn't require the memorization of trivia; one that offers practical principles but doesn't prevent students from applying them to their own situations in individual ways. A good course is clearly organized, fairly and appropriately evaluated, and interestingly presented. Fortunately, good courses are much more common than good teachers.

An unavoidable part of any course is evaluation. I have learned many techniques for doing well on tests, exams, and term papers, but there's no substitute for knowing the material thoroughly. This means taking careful notes in class and reading the text closely. Next, you can improve your chances of getting a good mark if you write well. I recently got back a paper from a teacher on which she had written, "You have misinterpreted or ignored most of the relevant material on this topic." But she gave me a mark of seventy-four per cent! The reason, as I see it, is that while I didn't say very much, I said it very well. A third key to success in essays or class tests is neatness. I suspect that neatness gains me the benefit of the doubt on questionable answers, and means the difference between eighty per cent and one hundred per cent on good answers. Finally, your success in a course can be favourably influenced if you appear interested in and enthusiastic about the course, without becoming a pest. I try once a week to ask a question in each course and often have the question thought out before class to make sure it's interesting and doesn't sound like a challenge to the teacher.

Some may consider all of this terribly cynical and unrelated to the purpose of education. I disagree. The system that has made me an expert on good teaching, good courses, and good grades has also taught me how to realize my potential as a student. And I believe the same principles will apply in any other career I enter. Most important is curiosity. I have discovered that I actually enjoy learning new things, exploring unfamiliar situations, once I get over my initial fear. Patience is important, too. Throwing your hands up and quitting in frustration is an easy "out," but the impatient student is the loser. There is something to be gained from the worst teacher, the dullest course, even if the gain is only increased self-discipline. Persistence is another important ingredient in success. There is so much to learn; why be satisfied with the minimum effort required to get by? By digging in at the library, I have managed to learn far more in some courses than the teacher required or my grades would indicate. And this leads me to my last and most important revelation. Education is *not* about marks; it's bigger than courses and teachers, more important than diplomas. It is the necessary foundation on which to build a successful career and a full life.

The Dimensions of a Complete Life[1]

Martin Luther King, Jr.

Many, many centuries ago, out on a lonely, obscure island called Patmos, a man by the name of John caught a vision of the new Jerusalem descending out of heaven from God. One of the greatest glories of this new city of God that John saw was its completeness. It was not partial and one-sided, but it was complete in all three of its dimensions. And so, in describing the city in the twenty-first chapter of the book of Revelation, John says this: "The length and the breadth and the height of it are equal." In other words, this new city of God, this city of ideal humanity, is not an unbalanced entity but it is complete on all sides.

Now John is saying something quite significant here. For so many of us the book of Revelation is a very difficult book, puzzling to decode. We look upon it as something of a great enigma wrapped in mystery. And certainly if we accept the book of Revelation as a record of actual historical occurrences it is a difficult book, shrouded with impenetrable mysteries. But if we will look beneath the peculiar jargon of its author and the prevailing apocalyptic symbolism, we will find in this book many eternal truths which continue to challenge us. One such truth is that of this text. What John is really saying is this: that life as it should be and life at its best is the life that is complete on all sides.

There are three dimensions of any complete life to which we can fitly give the words of this text: length, breadth, and height. The length of life as we shall think of it here is not its duration or its longevity, but it is the push of a life forward to achieve its personal ends and ambitions. It is the inward concern for one's own welfare. The breadth of life is the outward concern for the welfare of others. The height of life is the upward reach for God.

These are the three dimensions of life, and without the three being correlated, working harmoniously together, life is incomplete. Life is something of a great triangle. At one angle stands the individual person, at the other angle stand other persons, and at the top stands the Supreme, Infinite Person, God. These three must meet in every individual life if that life is to be complete.

Now let us notice first the length of life. I have said that this is the dimension of life in which the individual is concerned with developing his inner powers. It is that dimension of life in which the individual pursues personal ends and ambitions. This is perhaps the selfish dimension of life, and there is such a thing as moral and rational self-interest. If one is not concerned about himself he cannot be totally concerned about other selves.

Some years ago a learned rabbi, the late Joshua Liebman, wrote a book entitled *Peace of Mind.* He has a chapter in the book entitled "Love Thyself Properly." In this chapter he says in substance that it is impossible to love other selves adequately unless you love your own self properly. Many people have been plunged into the

---

[1]*From* The Measure of a Man *by Martin Luther King, Jr. (Philadelphia: Christian Education Press, 1959). Used by permission of the United Church Press.*

King originally wrote "Dimensions" as a speech and later published it in written form. As King's piece demonstrates, the principles of organization we have explained in unit 5 can be applied to oral presentations just as successfully as they can to writing.

"Dimensions" is a fairly challenging piece of reading, because King uses a very wide range of vocabulary. Don't let the unfamiliar words discourage you or throw you off track, however. If you read carefully, you'll notice that King frequently defines or explains difficult words as he uses them.

abyss of emotional fatalism because they did not love themselves properly. So every individual has a responsibility to be concerned about himself enough to discover what he is made for. After he discovers his calling he should set out to do it with all of the strength and power in his being. He should do it as if God Almighty called him at this particular moment in history to do it. He should seek to do his job so well that the living, the dead, or the unborn could not do it better. No matter how small one thinks his life's work is in terms of the norms of the world and the so-called big jobs, he must realize that it has cosmic significance if he is serving humanity and doing the will of God.

To carry this to one extreme, if it falls your lot to be a street-sweeper, sweep streets as Raphael painted pictures, sweep streets as Michelangelo carved marble, sweep streets as Beethoven composed music, sweep streets as Shakespeare wrote poetry. Sweep streets so well that all the hosts of heaven and earth will have to pause and say, "Here lived a great street-sweeper who swept his job well." In the words of Douglas Mallock:

> If you can't be a highway, just be a trail;
> If you can't be the sun, be a star,
> For it isn't by size that you win or you fail—
> Be the best of whatever you are.

When you do this, you have mastered the first dimensions of life — the length of life.

But don't stop here; it is dangerous to stop here. There are some people who never get beyond this first dimension. They are brilliant people; often they do an excellent job in developing their inner powers; but they live as if nobody else lived in the world but themselves. There is nothing more tragic than to find an individual bogged down in the length of life, devoid of the breadth.

The breadth of life is that dimension of life in which we are concerned about others. An individual has not started living until he can rise above the narrow confines of his individualistic concerns to the broader concerns of all humanity.

You remember one day a man came to Jesus and he raised some significant questions. Finally he got around to the question, "Who is my neighbour?" This could easily have been a very abstract question left in mid-air. But Jesus immediately pulled that question out of mid-air and placed it on a dangerous curve between Jerusalem and Jericho. He talked about a certain man who fell among thieves. Three men passed; two of them on the other side. And finally another man came and helped the injured man on the ground. He is known to us as the Good Samaritan. Jesus says in substance that this is a great man. He was great because he could project the "I" into the "thou."

So often we say that the priest and the Levite were in a big hurry to get to some ecclesiastical meeting and so they did not have time. They were concerned about that. I would rather think of it another way. I can well imagine that they were quite afraid. You see, the Jericho road is a dangerous road, and the same thing that happened to the man who was robbed and beaten could have happened to them. So I imagine the first question that the priest and the Levite asked was this: "If I stop to help this man, what will happen to me?" Then the good Samaritan came by, and by the very nature of his concern reversed the question: "If I do not stop to help this man, what will happen to him?" And so this man was great because he had the mental equipment for a dangerous altruism. He was great because he could surround the length of his life with the breadth of life. He was great not only because he had ascended to certain heights of economic security, but because he could condescend to the depths of human need.

All this has a great deal of bearing in our situation in the world today. So often racial groups are concerned about the length of life, their economic privileged position, their social status. So often nations of the world are concerned about the length of life, perpetuating their nationalistic concerns, and their economic ends. May it not be that the problem in the world today is that individuals as well as nations have been overly concerned with the length of life, devoid of the breadth? But there is still something to remind us that we are interdependent, that we are all involved in a single process, that we are all somehow caught in an inescapable network of mutuality. Therefore whatever affects one directly affects all indirectly.

As long as there is poverty in the world I can never be rich, even if I have a billion dollars. As long as diseases are rampant and millions of people in this world cannot expect to live more than twenty-eight or thirty years, I can never be totally healthy even if I just got a good check-up at Mayo Clinic. I can never be what I ought to be until you are what you ought to be. This is the way our world is made. No individual or nation can stand out boasting of being independent. We are interdependent. So John Donne placed it in graphic terms when he affirmed, "No man is an island entire of itself. Every man is a piece of the continent, a part of the main." Then he goes on to say, "Any man's death diminishes me because I am involved in mankind, and therefore never send to know for whom the bell tolls; it tolls for thee." When we discover this, we master the second dimension of life.

Finally, there is a third dimension. Some people never get beyond the first two dimensions of life. They master the first two. They develop their inner powers; they love humanity, but they stop right here. They end up with the feeling that man is the end of all things and that humanity is God. Philosophically or theologically, many of them would call themselves humanists. They seek to live life without a sky. They find themselves bogged down on the horizontal plane without being integrated on the vertical plane. But if we are to live the complete life we must reach up and discover God. H.G. Wells was right: "The man who is not religious begins at nowhere and ends at nothing." Religion is like a mighty wind that breaks down doors and makes that possible and even easy which seems difficult and impossible.

In our modern world it is easy for us to forget this. We so often find ourselves unconsciously neglecting this third dimension of life. Not that we go up and say, "Good-by, God, we are going to leave you now." But we become so involved in the things of this world that we are unconsciously carried away by the rushing tide of materialism which leaves us treading in the confused waters of secularism. We find ourselves living in what Professor Sorokin of Harvard called a sensate civilization, believing that only those things which we can see and touch and to which we can apply our five senses have existence.

Something should remind us once more that the great things in this universe are things that we never see. You walk out at night and look up at the beautiful stars as they bedeck the heavens like swinging lanterns of eternity, and you think you can see all. Oh, no. You can never see the law of gravitation that holds them there. You walk around this vast campus and you probably have a great esthetic experience as I have had walking about and looking at the beautiful buildings, and you think you see all. Oh, no. You can never see the mind of the architect who drew the blueprint. You can never see the love and the faith and the hope of the individuals who made it so. You look at me and you think you see Martin Luther King. You don't see Martin Luther King; you see my body, but, you must understand, my body can't think, my body can't reason. You don't see the me that makes me me. You can never see my personality.

Plato was right: "The visible is a shadow cast by the invisible." And so God is still around. All of our new knowledge, all of our new developments, cannot diminish his being one iota. These new advances have banished God neither from the microcosmic compass of the atom nor from the vast, unfathomable ranges of interstellar space. The more we learn about this universe, the more mysterious and awesome it becomes. God is still here.

So I say to you, seek God and discover him and make him a power in your life. Without him all of our efforts turn to ashes and our sunrises into darkest nights. Without him, life is a meaningless drama with the decisive scenes missing. But with him we are able to rise from the fatigue of despair to the buoyancy of hope. With him we are able to rise from the midnight of desperation to the daybreak of joy. St. Augustine was right — we were made for God and we will be restless until we find rest in him.

Love yourself, if that means rational, healthy, and moral self-interest. You are commanded to do that. That is the length of life. Love your neighbor as you love yourself. You are commanded to do that. That is the breadth of life. But never forget that there is a first and even greater commandment, "Love the Lord thy God with all thy heart and all thy soul and all thy mind." This is the height of life. And when you do this you live the complete life.

Thank God for John who, centuries ago, caught a vision of the new Jerusalem. God grant that those of us who still walk the road of life will catch this vision and decide to move forward to that city of complete life in which the length and the breadth and the height are equal.

appendix b

Answers

Chapter 1: Three Suggestions for Quick Improvement

1

1. desperately
2. crackling
3. conceivable
4. atonement
5. mating
6. rarely
7. elevator
8. emerging
9. positively
10. apologizing

2

1. gravely
2. heaving
3. defusible
4. generator
5. shapely
6. excitement
7. releasing
8. removable
9. consummately
10. assuring

3

1. operatively
2. interference
3. desirable
4. continuance
5. abridging
6. mangy
7. dissolutely
8. acquiring
9. shakable
10. aerating

4

1. apologizing
2. encouragement
3. noisy
4. issuable
5. famous
6. abridgement
7. movable
8. officiating
9. valuation
10. valueless

5

1. imaginary
2. wrangling
3. adversity
4. prancing
5. blameless
6. blaming
7. wavy
8. obtuseness
9. realizable
10. obliging

1. blotting
2. spanning
3. submitted
4. failing
5. blurred

1. fatter
2. getting
3. stopped
4. persisting
5. blotter

1. beguiling
2. demurred
3. referring
4. stripped
5. shooting

1. deferring
2. remittance
3. regrettable
4. cuddled
5. acquittal

1. tippable
2. wondering
3. regretful
4. rejected
5. corruptible

1. equipping
2. repelling
3. trapper
4. remitted
5. smearing

1. occurrence
2. persistence
3. emergence
4. recurrence
5. perseverance

7
6. plumper
7. admitting
8. abating
9. begging
10. entailed

8
6. mauled
7. pinned
8. lengthening
9. knitter
10. enlisted

9
6. expelling
7. grabbed
8. jarring
9. knitting
10. hindered

10
6. concurred
7. flagging
8. abettor
9. shining
10. referred

11
6. whipping
7. detained
8. extolling
9. reappearance
10. regrettable

12
6. blurring
7. occurring
8. allotting
9. accessible
10. petitioner

13
6. consistency
7. sufferance
8. resistance
9. concurrence
10. deterrence

15

1. brief
2. wield
3. deceive
4. achieve
5. relieve

6. retrieval
7. ceiling
8. besiege
9. receipt
10. grieve

16

1. pier
2. hygiene
3. hierarchy
4. deceit
5. fierce

6. pieced
7. tier
8. conceivable
9. receive
10. hieroglyph

17

1. thief, priest
2. surveillant, seized
3. freight, weighed
4. Neither, conceited
5. veins, Geiger

18

1. frontier, foreign
2. friendly, reigns
3. fierce, chief
4. siege, heir
5. heights, leisure

19

1. either, their, beliefs
2. deceived, perceive
3. conceivable, receive
4. relief, neither
5. neighbour, conceited, conceit

20

1. potatoes
2. mysteries
3. businesses
4. ghettos
5. leaves

6. theses
7. sheep
8. criteria
9. larvae
10. indexes *or* indices

1. loneliness
2. moneyed *or* monied
3. laziness
4. hazier
5. likeliest

6. denies
7. denying
8. twentieth
9. healthily
10. subtly

22

1. bet–ter
2. com–prise
3. pa–tience
4. ac–knowl–edg–ment
5. re–hearse

6. whip–ping
7. diph–the–ri–a
8. thrown
9. dis–tri–bu–tion
10. suc–ceed

Chapter 2: Sound-Alikes, Look-Alikes, and Spoilers

1

1. course, affect
2. Are, accept
3. then, dessert
4. you're, losing
5. quite, here

6. whose, conscience
7. fourth, than
8. It's, its
9. choose, course, advice
10. dining, does

2

1. principal's, principles
2. chose, fourth
3. Except, desserts
4. Your, conscious
5. quiet, hear

6. Except, minor
7. Morals, too, loose
8. You're, your, conscience, are
9. It's, stationery
10. woman, who's, does

3

1. hear, here
2. To, stationary
3. Losing, it's
4. you're, minor
5. Desert, peace

6. Council, except
7. coarse, effect
8. Peace, quiet
9. Women, whose
10. peace, forth

4

1. then, deserted
2. quiet, where, their
3. two, were, were, later
4. consul, principles
5. Many, lose

6. dose, your
7. quiet, their, principles, then
8. It's, latter, two
9. Later, accept
10. quite, women, lose

5

1. allot, dining
2. peace, our
3. Women, deserted
4. we're, where
5. fourth, chose, stationary

6. Are, conscious, you're
7. Their, course, choose, here
8. affected, morale
9. Whose, advice
10. principle, peace–

6

1. effects, moral
2. compliment, then
3. advise, personal
4. miner, does
5. There, their, morale

6. hear, your
7. personnel, whose, stationery
8. chose, latter, course, accept
9. deserted, quite
10. Too, too, where

7

1. It's, quite, personnel, course
2. their, hear, counsel
3. chose, advice
4. Then, than
5. where, effected

6. Whose, moral
7. Whose, conscience, affected, accept
8. course, does, your
9. deserts, personal
10. Too

8

Accept my advice: go immediately to Weight Watchers! Do not pass your home; do not collect one last dessert. Of course, it's all a matter of conscience — your conscience. Whether you choose to think of yourself as pleasingly plump or too fat is your business. There are always those friends without principle who will tell you anything you want to hear — for instance, how your gently curving middle (read, bulging stomach) complements your tall frame and large bones. But then, are those friends? I'm your friend, so please believe me: dining heavily six or seven times daily is not only not for you, it's not for anyone. You really must lose weight. Two hundred pounds on a five-foot-two frame is big-league fat. I beg you, join the minors!

9

There must be a better way to cope with house renovations. If I were to describe my personal agony during the months it took for the construction workers and contractors to achieve their final effect your heart would bleed. Plaster dust was the worst problem, because it gets into everything, making even dining an uncomfortable experience. As the walls were torn loose and the house was gradually reduced to its skeleton, plaster dust found its way into every crack and corner. The noise and confusion affected my morale, and I became inclined to use coarse language, particularly with those who insisted on giving me advice. Later, when my conscience got the better of me, my feeble attempts at apology were not accepted. In the end, the renovations cost me my peace of mind, my friends, and more money than I dreamed possible.

10

By the time we discovered that there was too much cholesterol in fried foods, we were already addicted. French fries and chicken wings, battered fish and doughnuts were an <u>accepted</u> part of our diet. The <u>effect</u> that <u>dining</u> on such foods has on us is evident in our <u>waist</u>lines and in the nation's heart disease statistics. The <u>desserts</u> we tend to <u>choose</u> are the worst offenders, according to diet <u>counsellors</u>, but <u>our</u> main <u>course</u> can be equally dangerous if <u>its</u> cholesterol count is high. Experts now <u>advise</u> us <u>to</u> be guided by the <u>principle</u> that "less is more." But this <u>advice</u> is more difficult to follow than one might expect in a society that has been conditioned to <u>believe</u> "bigger is better". The <u>moral</u> seems to be that we must <u>choose</u> between foods that taste good and foods that do good.

Chapter 3: The Apostrophe

1

1. it's
2. hasn't
3. they're
4. there's
5. won't
6. it'll
7. he's
8. we'll
9. you're
10. she's

2

1. he'll
2. you've
3. I'm
4. don't
5. who's
6. wouldn't
7. we're
8. who'll
9. you'll
10. didn't

3

1. can't
2. you're
3. they're
4. shouldn't
5. who'll
6. don't
7. you'll
8. we're
9. they've
10. it'll

4

1. Yes, it's a long way from Halifax to Vancouver, but we've been in training for three months.
2. We're taking the train to Antigonish and we're biking to Halifax; then we'll begin the big trip west.
3. Can't you stop your poodle from chasing its tail?
4. Don't the maps you've packed show secondary roads?
5. Let's get some others; I haven't the courage for highways.
6. What's the plan for the rest of the club?
7. Who's detouring through Manitoulin? Shouldn't the officials know?
8. I'd prefer my own bike for the trip; wouldn't you?
9. There isn't a dry eye in the theatre when Spielberg's film reaches its climax.
10. Won't we take our down jackets? We'll still be travelling in October, and it's quite cool then.

5

The loudest complainer about smoking isn't the person who never started; it's the person who's recently quit. There are many reasons for this phenomenon, including the fact that recent non-smokers aren't really convinced that they've kicked the habit. They don't want temptation blown in their faces. You've probably noticed that someone who's never smoked can refuse an offered cigarette with "No thanks," while the recent convert can't resist adding "No, I've given them up," or "No thanks, I don't touch them; they're bad for you!" Reformed smokers are surprisingly unsympathetic toward others who're still addicted, providing little support for those who can't break the habit as they've been able to do. On the other hand, there's no one as belligerent and full of excuses as a person who's fallen off the wagon and resumed smoking after a short period of "reformation." We'd do well to remember the words of Mark Twain: "It's easy to stop smoking; I've done it dozens of times."

6

1. tractor's
2. Lee's
3. somebody's
4. dove's
5. Beatrice's

6. course's
7. Norsemen's
8. loss' *or* loss's
9. glass' *or* glass's
10. bandits'

7

1. salesmen's
2. purses'
3. our
4. yesterday's
5. no one's

6. Hopkins' *or* Hopkins's
7. Fenelon Falls' *or* Fenelon Falls's
8. man's
9. actress' *or* actress's
10. Judy's

8

1. their
2. Chris' *or* Chris's
3. her
4. gentlemen's
5. strawberries'

6. mystery's
7. one's
8. Burgess' *or* Burgess's
9. chairmen's
10. ladies'

9

1. week's, his
2. fish's, its
3. day's, dogs'
4. church's, its, minister's
5. Sandy's, Lewis' *or* Lewis's
6. children's, his, their, mother's
7. hoses', salesmen's, their
8. Today's, producers', tomorrow's
9. minute's, year's
10. United States', terrorists', countries'

10

1. A floppy disk's quality is measured by its ability to store information without error.
2. Expo 86 owed much of its success to Vancouver's natural beauty and its citizens' natural friendliness.
3. Diplomatic ambassadors' wives or husbands are often as important to a mission's success as the ambassadors themselves.
4. Near Chicoutimi is one of the country's most beautiful parks, where the skills of canoeists, fishermen, and wildlife photographers can all be put to the test on a summer's day.
5. The Leafs' forward and the Oilers' defenceman were exchanged during the last day's trading at the NHL meetings.
6. Women's clothing styles have changed more than men's over the last thirty years, but men's fashions are becoming more interesting as we enter the twentieth century's last decade.
7. The Metro Toronto Zoo's care for its animals is world famous; it was the first zoo to employ a nutritionist's services for the maintenance of the animals' diets.
8. My grandparents' wedding picture sits on the desk next to my computer manuals to help me keep a perspective on life's changes and challenges.
9. Janis' career got its start when she sang fishermen's songs in the yacht club's dining lounge.
10. Many movies' plots are criticized for violence, but our censors' scissors are usually reserved for scenes involving sex.

11

1. It's, its, turtle's, turtle's
2. It's, they're
3. you're, your, your
4. Joan's, Society's, province's
5. Someone's, whose
6. There, Jones' *or* Jones's, their, it's
7. Countries, their, they're, powers'
8. Brothers', today's
9. father's, uncle's, fox's, woods
10. people's, workers', sides', strike's

12

1. Garlic's effects should not be forgotten by those whose aim is to impress their friends with close-up wit.
2. Noticing the customer's suspicious behaviour, David questioned her about her purse's contents.
3. You're playing well already, with only a year's study.
4. Fort Gary's history is revealed in the books, documents, and historical artifacts on display at the Art Gallery's special show.
5. Admissions to the journalism program are down this term, but it's not the director's fault; she toured the city's high schools to find interested students.

6. You're not going to improve your playing beyond this point unless you concentrate on making the most of your instrument's projection capabilities.
7. After all, audiences shouldn't have to strain to hear what they've paid good money to hear with ease and pleasure; it's a different matter if the concert hall's acoustics are at fault.
8. The concertmaster's patience gave out when his two solos were suddenly cut from the score; he'd been practising them daily for several weeks.
9. Jerry Smith built a house that became known to our area's residents as Smith's Folly, thanks to its strange design and its owner's even stranger decorations.
10. Canada's opportunities for its professional musicians are numerous. From coast to coast there are symphony orchestras, opera and ballet companies, rock groups, pop groups, and music-teaching facilities, all requiring talented professionals.

13

1. girls'
2. life's
3. fence's
4. its
5. activities'

6. we're
7. who's
8. it's
9. they're
10. shouldn't

14

1. women's
2. violinist's
3. someone's
4. intermediary's
5. intermediaries'

6. can't
7. he's
8. there's
9. couldn't
10. haven't

Chapter 4: Cracking the Sentence Code

1

1. Marie types slowly.
2. Her essays are always late.
3. Marie's essays usually get high marks, though.
4. Henri is a fast typist.
5. His marks, however, are disappointing.
6. Henri asked Marie for a date.
7. Finally she agreed to go out with him.
8. Suddenly, Henri's marks improved dramatically.
9. Coincidentally, Marie began to submit her work on time.
10. How these events relate to one another is fairly obvious.

2

1. Canoeing the old voyageurs' route was exciting.
2. More than the common cold and car accidents, sugar is your body's worst enemy.
3. Was that nice?
4. Up on the display wall was the famous blue bicycle.
5. Here is the officer from Station 52.
6. Are the other teachers as helpful?

7. On every weekend in the summer, Québec's <u>highways</u> <u>are</u> crowded.
8. On Hallowe'en, <u>soaping</u> windows <u>is</u> mischievous but not destructive.
9. (<u>You</u>) Please <u>write</u> in the spaces provided.
10. <u>Saskatoon</u> almost <u>became</u> the home of a National Hockey League team a few years ago.

3

1. <u>Pierre Trudeau</u>, like Jack Benny, <u>is</u> perennially middle-aged.
2. Here <u>is</u> an <u>idea</u> to consider.
3. <u>Lucy Maud Montgomery</u> <u>was born</u> in Ontario's Durham County before Confederation established Canadian unity.
4. <u>Who</u> <u>will eat</u> the last pickle?
5. (<u>You</u>) <u>Eat</u> slowly.
6. Physical <u>activity</u> <u>builds</u> strong bodies and healthy minds.
7. (<u>You</u>) <u>Keep</u> your body fit.
8. Far behind the Liberals and New Democrats <u>trailed</u> the <u>Conservatives</u>, bringing up the rear.
9. <u>Pride</u> <u>goes</u> before a fall. (Biblical proverb)
10. Only in Canada <u>is</u> a so-called <u>lack</u> of national identity a distinctive national characteristic.

4

1. <u>Toronto</u> <u>is</u> a metropolitan centre with scores of distinct neighbourhoods.
2. The <u>word</u> "Toronto" <u>is</u> the Anglicization of the Indian term for "meeting place."
3. The <u>Toronto Islands</u> <u>were</u> originally a part of the mainland.
4. <u>Are</u> <u>you</u> a year-round island resident?
5. At a joint meeting of the councils, the city <u>mayor</u> <u>opposed</u> the Metro Council on behalf of island residents.
6. No <u>evictions</u> <u>occurred</u> last year.
7. The islanders' <u>cohesiveness</u> <u>is</u> the product of both genuine neighbourliness and common community concerns.
8. There <u>is</u> surprisingly little <u>vandalism</u>, the plague of other downtown areas.
9. For the average visitor to the Toronto Islands, the <u>combination</u> of private and public properties <u>is</u> acceptable and even enjoyable.
10. Minutes from the middle of the city <u>nestles</u> my sunny, serene island <u>retreat</u>.

5

1. <u>He</u> <u>has talked</u> nonstop for three hours.
2. <u>She</u> <u>should have been examining</u> each package.
3. <u>Could</u> <u>they</u> <u>return</u> the goods tomorrow?
4. In the winter, the <u>car</u> <u>starts</u> more easily inside the garage than outside.
5. Where <u>is</u> the nearest gas <u>station</u>?
6. <u>He</u> <u>is</u> not <u>going</u> to drive.
7. Which horse <u>does</u> <u>she</u> <u>prefer</u>?
8. <u>Parents</u> <u>will</u> always <u>perceive</u> their offspring as small children.
9. The <u>barometer</u> <u>has</u> just <u>fallen</u> alarmingly.
10. Patiently and painstakingly, against all odds, <u>struggled</u> the little <u>army</u>.

6

1. In a couple of years, <u>you</u> <u>will be</u> a professional dancer.
2. By noon, <u>he</u> <u>will have been sleeping</u> for eighteen hours.
3. How <u>are</u> the different cycling clubs' <u>members</u> <u>identified</u>?

4. The <u>police</u> <u>will</u> certainly <u>stop</u> all yellow cars on the road tonight except their own.
5. Salad <u>suppers</u> <u>were</u> sometimes <u>supplied</u> secretly to the sufferers.
6. To some small degree at least, accidentally or purposely, in the schools personal <u>opinion</u> <u>is</u> often <u>presented</u> as fact.
7. <u>Could</u> <u>you</u> <u>have taught</u> your personal philosophy objectively and without prejudice?
8. <u>Have</u> <u>you</u> ever <u>been seen</u> at the Zanzibar tavern?
9. <u>Little</u> <u>is known</u> about his past, except that <u>he</u> <u>visited</u> here twice.
10. Isn't <u>she</u> <u>going</u> to go home now?

7

1. The new member's <u>idea</u> <u>was accepted</u> eagerly by the committee.
2. How <u>should</u> the <u>committee</u> <u>introduce</u> this concept to management?
3. <u>Management</u> <u>is</u> increasingly <u>concerned</u> with income over product quality.
4. Time and time again <u>had</u> <u>they</u> <u>demonstrated</u> that fact.
5. The <u>committee</u> <u>cannot</u> <u>make</u> things true, but <u>it</u> <u>must</u> <u>prove</u> things true.
6. There <u>have been</u> several unconvincing <u>presentations</u>.
7. <u>Management</u> <u>must become convinced</u>; superior product <u>quality</u> <u>will</u> ultimately <u>ensure</u> greater income and profit.
8. Why <u>could</u> <u>he</u> <u>convince</u> management? The <u>committee</u> <u>could</u> not <u>do</u> it.
9. <u>Has</u> the <u>committee</u> completely <u>understood</u> his idea?
10. Only through his presentation <u>did</u> <u>management</u> <u>understand</u> and <u>accept</u> the new program.

8

1. <u>Charlie Chaplin</u> ~~on film~~ <u>is</u> funnier than <u>Eddie Murphy</u> <u>is</u> ~~in person~~.
2. <u>Some</u> ~~of them~~ <u>are staying</u> for the matinée ~~on Saturday~~.
3. <u>All</u> ~~of your friends~~ <u>are</u> welcome here.
4. <u>Can</u> <u>you</u> <u>use</u> either ~~of these two ingredients in the recipe~~?
5. <u>(You)</u> <u>Follow</u> me out ~~to the highway~~.
6. A <u>couple</u> ~~of pounds of bananas~~ now <u>costs</u> more than a dollar.
7. A dozen cigarette <u>butts</u> ~~of several kinds~~ <u>littered</u> the floor ~~of the burnt-out room~~.
8. Here <u>is</u> an <u>example</u> ~~of successful career change at mid-life~~.
9. Creative <u>thought</u> ~~without action~~ <u>is</u> not productive.
10. Two <u>occurrences</u> ~~of vandalism in three years~~ <u>do</u> not <u>constitute</u> a crime wave.

9

1. ~~According to the old proverb~~, a <u>stitch</u> ~~in time~~ <u>saves</u> nine.
2. <u>I</u> <u>have had</u> a stitch ~~in my side~~, and <u>I</u> <u>have</u> often <u>been</u> ~~in stitches~~.
3. <u>Stitching</u>, ~~in my opinion~~, <u>is</u> best <u>left</u> ~~to tailors and surgeons~~.
4. ~~For today's prices~~, clothing <u>manufacturers</u> <u>should be sewing</u> triple seams ~~in their clothing~~, all ~~by hand~~.
5. ~~From the beginning~~, each <u>item</u> ~~of clothing~~ <u>should be</u> separately <u>designed</u>.
6. ~~After that~~, every pattern <u>piece</u> <u>should be hand cut</u>.
7. Each <u>piece</u> ~~of cloth~~ <u>should</u> then <u>be sewn</u> ~~with great care to the other appropriate pieces, by one person~~.
8 The same <u>craftsperson</u> <u>should</u> then <u>pay</u> attention ~~to double seaming~~ and ~~to details of hand finishing~~.
9. <u>Items</u> ~~of clothing~~ <u>produced</u> ~~in this way~~ <u>might justify</u> today's high prices.
10. ~~In this kind of manufacturing procedure~~, the individual <u>maker</u> ~~of the item~~ <u>should receive</u> a specified percentage ~~of the wholesale price~~.

10

1. ~~After years of arguing politics over a few beers,~~ <u>I</u> <u>started</u> <u>campaigning</u> ~~for the NDP~~.
2. The <u>idea</u> ~~of actually fighting the issues~~ <u>originated</u> ~~with you~~.
3. ~~Around my right ankle, on the palms of both hands,~~ and ~~in my left ear,~~ the dreaded green <u>pox</u> <u>appeared</u>.
4. ~~Over a period of three months,~~ <u>most</u> ~~of the springs~~ <u>dried up</u>.
5. ~~During the winter months,~~ every weekend, this <u>sportsman</u> <u>curled up</u> ~~at the fireside with a book~~.
6. His wife's <u>ideas</u> ~~of winter fun~~ <u>are</u> skiing, skiing, and skiing.
7. ~~Despite their differences~~ of temperament ~~and interest,~~ their <u>marriage</u> <u>is</u> quite stable.
8. ~~At the time of Marco Polo's explorations,~~ vast <u>China</u> <u>was ruled</u> ~~by its warlords~~.
9. Why <u>wouldn't</u> you <u>ride</u> ~~with him in the Jaguar~~?
10. <u>One</u> ~~of Alcoholics Anonymous' members,~~ a distinguished show-business personality, <u>will speak</u> ~~on television on Tuesday night about the organization~~.

11

1. ~~In the cage next to my dog's at the kennel~~ <u>lay</u> the saddest-looking basset <u>hound</u> ~~in dogdom~~.
2. Having realized the dangers, <u>Rudolf,</u> ~~along with the rest of the club members,~~ <u>requested</u> a change ~~in the route of the race~~.
3. <u>(You)</u> Please <u>send</u> me the quotations ~~on the construction of sprung floors for the three studios~~.
4. ~~In the past,~~ barefoot and pregnant ~~in the kitchen,~~ women's only <u>authority</u> <u>was</u> ~~over their stoves and sinks~~.
5. <u>Experiments</u> ~~in consciousness-raising~~ sadly <u>demonstrated</u> some women's preference ~~for the status quo~~.
6. ~~On the seventeenth hole, at the right edge of the fairway,~~ there <u>is</u> a marshy <u>spot</u> as big and inviting as ten bathtubs.
7. Here <u>is</u> a <u>list</u> ~~of the public schools in the area~~.
8. ~~According to the LaMarsh Commission's report,~~ <u>children</u> already predisposed ~~to violent behaviour~~ <u>are incited</u> ~~to increased violent behaviour by its portrayal on television~~.
9. There, ~~on an island off Scotland's rocky coast,~~ the <u>Canadian</u> ~~with the dark auburn hair~~ <u>traced</u> her immediate and ancient family tree.
10. Unacceptable ~~to both sides,~~ the UN Security Council's <u>plan</u> <u>had made</u> no recommendations ~~about what was so important to both sides,~~ the sovereignty issue.

12

1. ~~In the next twenty years,~~ the average <u>age</u> ~~of the Canadian population~~ <u>will increase</u> significantly.
2. ~~For those of us~~ now ~~in our forties,~~ this <u>trend</u> <u>is</u> good news.
3. ~~For those in their teens,~~ however, the <u>news</u> <u>is</u> not so good. <u>They</u> <u>will have to carry</u> the burden ~~of caring for the increasing numbers of elderly persons in society~~.
4. ~~On the positive side,~~ the <u>leaders</u> ~~of tomorrow~~ <u>will have</u> the experience and wisdom ~~of a large segment of the population~~ to <u>draw</u> on ~~in their planning and decision making~~.

5. ~~Throughout history~~, <u>cultures</u> ~~around the world~~ <u>have</u> traditionally <u>associated</u> age ~~with wisdom~~.
6. Ironically, however, this <u>assumption</u> <u>is</u> not always <u>supported</u> ~~by the evidence~~.
7. There <u>are</u> many <u>examples</u> ~~from the past~~ and ~~in the present of young leaders with more wisdom and maturity~~ than their aged counterparts.
8. (<u>You</u>) <u>Consider</u>, ~~for example~~, Alexander the Great. He <u>had</u> <u>conquered</u> the known world ~~by the age of 19~~.
9. ~~For a contemporary example~~, (<u>you</u>) <u>consider</u> the success stories ~~of youthful entrepreneurs like Bill Gates~~. Many young <u>people</u>, just ~~out of college~~, <u>have</u> <u>launched</u> hi-tech ventures to compete ~~with old, established companies~~.
10. ~~Over the next two decades, with the maturing of the "baby boom,"~~ <u>Canadians</u> will <u>encounter</u> changes ~~in lifestyle, in political focus~~, and ~~in cultural attitudes toward the "young" and the "old."~~

14

1. The <u>prime minister</u> and the provincial <u>premiers</u> <u>met</u> at Meech Lake.
2. <u>They</u> <u>debated</u> and <u>drafted</u> amendments to the Constitution.
3. The <u>anaesthetist</u> and the <u>surgeon</u> <u>scrubbed</u> for surgery and <u>hurried</u> to the operating room.
4. <u>Blue spruce</u> and <u>hemlock</u> <u>are</u> both northern imports to southern Ontario.
5. <u>I</u> <u>tried</u> and <u>failed</u> once, and then later <u>tried</u> again and <u>succeeded</u>.
6. My <u>son</u> or my <u>daughter</u> <u>will drive</u> me home.
7. The two <u>dogs</u> and the <u>cat</u> <u>travelled</u> a thousand miles in three months.
8. My retired <u>father</u> <u>reads</u>, <u>travels</u>, <u>golfs</u>, <u>walks</u> the dog, and <u>loves</u> all these activities.
9. (<u>You</u>) <u>Knock</u> three times and <u>ask</u> for Joe.
10. <u>Sight</u> <u>reading</u> and <u>improvising</u> <u>are</u> necessary skills of the small-band musician.

15

1. Fortunately for Sean, <u>Dan</u> <u>listened</u> sympathetically and <u>understood</u> clearly.
2. During his bouts of drunkenness, <u>Sean</u> <u>talked</u> compulsively and complainingly about everything under the sun.
3. In response, <u>Dan</u> sometimes just <u>put up</u> with the whining and sometimes <u>suggested</u> a visit to AA.
4. Drunk and depressed one night, <u>Sean</u> <u>phoned</u> Dan and <u>asked</u> him to go drinking.
5. <u>Dan</u> and his friend <u>Robert</u> <u>answered</u> no to the request and <u>suggested</u> AA to Sean.
6. On this occasion, <u>Sean</u> actually <u>listened</u> to his friend and <u>thought</u>, "Maybe <u>I</u> <u>should give</u> it a try."
7. Sean's new <u>friends</u> <u>encouraged</u> and <u>helped</u> him: "(<u>You</u>) <u>Live</u> one day at a time, and (<u>you</u>) <u>let</u> the higher power help you."
8. His special <u>sponsor</u> <u>had entered</u> the program five years earlier and <u>had been</u> dry for the same amount of time.
9. (<u>You</u>) <u>Stay</u> dry: (<u>you</u>) <u>don't</u> <u>take</u> the first drink.
10. The <u>suggestion</u> of one friend, the <u>support</u> of new friends, his own <u>determination</u> and, according to him, a higher <u>power</u>, all <u>helped</u> Sean in the climb back to sobriety and sanity.

16

1. (You) Consider the lilies of the field. (Biblical proverb)
2. Melanie and Morris adjusted their chains, checked their earrings, and patted their spiked hair into place before stomping off to their job interviews.
3. I asked the necessary questions and recorded the householders' answers but was puzzled by one most unusual response.
4. In my house live my wife and I, our two teenagers, two dogs, one cat, and one ghost.
5. No other researcher got such a startling answer or finished a questionnaire so quickly.
6. On King Street, between St. Andrew's Church on the east and assorted small buildings on the west, lies Toronto's Roy Thomson Hall.
7. Ragweed, goldenrod, and twitch grass formed the essential elements in the bouquet for his English teacher.
8. He spun around the corner, whirled into a doorway, and careened up the stairs, with the police in hot pursuit.
9. Today's artists must mirror the real world rather than create an ideal one.
10. This theory of art produces ''slice-of-life'' drama, encourages representational painting and visual art, engenders atonal music, and sells computers.

Chapter 5: Still More about Verbs (For Those Who Need It)

1

1. were
2. struck
3. sold
4. hid
5. swam

6. forgave
7. ridden
8. built
9. swore
10. paid

2

1. came
2. spent
3. made
4. been
5. lost

6. spoke, found
7. knew
8. had
9. chosen
10. told, led

3

1. slid, slid
2. tore, torn
3. shone, shone
4. thrown, threw
5. drawn, drew

6. hurt, hurt
7. eaten, ate
8. slept, slept
9. sat, sat
10. thought, thought

4

1. won, won
2. worn, wore
3. did, done
4. forgotten, forgot
5. became, become

6. seen, saw
7. set, set
8. fallen, fell
9. met, met
10. kept, kept

5

1. burst, burst
2. sung, sang
3. run, ran
4. shaken, shook
5. brought, brought

6. wound, wound
7. hit, hit
8. risen, rose
9. blew, blown
10. chosen, chose

6

1. heard, heard
2. come, came
3. gotten (or got), got
4. hung, hung
5. stolen, stole

6. meant, meant
7. rung, rang
8. put, put
9. bore, borne
10. stood, stood

7

1. lay, lain
2. said, said
3. left, left
4. written, wrote
5. lent, lent

6. flung, flung
7. flown, flew
8. given, gave
9. caught, caught
10. bought, bought

8

1. dealt, dealt
2. driven, drove
3. fought, fought
4. grown, grew
5. bid, bid

6. began, begun
7. felt, felt
8. cost, cost
9. left, left
10. swung, swung

9

1. taught, taught
2. hanged, hanged
3. held, held
4. drunk, drank
5. sped, sped

6. laid, laid
7. gone, went
8. frozen, froze
9. dived, dove (or dived)
10. broke, broken

Chapter 6: Solving Sentence-Fragment Problems

We have made the sentence fragments into complete sentences only for the first set and only to give you an idea of how the sentences might be formed. Many different sentences can be made out of the fragments given; just be sure each of your sentences has a subject and a verb.

I

1. F <u>He</u> <u>is</u> the college's expert regarding myths and fairy tales.
2. F <u>It</u> <u>is</u> silly to decide on the basis of rumour, not facts.
3. F Coming home, <u>he</u> <u>was</u> sad to hear of the many occurrences of vandalism.
4. F Those <u>students</u> <u>were writing</u> exams all evening, after working all day.
5. F The party <u>members</u> gathering in the campaign office <u>called</u> for a recount of the ballots.

6. S
7. F The air <u>attack</u> <u>was cancelled</u> because of cloud cover.
8. F The young <u>artists</u> <u>were painting</u> in a studio with bad lighting.
9. F Having worked outdoors all his life, upon retirement <u>he</u> <u>spent</u> his time in his garden.
10. S

1. F
2. F
3. F
4. F
5. F

2
6. F
7. S
8. F
9. F
10. S

1. S
2. F
3. S
4. F
5. F

3
6. F
7. F
8. F
9. F
10. F

1. F
2. S
3. F
4. F
5. F

4
6. F
7. S
8. S
9. F
10. S

1. F
2. F
3. S
4. F
5. F

5
6. F
7. F
8. F
9. F
10. F

1. F What
2. F As
3. F Where
4. F If
5. F So that

6
6. F Although
7. F Since
8. S
9. F Whichever
10. F Before

1. F Who
2. F Unless
3. F When
4. F Even if
5. S

7
6. S
7. F Whatever
8. F Because
9. F who
10. F After

8

Before the curtain went up on the lavishly decorated and beautifully lit set. The actor playing Frankie could be seen pacing up and down nervously. Although he was a veteran of many stage performances and several popular movies, and was accustomed to appearing before large audiences. Which made it very strange that he would demonstrate the symptoms of stage fright so clearly. Looking closely, a careful observer might have noticed, however, that he wasn't studying his lines or rehearsing his role. In fact, unless one were right beside him and watching very closely. The real purpose of his pacing could easily be missed. Although he appeared to be alone. He was, in reality, exercising his pet cockroach.

9

Our fishing trip turned out to be a huge success. Although it started out very poorly. After awakening to an overcast, blustery day. We left the house at 6 A.M. to be the first on the lake. After four hours of driving in weather which alternated between heavy rain and wet snow. We concluded that we were lost. We tried to fix the blame on each other and quarrels soon broke out in the car, almost leading to a fist fight. Even before the first morning of the week was over. We were at each other's throats! Which of my friends it was, I don't know. One of them began laughing, and soon we were all helpless with laughter. That broke the ice. From then on, whenever things looked their worst, and we were on the edge of disaster. Someone would recall that moment.

10

Photographing wildlife can be a rewarding and entertaining experience. Provided that one is very careful and has the right photographic equipment. Where some photographers try to capture the essence of a bowl of fruit, and others aim for a spiritual quality in family portraits or wedding pictures. I prefer to capture on film an accurate reflection of true wild-life. So that I can achieve this goal, I follow some of my crazy friends around from party to party, recording their antics with my pocket camera. Since so many of my friends are, by any definition, wild. The reproduction of wildlife in my photo albums is quite remarkable. Whether it is Jayne trying to play baseball in an evening gown, or Tessa going to a ballet opening in her jeans. As long as I have friends like Terry, who carries a pair of scissors to cut off people's ties, or Phyllis, who insists that she is Princess Di. I will always have plenty of subject matter for wildlife photography.

12

The attitude to Toronto takes two forms. There is first the attitude of the non-Torontonians, who live in places like St. John's, Maple Creek and Vancouver. Then there is the attitude of the Torontonians themselves.

The attitude of the outsider is compounded of envy, malice and pity in about equal quantities. It is admitted that Torontonians make large sums of money, but not much else. Certainly they never have any fun. There is none of the leisurely gracious living that is to be found in Montreal, say, or Halifax, or Okotoks, Alberta. When a young man sets out for Toronto, he is surrounded by a covey of friends, all commiserating with him and whispering to him to look about for a job for them in the big city. It is generally acknowledged that the bereaved young man will return, but he rarely does. If he sees his friends again, he sees them in Toronto where they all have a good cry, and talk over the grand old days when they were poor in Pelvis or West Webfoot.

The attitude of the Torontonians is that they simply do not care what people think of them. They live in Toronto and that is good enough for them. For years a host of magazine articles, newspaper editorials and commentators have baited Toronto. Toronto refuses to swallow the bait. One mayor tried to launch a campaign to make the city popular, but it fizzled out after a few days. Torontonians do not really care about being popular; in fact, about half the criticism about the city comes from its own people. Nobody baits Toronto quite as much as those who live there.

Chapter 7: Solving Run-On Problems

1

1. The teacher's late; let's go!
2. Just let me do the talking; you'll get us a ticket if you open your mouth.
3. correct
4. My parents golf and swim every day; they're both quite fit. They're only in their fifties.
5. correct
6. correct
7. Students today need summer jobs. Tuition and living costs are too much for most families.
8. Bryan will be going to college if he is accepted. His parents have lots of money.
9. correct
10. I am seeking a hero after whom I can model my life; so far I've rejected Sly Stallone, Madonna, and Hulk Hogan.

2

1. The comma splice gets its name from the film splice; two pieces of film are taped, or spliced, together.
2. Old movies are sometimes choppy and disconnected because they have been spliced badly or too often.
3. Two sentences cannot be spliced together with a comma; you need to use a semicolon or a period or a linking word between them.
4. You should be particularly careful when using linking words like "however," "consequently," "therefore," and "moreover." These words need a semicolon before them and a comma after.
5. This isn't a very difficult rule; in fact, it's one of the easiest rules to learn because it has no exceptions.
6. With one minute to go, the opposing team scored the winning goal; consequently, no one on our team felt much like celebrating the end of the season.
7. The anti-smoking bylaw doesn't seem to have done much good. I often see people smoking in restaurants, stores, and even elevators.
8. One of the things I hope to learn at college is French; however, I doubt if I'll ever learn to speak it fluently.
9. It's a pity that burning coal contributes to acid rain since we have an almost inexhaustible supply of coal in Canada.

10. Our country's culture, attitudes, and even politics are strongly influenced by television. That is why the CRTC insists on a high level of Canadian content in television broadcasting.

3

1. correct
2. She spent most of the term playing pinball in the lounge; it's not surprising she failed.
3. Please close the door gently. Don't slam it; one hinge is loose.
4. correct
5. If you find it hard at first to recognize run-ons, don't give up in despair. Read the explanation again, and then do the exercises slowly and carefully.
6. Frances thought her interview had gone very well; however, she wasn't offered the job.
7. General education courses may be broadening and even interesting; on the other hand, they don't have any relevance to the job I'm training for.
8. Keep working on your daily exercise program; you'll get over the stiffness in a week or so.
9. If you really want to stay healthy, quit smoking and drinking; cut out junk food and eat a balanced diet; exercise at least three times each week; and finally, get the brakes on your car fixed.
10. Americans like to tell jokes about Canada's climate. For example, here's an old favourite: a Miami businessman, returning to Florida after a prolonged stay in Toronto, was asked, "What was the summer like in Canada?" He replied, "I've no idea; I was there only eleven months."

4

1. A Canadian who speaks three languages is called multilingual; one who speaks two languages is called bilingual; and one who speaks only one language is called an English Canadian.
2. I'm sure the job couldn't have been as bad as he claims; maybe he just didn't try hard enough. *Or*: I'm sure the job couldn't have been as bad as he claims. Maybe he just didn't try hard enough.
3. Meetings such as this are fine for small groups, but large groups have to be handled in a different way.
4. I'll be glad to help you out. When you need me just call; I'll be here all day.
5. In Canada, winter is more than a season; it's a bad joke.
6. correct
7. It may seem foolish, especially after all the wrangling over our new constitution, but I still believe in a unified Canada. I believe in one nation extending from sea to sea. The Fathers of Confederation were right; a federation of provinces can work.
8. Sales of video cassette recorders have really taken off in the last few months; about 150,000 were sold in Canada in 1987.
9. They're expensive; the average selling price is $1200 to $1500 a unit.
10. VCRs can be preset to tape television programs; they can play prerecorded tapes of movies; moreover, they can also record through a video camera.

5

1. Career opportunities appear very good for students in a wide range of technical programs; however, most employers are looking for people with experience as well as training.

2. The demand for technicians and technologists is highest in resource fields. Industries based on oil, petrochemicals, mining, and pulp and paper cannot find enough experienced people to fill available jobs.
3. Job prospects should be bright for those in energy-related industries; moreover, if the proposed offshore drilling projects get underway, demand for trained technologists will far exceed supply.
4. correct
5. correct
6. People with high-technology skills are urgently required in several fields; plastics processing, mouldmaking, and tool- and die-making are three examples.
7. The Ontario government has made millions of dollars available for the establishment of CAD/CAM centres at community colleges. These are centres for instruction in computer-aided design and computer-aided manufacture.
8. Even small manufacturers are showing an interest in robotics and other sophisticated computer-controlled systems. Hence, an increasing number of engineers, technologists, and designers are going back to school to find out what CAD/CAM can do for them.
9. For community college students in technology programs, then, the future looks bright; however, a diploma does not necessarily guarantee job security.
10. As a group, technicians and technologists are less likely than engineers to find their skills obsolete; nevertheless, electronics and aeronautics are changing rapidly, and so people must expect to retrain every few years.

7

1. Beagles, which are a kind of small hound, make excellent pets because of their cheerful, affectionate nature. I know, because I have one.
2. In the past fifteen years, we have seen a remarkable increase in the health consciousness of the average North American. The result has been a huge and growing industry that attempts to make fitness painless or even fun. From health clubs and aerobics classes to weight lifting and diet plans, we have an almost limitless choice of ways to spend our money on our bodies.
3. Since you are interested in both careers, you should probably play hockey now and take up teaching in the future. Usually the legs give out before the mind does.
4. I look back with real nostalgia on winter in the small Manitoba town where I grew up with the softly falling snow, the excitement of the year's first snowball fight, and the crunch of snow beneath my boots on those *really* cold prairie mornings. This is all proof that the mind remembers the pleasant and blots out the painful as one gets older.
5. As farm animals, pigs leave a great deal to be desired. As pets, however, they are very clean, intelligent, obedient, and even cute, or so I am told. I suspect I shall never personally discover if there is any truth to this notion.
6. Joan is a complete hypocrite now that she is wealthy. Insisting with every other breath that she hasn't changed a bit, she drives a Rolls, flaunts her furs, and wears diamonds in bunches.
7. When I woke up this morning, I had a hard time getting out of bed. I knew I ought to eat some breakfast, but I didn't have time. Then I realized I had to finish an essay for a nine o'clock class. I thought my car probably wouldn't start because of the cold, and I wouldn't be able to get to school anyway, so I just stayed in bed.

8. The hockey season now extends well into the baseball season, which, in turn, encroaches on the football season. Football, being a fall and winter sport, extends halfway into the hockey schedule. So it goes, with basketball overlapping the other three.
9. Nothing is so relaxing as a whirlpool after a hard day at work. It soothes sore muscles and eases the accumulated aches and pains of the day, while at the same time providing the emotional therapy of a hot bath.
10. Following the high speed chase and subsequent arrest of the car's driver, the police learned that the vehicle had been stolen. They added a charge of theft to the reckless driving charge, and the young man spent the night in jail. There he came to realize the seriousness of his predicament, and he asked for permission to make a telephone call so he could get in touch with his parents' lawyer.

8

1. Foster Hewitt, the original voice of hockey, died in 1985.
2. correct
3. Learning to ride horseback without instruction must be difficult. I have a friend who taught himself to ride by watching Clint Eastwood movies.
4. At least fifteen people were casting for salmon in the running water just above the dam on the Kennisis River, which is only one-half mile from my home.
5. Her friends say she has a heart of gold. However, her children claim she has ruined their lives.
6. correct
7. Margaret expressed her wish to see them visit Canada. They will probably come despite the difficulties that air travel from New Zealand poses.
8. The campers are given recipes and supplies for the meals that they must cook themselves and are made responsible for maintaining their own cabins and establishing their daily routine.
9. correct
10. Given his excellent reputation in civil engineering in his own country, his rise through the ranks of the company since his arrival in Canada, and the fact that he now makes more than $100,000 a year, it is not surprising that he seems contented with his life.

9

Fourteen people live in Punkeydoodle's Corner, Ontario, a town famous for its funny name. Twenty-five kilometres west of Kitchener, Punkeydoodle's Corner was a stagecoach stop on the Huron Trail during the nineteenth century, when it was a bustling town of more than one hundred people. But, as stagecoaches gave way to trains, which, in turn, gave way to automobiles, the little town dwindled and shrank until only three families were left to call it home.

Several different stories account for the origin of the town's name. The hero of one of these stories was a man called John Zurbrigg, who was a Swiss settler and pumpkin farmer. According to the tale, Zurbrigg was a rather lazy man, preferring to "doodle" his time away rather than tend to his pumpkins. One of his neighbours, furious at Zurbrigg's idleness, is said to have labelled him "punkey doodle" during an argument; history does not record Zurbrigg's response.

Another story claims the town got its name from John Zurbuchen, the chubby, genial host of the old hotel in the town who had been born in Germany, then moved to Ontario in the 1860s with his family. Apparently, Zurbuchen never quite mastered English pronunciation. He loved to sing, though, and frequently entertained his beer-drinking customers with his version of "Yankee Doodle," which he mispronounced "Punkey Doodle." Both of these stories seem a bit farfetched, if you ask me.

Its unusual name attracts hundreds of visitors to Punkeydoodle's Corner every year; however, being a tourist attraction has one disadvantage, according to the townspeople. Every time a sign is put up to identify their village, the sign is stolen within a few weeks, even when it is firmly embedded in concrete.

10

Until I moved to the country, I could never see the attraction of bird-watching as a pastime. My parents had enjoyed bird-watching as a hobby for years, frequently boring me numb with their enthusiastic tales of warblers heard or kingfishers sighted. While I lived in the city I saw birds so infrequently that I was completely indifferent to my parents' enthusiasm; those birds I did see were always pigeons, sparrows, or starlings, anyway. Within a week of moving out of the city to take a new job, I began to take notice of my feathered neighbours. I was awakened three mornings in a row by squawking blue jays. Three days later a convention of crows descended on my property, sending everyone indoors for two days. My bird-watching really became an obsession when I was dive-bombed repeatedly by an irate woodpecker which I had offended in some mysterious way. Now, protected by a surplus army helmet and armed with binoculars, I go on excursions with the most dedicated birders; however, where they creep silently through the underbrush, and meticulously record each sighting in a log book, I crash about, threatening and cursing any birds I encounter. Now everyone regards me with pity or contempt, and more than one former friend has suggested that I've gone "cuckoo."

Chapter 8: Solving Modifier Problems

I

1. On the third floor there is a library that has a washroom.
2. He told us no one works hard on the first day.
3. correct
4. Why did you give the fruit in that flimsy bag to the customer?
5. We applied for almost every job that was posted.
6. He played the piano beautifully all the time I was there.
7. There are just enough pieces to go around.
8. When they drove down his street, they couldn't remember which house Sean was living in.
9. These language teachers have no use for dictionaries unless they're French or German.
10. By working night and day, he managed to pay for almost all the damage for which his brother had been charged.

2

1. Only the waitress who normally serves us was on duty.
2. Brian Linehan, the CITY-TV interviewer, doesn't easily get his guests to open up as they do.
3. The dogs in that kennel were healthy looking, lively, and well-behaved.
4. In May, my supervisor told me I would get a raise. (*or*: My supervisor told me I would get a raise in May.)

5. One usually finds the best Chinese cuisine in those restaurants frequented by Chinese people.
6. Using his new binoculars, he caught sight of a killdeer and several finches.
7. He had played ball professionally for several major American teams before coming to the Blue Jays.
8. correct
9. The football practices have been organized as a keep-fit measure for players who are not with a team in the summertime.
10. In a large laundry basket in a dark corner behind the automatic washer huddled a small cat gripping a kitten in its mouth.

3

1. Vancouver is a wonderful city to live in for anyone who likes rain and fog.
2. correct
3. Some games, such as tiddlywinks, are less demanding in terms of time and equipment.
4. The Human Rights Code prohibits discrimination on the basis of race, sex, or age against anyone who is applying for a job.
5. With a screwdriver, I was able to loosen the clamp that held the broken cable in place.
6. The piece of chalk that my English teacher threw at me hit me on the head.
7. Mile after mile, town by town, Terry Fox uncomplainingly fought his battle against time, space, and pain.
8. With an open can of tomato juice, they waited breathlessly under the trees for the return of their dog, that had been sprayed by a skunk.
9. correct
10. Tonight Dr. Brothers will lead a panel discussion on relaxation through sex, including how to tone and stretch muscles, how to relieve tension, and even how to sleep.

5

1. Cutting the wire for the cable, I broke the pliers.
2. We should vacuum the floors before polishing the furniture.
3. We felt that, being small-town people, we might not be accepted by Torontonians.
4. Leaving the building, we noticed it had gotten dark.
5. Although adults now, we still need time to play.
6. Recognizing it as the ring of the telephone, I wasn't bothered by the noise.
7. After criticizing both my work and my attitude, my boss fired me.
8. Trying to bunt, the batter hit the ball over the fence at centre field for a home run.
9. Trying to focus his binoculars, he couldn't see the eclipse because of the obscuring clouds.
10. As a jogger, I consider that well-fitting shoes are important.

6

1. Considering Michael's charm and good manners, I think his good looks are unimportant.
2. My supervisor gave me a lecture about punctuality after I was late twice in one week.

3. After spending all my money, I was disappointed that the flowers were delivered to the wrong house.
4. After supplying them with seeds all winter, we found that the wild birds wouldn't forage for insects in the summer.
5. When looking over their résumés, you can see that Carol and George have completely different backgrounds but that both could do the job.
6. correct
7. correct
8. Fifteen minutes after setting sail for the island, they were struck by the storm.
9. After struggling desperately for almost two hours with high winds and torrential rains, they were relieved by the storm's stopping as suddenly as it had begun.
10. Even in hot weather, runners should warm and stretch the legs and feet before doing any serious jogging.

7

1. As I cut the wire for the cable, the pliers broke.
2. The floors should be vacuumed before we polish the furniture.
3. We felt that, since we are small-town people, Torontonians might not accept us.
4. When we left the building, it had gotten dark.
5. Although we are adults now, finding time to play is still important.
6. Because I recognized it as the ring of the telephone, the noise didn't bother me.
7. After my boss criticized both my work and my attitude, I was fired.
8. When Ziggy tried to bunt, the ball went over the fence at centre field for a home run.
9. Just as he tried to focus his binoculars, the eclipse was obscured by clouds.
10. Because I am a jogger, well-fitting shoes are important to me.

8

1. When you consider Michael's charm and good manners, his good looks are unimportant.
2. My supervisor gave me a lecture about punctuality after I was late twice in one week.
3. After I had spent all my money, the flowers were delivered to the wrong house.
4. After we supplied them with seeds all winter, the wild birds wouldn't forage for insects in the summer.
5. When you look over their résumés, you realize that Carol and George have completely different backgrounds but that both could do the job.
6. correct
7. correct
8. Fifteen minutes after they set sail for the island, the storm struck.
9. After they had struggled desperately for almost two hours with high winds and torrential rains, the storm stopped as suddenly as it had begun.
10. Even in hot weather, the legs and feet should be warmed and stretched before one does any serious jogging.

9

1. As a college student constantly faced with new assignments, I find the pressure is sometimes intolerable.
2. Being horribly hung over, I realized that the only problem with a free bar is knowing when to quit.
3. Since their dog is allowed to run free, there is great danger it will be run over.
4. H. Salt's best dish is deep-fried giant shrimp in their special seafood sauce.
5. The villagers no longer drive cars or ride bicycles over the bridge that has been rotting slowly over the years.
6. As it burrowed into the wood shavings in the cage that night, Stephen could tell that his gerbil already felt at ease in its new home.
7. The driver whose license had been suspended who hit my car left the scene of the accident.
8. The Canadian Brass receives enthusiastic acclaim from Vancouver to Halifax for its witty presentation, its wide repertoire, and its clarity of tone.
9. For the classical pianist who possesses a natural instinct for rhythm and a good musical ear, it is easy to switch over to jazz.
10. Because Sean had obviously drunk too much, I drove him to his apartment, made him a pot of coffee, and phoned his AA friend.

10

1. Our hearts were wrung by the frail, unkempt little woman carrying two shopping bags full of old clothes and several other bags.
2. One passenger said that from her window seat she saw the engine catch fire and begin spewing smoke.
3. When it had all the stops pulled out, the organ had all the power of a full-sized symphony orchestra.
4. I learned in the *Toronto Star* that the provincial premiers will meet in July.
5. In the crowd and the confusion at Jon's Hallowe'en party, although costumed and masked, they recognized each other.
6. When I finally got to the shop on payday, the gorgeous dress I had been looking at all week had been sold.
7. On the day I was demonstrating how to make a Caesar salad, I left the Parmesan cheese, my favourite ingredient, in my locker.
8. Barry will serve his guests a Japanese sukiyaki dinner cooked in a wok and served with steamed rice.
9. In most cases, the person who has lived for a long time has lived a simple life.
10. Thirteen couples who have newborn twins are participating in Dr. Gemini's research program on families of twins.

11

1. Walking along the branch of a tree and singing, a worm-eating warbler was spotted by Hazel Miller.
2. When you try for your Red Cross bronze medal, your examiner will consider speed, endurance, and resuscitation techniques.
3. The University of Toronto's research in heart disease will be summarized this month in a special issue of the *Canadian Medical Journal*.
4. His guests observed that most despised of uninvited dinner guests, a cockroach, trapped under a delicate crystal wine glass on the elegantly set table.
5. Since she is not reliable about arriving on time, I can't hire her to supervise others who *are* punctual.

6. On Friday at the Toronto conference, the parks superintendent explained that reforestation was urgent in Ontario's northernmost provincial parks.
7. Just like his father, he maintains the tack, grooms the horses, and shovels manure.
8. When he was five, his mother took Scott for the first time to the movie theatre that had been in the neighbourhood for many years.
9. We always pay our respects in a funeral parlour to our friends and relatives who have passed on.
10. This bus has a seating capacity of 56 passengers and a maximum height of 14 feet, 6 inches.

Chapter 9: The Parallelism Principle

I

1. Food and shelter are the minimum requirements for survival.
2. My name is difficult to pronounce and to spell.
3. correct
4. Slowly, haltingly, and tearfully, she told them what had happened.
5. This year I intend to go to the Stratford Festival, the Shaw Festival, and the Mariposa Folk Festival.
6. Make sure that the people you hire are intelligent, articulate, and hardworking.
7. My wife told me to stay home and paint the basement.
8. I had a hard time deciding whether to continue my education in a college or university, or to plunge right into a job.
9. Lots of swimming, tennis, and sightseeing are what I plan to do in Bermuda.
10. Turn right at the first stop sign, left at the first traffic light, and right at the doughnut shop.

2

1. I'm looking for a babysitter who is intelligent, patient, and kind.
2. Make sure your report is comprehensive, readable, and accurate.
3. Those in community-service fields must be loving, patient, objective, and understanding.
4. Its location, staff, and appearance made that hospital a more pleasant place to stay than most.
5. We were told to study the report carefully and make our recommendations in writing.
6. Their chances for a lasting relationship aren't good, considering their differences in goals, temperament, and culture.
7. Her small build, quick temper, and criminal record will disqualify her from becoming a corrections officer.
8. Barry is everything a girl could want: handsome, intelligent, successful, and kind.

9. The space-age kitchen, the pool and sauna, and the burglarproof security system were what sold us on the apartment.
10. Mr. Redfern explained how to use the tape recorder, the microphone and camera, and the video cassette recorder.

3

1. Body-building has made me what I am today: physically perfect, financially prosperous, and practically friendless.
2. If there is no heaven, then there is no hell.
3. In my tiny home town, two significantly related crimes prevail: vandalism and drug-trafficking.
4. I'd like to help, but I'm too tired, too poor, and too busy.
5. I wanted either a Mother's pizza or a McDonald's Big Mac.
6. Every hour each guard counts the prisoners in his care, and twice a day the prisoners answer the guard's roll call.
7. My sister, who's trying to teach me to play tennis, says that my forehand and serve are all right, but that my backhand needs strengthening.
8. The two factors thought to be most important in a long-lasting marriage are the commitment of each partner to the marriage and the willingness of each partner to compromise.
9. Barry claimed that, through repetition and firmness, he had trained his guppy to be obedient, quiet, and loyal.
10. The new budget must deal with several major problems, two of them being the devalued Canadian dollar and the high rate of inflation.

4

1. Feeling discouraged and hopeless, Sarah and Peter went to the employment office to see if any new jobs had been posted.
2. Here we are, stranded in the middle of the jungle, without food or water. We're sure to die of exposure, starvation, or thirst.
3. correct
4. In tournament play, good golfers require patience, stamina, and nerves of steel.
5. Lawn-mowing, painting, carpentry, and cookie-baking are some of the many odd jobs George is doing this summer.
6. Like many politicians, he is fully aware of his capabilities but not of his limitations.
7. Times have changed: we work fewer hours than our parents did, and we enjoy more leisure activities.
8. Get the ball either to your right forward or to your guard.
9. In order to guarantee a painless annual visit to your dentist, you should clean your teeth with a brush and dental floss after every meal, and cut down significantly on sugar consumption.
10. An experiment that removed the TV sets from 100 homes for a month proved to be a good test of human creativity and ingenuity. One-third of the families in the experiment read books, played games, and talked with other family members; one-third attended twice as many movies, sports events, and other entertainments; and one-third went to the homes of friends or to pubs and watched even more television at home than they had before the survey period.

5

1. wine   women   song
2. privately   publicly
3. employers   employees
4. lying about all morning   doing whatever I please
5. as individuals   as a group
6. happy   healthy   wise
7. do your best   don't give up
8. information   education   entertainment
9. not enough time   not enough money   not enough staff
10. French is the language of love
    English is the language of business
    German is the language of profanity

Chapter 10: Subject-Verb Agreement

1

1. two
2. anyone
3. tasks
4. attraction
5. printouts

6. kinds
7. writer
8. anyone
9. One
10. Drugs, alcohol, and video games

2

1. They sell used essays to other students.
2. He often spends the weekend on his sailboat.
3. The women maintain that their boss has been ogling them.
4. Their flights have been delayed because of the storm.
5. Those new computers affect the entire office procedure.
6. They like to work with children, so they are looking for jobs in a day-care centre.
7. All those who shop at Pimrock's receive free cans of tuna.
8. Those girls' fathers are looking for rich husbands for them.
9. Civil servants with indexed pensions stand to gain from future inflation.
10. Both of her sons are successful in their own ways.

3

1. Atari games are Vince's first love in life.
2. Movies are what Marcia spends most of her time on.
3. The only junk food Tim eats is Hostess Twinkies.
4. The cause of his downfall was frequent nights of debauchery.
5. A good pitcher and outfielder are what the team needs now.
6. Clean living and Lois Lane are the sources of Superman's strength.
7. Frequently, the cause of failure is absences from class and failed exams.

8. What I least like to eat is brown rice and tofu.
9. Accounting procedures were something that I didn't understand.
10. The reason for your success in the aluminum-siding business is your stunning good looks.

4

1. were
2. is
3. are
4. know
5. is

6. is
7. are
8. repel

5

1. is
2. has
3. inflicts
4. is

5. unravels
6. is
7. is
8. keeps

6

1. is
2. loves
3. was
4. is

5. wants
6. is
7. was
8. is

7

1. is
2. was
3. works
4. likes

5. is
6. involves
7. has
8. wants

8

1. is
2. prefers
3. leave
4. is

5. Was
6. brawl
7. was
8. flies

9

1. is
2. was
3. is
4. seems

5. is
6. seems
7. is
8. seems

10

1. Do you know everyone who comes . . .
2. The whole team was . . .
3. The largest breed of domestic rabbits is . . .
4. Tim hopes he never meets . . .
5. correct

6. Neither Roger nor I am ...
7. The rust problem ... was ...
8. Everyone attending this series of meetings has ...
9. correct
10. When there are ...

II

1. My sense of the schools is that none of them is ...
2. Neither of them remembers ...
3. Every one of the SUNshine Boys appeals . . .
4. My whole family, with the exception of Fido, dislikes ...
5. Popular belief notwithstanding, quicksand does ...
6. It is the suction created by the victims that is ...
7. correct
8. Eight hundred dollars per term, all students agree, is ...
9. The birth of quintuplets was ...
10. Everything that we agreed to last night seems ...

12

Quebec City, along with Montreal, Toronto, and Vancouver, *is* among Canada's great gourmet centres. While Toronto is a relative latecomer to this list, neither Quebec City nor Montreal *is* a stranger to those who *seek* fine dining. Indeed, travel and food magazines have long affirmed that the inclusion of these two cities in a Quebec vacation *is* a "must." While Montreal is perhaps more international in its offerings, Quebec City provides exquisite proof that French Canadian cuisine and hospitality *are* second to none in the world. Amid the old-world charm of the lower city *are* to be found some of the quaintest and most enjoyable traditional restaurants, while the newer sections of town *boast* equally fine dining in more contemporary surroundings. The combination of the wonderful food and the city's fascinating charms *is* sure to make any visitor return frequently. Either the summer, when the city blooms and outdoor cafes abound, or the winter, when Carnaval turns the streets into hundreds of connecting parties, *is* a wonderful time to visit one of Canada's oldest and most interesting cities.

13

1. singular
2. plural
3. singular
4. singular
5. singular

6. plural
7. singular
8. singular
9. singular
10. could be singular or plural

14

1. singular
2. singular
3. plural
4. singular
5. could be singular or plural

6. singular
7. singular
8. plural
9. singular
10. singular

16

The interest in wrestlers and their managers, fans, and friends *is* fascinating proof that our society needs cheap thrills. The concept of good and evil fighting it out in epic battles *is* an enduring one. In simpler times, everyone who felt the need to witness such struggles *was* able to watch westerns on TV and see the Bad Guy (wearing the black hat) gunned down at high noon by the reluctant Good Guy (wearing the white hat). The complexity of our society, where good and evil *are* constantly redefined, *means* that we seldom get a clear decision in the battles we see each day on the news, let alone witness the triumph of good over evil. Into this frustrating world *come* Rowdy Roddy Piper, Hulk Hogan, The Junk Yard Dog, and King Kong Bundy. The variety of names, personalities, and "show biz" tricks *is* bewildering. Though the staging of the various moves and even the outcomes of the matches *are* obvious, the immense popularity of the matches, both on television and in the arenas, *is* undeniable. Like Rambo and Dirty Harry, the professional wrestler cuts through frustrating complexity and represents good or evil in its simplest most dramatic form. To a great many people, wrestling — not to mention wrestlers — *is* irresistible.

17

1. Cloud seeding to enhance rainfall and prevent snowstorms is . . .
2. The bizarre lives of many rock stars captivate . . .
3. Everybody we see at the wrestling matches roots . . .
4. Many cities in Russia have a "Kremlin" because the word simply signifies . . .
5. The rate of business bankruptcies is . . .
6. All of us at the college feel that cheating and plagiarism are serious offences.
7. Either French dressing or mayonnaise goes . . .
8. By the time we reached the Festival Theatre at Stratford, there were . . .
9. correct
10. The variety of Richard's money-making activities is . . .
11. One can't help noticing that the orchestra is . . .
12. At lunchtime our cafeteria, with its dreary salad bar, greasy chips, and soggy burgers, takes . . .
13. Both of Canada's native groups, the Indian and the Inuit, are . . .
14. Neither subject-verb agreement nor run-on sentences present . . .

Chapter 11: Pronoun-Antecedent Agreement

1

1. Yesterday's lecture was given by the English teacher who has a large wart on her nose.
2. Curling's most durable player is a man named Howard "Pappy" Wood, who competed in sixty-five consecutive bonspiels between 1908 and 1972.
3. Is this the car that was stolen by the man who escaped last night?
4. We are often attracted to people who are completely opposite to ourselves.
5. When I entered the locker room, I knew the team that had lost had been there before me.
6. Liona Boyd is the musician who is scheduled to perform tonight.
7. correct
8. Rudolf's grandmother always told him that people who couldn't fly as well as eagles should stay out of airplanes.

9. He remembered that sage advice the stormy night when the DC-9 in which he was flying went into a sickening tailspin over Great Slave Lake.
10. The math problems which we worked out last night would have stymied anyone who hadn't attended class regularly.

2

1. his
2. himself
3. her
4. his
5. their
6. his
7. itself
8. her
9. their, they
10. himself, he, he

3

1. Everyone who works in this car wash should pick up his cheque on Monday.
2. Women are treated as equals when they work in the fields.
3. A good manager must have an understanding of every employee and what makes her tick. (*or* ... what makes him tick.)
4. Do you know whether anyone in this neighbourhood wants to have his windows washed?
5. correct
6. Virginia claims that every one of her male friends has a room of his own.
7. It is now time to listen to the voice of your conscience and what it has to say.
8. No one living in Canada today believes the country is thriving economically.
9. Bob and Doug bring their own brand of zany humour to "The Great White North."
10. Whenever they appear on the screen, one or the other is holding a bottle of beer in his hand.

4

1. The gorilla was mean and thirsty because he had finished all the water in the morning.
2. If your pet rat won't eat its food, feed the pellets to the kitty.
3. Hockey is his favourite game, and he badly needs new skates.
4. Tim told Rocco, "My teeth are falling out."
5. Whenever Dennis and Bob played poker, Bob stacked the deck.
6. Every time Rudolf sat on the frog it croaked.
7. You know that smoking is very bad for your health, but you won't throw your cigarettes away.
8. Daphne dented her car by backing it into a garbage truck.
9. Lefty was suspicious of handgun control because he thought everyone should have a pistol for late-night subway rides.
10. If Pierre and Joe begin to argue, Pierre will tell him that he's never had any use for Joe and that Joe ought to keep his crazy ideas to himself.

5

1. I would like to apply for the advertised clerk/typist position, male or female, because I have experience as both a clerk and a typist.
2. Watching television requires little mental or physical effort, but we need to use both our minds and our bodies more than we do.
3. The only used motorcycles we found were all scratched up because they had been driven by young punks.

4. She told her mother, "You'll soon win some money."
5. This comment says that I use too many pronouns.
6. At the Nifty Burger, the employees play old Beach Boys albums in the evening.
7. These records remind me of my California surfing days, but the Pacific is a long way from Mississauga.
8. The first chapter of Pierre Berton's book mentions life in the Klondike.
9. Tim sat down next to Chuck and ate lunch.
10. My boss said that if any shoplifters were caught the store would press charges against them, even if they were cabinet ministers.

6

1. Anyone who has completed introductory sociology should know what a "peer group" is.
2. The team took their positions on the baseball diamond and outfield.
3. Employees must arrive early if they want to find parking places.
4. correct
5. All the people we saw were running as though something had terrified them.
6. When the collection agent called, my friends told him to "Take off, eh."
7. Someone who saw the crime had been lying to protect himself.
8. Most people know Gordie Howe is the man who played twenty-five years in the NHL, but do they know he also collected 500 stitches on his face?
9. Unscrupulous preachers try to convince people that they can't go to heaven without paying the preachers money.
10. We fed popcorn, which we had been munching on all afternoon, to the elephant.

7

Reading the newspaper the other day, I found the following advertisement intriguing: "Wanted to rent by young couple: modern apartment with view of the river." I wondered why the couple *who* had placed the ad had wanted it known that they were young. Perhaps they thought *a landlord* would be more likely to rent to people *who* did not have teenage children. Everyone *who* has *a* choice would like a view of the river, but *these apartments* are expensive. My friends Conrad and Barry have *such an apartment*. It's on the eighth floor, but Barry won't even look out of the windows of the apartment they are paying so much for. Conrad advised *Barry* to get his finances in order so he could afford a good psychiatrist *who* could help him with his phobia. But *Barry* refuses to believe that not everyone with an apartment above ground-floor level suffers from a fear of heights.

Chapter 12: Tense Agreement

I

1. Rolly goes home and <u>kicks</u> his cat.
2. Hank Aaron broke Babe Ruth's record of 714 home runs in a lifetime when he <u>hit</u> number 715 in 1974.
3. Children are quite perceptive and <u>know</u> when you are lying to them.
4. We had just finished the floor when the dog <u>ran</u> through.
5. When Knowlton Nash walked into the room, the ladies <u>went</u> crazy.
6. correct

7. Tim walked into the room, took one look at Lefty, and <u>smashed</u> him right through the wall.
8. First you will greet your guests; then you <u>will show</u> them to their rooms.
9. The largest cheese ever produced took 43 hours to make, and it <u>weighed</u> a whopping 15 723 kilograms.
10. He watches television all evening until he finally <u>goes</u> to sleep.

2

1. The goons in hockey kept ruining the sport for those who <u>wanted</u> to play it the way it <u>was intended</u> to be played.
2. Whenever he skipped his chemistry class, it <u>seemed</u> old Mr. Bunsen was lurking in the halls to apprehend him.
3. If you will lend me $300, I <u>will</u> double your money in Atlantic City.
4. First the gorilla looks me over; then he <u>turns</u> his back and walks away.
5. Our friends in the country had a prize bull that <u>cost</u> a fortune.
6. Many people think that drowning persons rise three times before they sink, but this <u>is</u> not true all the time; how many times they surface <u>depends</u> only on how much they struggle.
7. Because Tim assaulted an officer, he <u>got</u> a jail sentence.
8. Candy
   Is dandy
   But liquor
   <u>Is</u> quicker
9. The little boy looked so innocent while he <u>slept</u>.
10. While the Argonauts lost game after game, the loyal fans <u>kept</u> coming.

3

1. correct
2. I tried to warn him about her evil ways, and what thanks <u>did</u> I get?
3. The embarrassed girl didn't say anything. She just <u>blushed</u> and <u>ran</u> from the room.
4. Before Roger noticed the snowstorm, he <u>was</u> already up and dressed.
5. They agreed to our living here after we <u>paid</u> them a substantial bribe.
6. In the interests of good community relations and to prevent them from blowing up our house, I vote that we <u>pay</u> what they asked for.
7. Drusilla looks like a sweet young thing; when she <u>speaks</u>, however, the toughest truck drivers blush.
8. Lefty had wanted to <u>quit</u> drinking many years earlier.
9. It is surprising to learn that the High Arctic is like a desert in terms of precipitation; much more snow <u>falls</u> in Northern Ontario than on Baffin Island.
10. We attempted to change Rudolf's mind all day, but we didn't know he <u>had</u> already voted.

4

1. Are you going to see *The Blob*? It <u>is</u> a great movie!
2. *Prince of Space* and *The Blob* are the best movies I <u>have</u> ever seen.
3. The film begins with a clever sequence in which a girl <u>meets</u> a boy and his dog.
4. Little do we realize what kind of dreadful creature our young lovers will encounter, or that it <u>will</u> terrify the whole town.
5. The Blob originates in a test tube as a tiny bit of green ooze that then <u>grows</u> to enormous proportions.

6. The slimy, pulsating mass gathers both speed and size as it <u>moves</u> toward our young lovers necking in a pick-up truck.
7. They repel the fearsome Blob with the defrost button and <u>realize</u> the monster <u>can't</u> stand heat, so they <u>rush</u> off to save the town.
8. The Blob is devouring patrons at a local bowling alley, and its increasing girth <u>indicates</u> that it <u>enjoys</u> every morsel. What gruesome sights <u>does</u> this movie have in store for us next?
9. Much to our relief, our hero arrives and <u>builds</u> a huge bonfire out of five-pins; the Blob <u>withers</u> and <u>shrinks</u> away before our very eyes. The town <u>is</u> saved!
10. Is it any wonder why this movie <u>is</u> my favourite? I only wish we <u>could</u> see it with 3-D glasses.

5

Ken tried his best to understand the reasons for the constant unrest in Candeloro, but he finally *came* to the conclusion that he *didn't* have enough reliable information. The reports in the newspapers *gave* him the impression that most of the problems were caused by external forces. In some papers, communist rebels supported by Cuba *were* blamed for the trouble; in other papers, the United States' support of the corrupt regime in power *was seen* as the cause. Ken *decided*, after much consideration and discussion, to visit Candeloro and find out for himself what *had created* the tragic situation. His friends *tried* to dissuade him from going to such a dangerous place, but the need to know *was* too strong in Ken. "It *is* more dangerous to stay here without knowing," he *said*, "than to go and find the truth."

6

Having done everything he had ever wanted to do by the time he *was* 23 years old, Jeffrey tried to find new goals in life. At age 7, he *predicted* to anyone who would listen that he would be a millionaire by the time he *was* old enough to vote. When he *was* 11, he *predicted* that he *would star* in a major motion picture by the time he could legally drive. At 14, he *prophesied* that he *would be* elected mayor before his 23rd birthday. Incredibly, his predictions came to pass, one after the other. At 16, he *became* the youngest person ever to play James Bond in a movie; this role *led* to other pictures and a salary well into six figures. Careful investing *made* him a millionaire within two years. With all that money behind him, there *was* no stopping Jeffrey's campaign to become, at 22, the youngest mayor in Moose Factory's history. However, his amazing early successes *were* not repeated and Jeffrey *became* a has-been by the time he *turned* 25.

7

Once he has invested in a telescope and star map, the novice astronomer is ready to begin exploring the wonders of the night sky. It *is* necessary first *to find* a place to set up the telescope where light *does* not interfere. For the best viewing, one *needs* to find a spot well out in the countryside, away from street lights and the diffuse light of the town. Adequate sightings are possible, however, in large city parks or on college campuses. The most interesting heavenly bodies to study *are* the moon and the planets, of course. Seen through a telescope, the moon *reveals* craters, mountains, and valleys invisible to the unaided eye. The planets *are* usually easy to find since, except for the moon, they *are* the brightest objects in the sky. A fairly small telescope *is* able to reveal the rings of Saturn and at least four of Jupiter's moons. Amateur astronomy *is* an educational and enjoyable pastime if one invests enough patience and study in it.

Chapter 13: Person Agreement

I

1. he
2. you
3. you, your
4. he
5. they, themselves
6. she
7. he
8. he
9. we
10. she, her

2

1. When you have completed all of the sentences in one exercise, you should check your answers in the back of the book.
2. Everyone graduating this spring should order his cap and gown now.
3. You should always wear garlic around the neck if you fear vampires.
4. Any girl who does so won't have to worry about men bugging her, either.
5. In fact, everyone wearing a garlic necklace may find himself suddenly alone.
6. correct
7. If one attends enough Blue Jays games, one is bound to see a win eventually.
8. correct
9. If you don't come to class regularly, you run the risk of failing the course.
10. One shouldn't always look for a scapegoat when one makes a mistake.

3

1. After the unfortunate brawl, Tim learned that if a person stomps on policemen, he can expect to end up in jail.
2. People can expect to experience the horrors of nuclear war unless they raise their voices against nuclear proliferation.
3. If you leave garbage at your campsite, you may well have bears as midnight callers.
4. correct
5. One will always think about the opportunities he's missed, even if he's happy with what he has.
6. Canadians who worry about street violence should keep in mind that, in comparison to New York, they are safe in downtown Toronto after dark.
7. You know that a young kangaroo is called a joey, but do you realize that a baby eel is called an elver?
8. correct
9. Can you really know another person if you have never been to his home?
10. A sure way to lose your friends is to eat all the Baskin-Robbins ice cream yourself.

4

You can enjoy classical music if you are willing to give it a chance and really listen. If *you* listen closely, you will find relaxation and enjoyment quite different from that which *you* might experience when listening to "pop," rock, country and western, or any of the other varieties of music. Of course, not all classical music appeals to everyone, but then, everyone doesn't find all rock music *enjoyable* either. Nevertheless, there are some classical selections *you* are sure to enjoy. Go to the public library and borrow one or two of the following records and put them on your turntable. If *you* then *relax*, put *your* feet up, and really listen, you will be guaranteed an enjoyable experience. For your introduction to classical music, *you* might try Beethoven's Sixth Symphony (*Pastoral*), Grieg's *Peer Gynt Suite*, and Tchaikovsky's *Romeo and Juliet*. These pieces appeal to almost everyone and are ideal selections with which to begin *your* exploration of a new musical world.

5

1. If you're ready to learn how to operate a motorcycle, you should involve yourself in lessons, especially if you are interested in safety.
2. We often go to wrestling matches at the Gardens, and we're always sure of having a stimulating evening as we watch the Sheik make mincemeat of the Masked Marvel.
3. I don't know whether I can complete the program on time because it always seems either I must wait for a terminal, or the machines are down.
4. Until last week Marcia had us all believing her unlikely story; then we realized that she was lying.
5. You know that Cindy Nicholas holds the record for completing a double crossing of the English Channel, but are you aware that she has swum it a total of six times?
6. You know Orville is a troublemaker when you see his sneaky little face.
7. When we considered the issue carefully, we thought better of the more expensive proposal. After all, quality workmanship was what we were looking for.
8. When summer arrives, our patio is where you find us, relaxing and enjoying our leisure hours.
9. Many women think that the only way they can succeed in the business world is by wearing conservative three-piece suits similar to those men wear.
10. Actually, while you should dress appropriately, you needn't spend undue amounts of time and money trying to ape "the executive look." Ability and competence have always had more impact than appearance.

6

1. them		6. we
2. themselves		7. we
3. people		8. our
4. they		9. we
5. their		10. our

7

When you see dreadful occurrences like wars, earthquakes, or mass starvation on television, it does not always affect you. It is one thing for you to see the ravages of war yourself and another thing to see a three-minute newsclip of the same battle, neatly edited by the CBC. Even the horrible effects of natural catastrophes that wipe out whole populations are somehow minimized or trivialized when you see them on TV. And while you may be shocked and horrified by the gaunt faces of starving children on the screen, you can easily escape into your familiar world of Egg McMuffins, Shake 'n Bake, and Sara Lee Cheesecakes portrayed in commercial messages.

Thus, the impact of television on people is a mixed one. It is true that they are shown events, tragic and otherwise, which they could not possibly have seen before television. In this way, <u>their</u> world is drawn together more closely. However, the risk in creating this immediacy, and perhaps the most tragic consequence of all, is that <u>people</u> may become desensitized and cease to feel or care about *their* fellow human beings.

Chapter 14: Question and Exclamation Marks

1

1. incorrect
2. correct
3. correct
4. incorrect
5. incorrect
6. incorrect
7. correct
8. incorrect
9. correct
10. incorrect

2

1. correct
2. incorrect
3. incorrect
4. correct
5. incorrect
6. incorrect
7. correct
8. incorrect
9. incorrect
10. incorrect

3

1. question mark
2. question mark
3. period
4. period
5. question mark, question mark
6. period
7. period
8. question mark
9. period
10. question mark

4

1. exclamation mark
2. period or exclamation mark
3. exclamation mark
4. exclamation mark
5. exclamation mark, exclamation mark
6. question mark
7. exclamation mark and period
8. period or exclamation mark
9. exclamation mark or period
10. exclamation mark

5

1. two exclamation marks or exclamation mark and period
2. exclamation mark
3. exclamation mark
4. two exclamation marks or exclamation mark and period
5. question mark
6. exclamation mark
7. exclamation mark, exclamation mark
8. exclamation mark or period
9. exclamation mark or period
10. exclamation mark or period

6

1. period
2. period
3. question mark
4. period
5. question mark

6. exclamation mark
7. question mark
8. exclamation mark
9. Dr. and Mr. and period
10. exclamation mark and period

7

1. The question was whether we would spend the night in Cornwall or push on for Montreal.
2. "Help!" he screamed. "The piranha has my finger!"
3. Just think! We have two glorious weeks free of English class.
4. Tim thought he looked lovely in his new sharkskin suit.
5. If you think you're confused, just imagine how I must feel.
6. correct
7. Catherine asked Arthur if he would like to stay over.
8. Her Ph.D. didn't seem to impress her co-workers at the doughnut shop.
9. Despite the fact that he was busy with his weightlifting, jogging, swimming, tumbling, etc., Jacques always had time for a little drinking.
10. We studied the poems of Irving Layton, who was born in Romania, I think.

8

Gordon and I have often questioned the meaning of life as it relates to fishing. Are there fish? Why are there fish? What do fish think about? Why do people try to catch fish? Our last fishing expedition was no less successful than most, but it got us thinking about these great philosophical questions more intensely than usual. With my brand-new and very expensive fishing gear, I caught a clam. Gordon was only slightly more successful, catching three small bass. He later confessed, however, that he had sat for an hour with one of those fish on his line, because he was embarrassed to be catching fish with his bamboo pole, while I thrashed about unsuccessfully with my high-tech rod and reel. There is no justice!

The cry of "Fish on!" fills me with loathing for the successful fisherman. "Why him?" I cry. "What an idiot! Look at the lure he was using! No one can catch a fish at this time of year using one of those!" But the fact remains: the fish has selected his offering and not mine. By my calculations, the few fish that have managed to impale themselves on my hooks have made it to the table at an average cost of some $137.67 per kilo. I'd be better off dining on lobster every night! What a ridiculous sport!

9

Lady Macbeth (sleepwalking): Out, damned spot! Out, I say! One: two: why, then 'tis time to do't. Hell is murky! Fie, my lord, fie! A soldier, and afeard? What need we fear who knows it, when none can call our pow'r to account? Yet who would have thought the old man to have had so much blood in him?

Doctor: Do you mark that?

Lady Macbeth: The thane of Fife had a wife; where is she now? What, will these hands ne'er be clean?

Chapter 15: Quotation Marks

1

1. "Pardon me, boys, is this the Transylvania Station?" asked the man in the black cape.
2. Every day Rudolf asked the same question: "When do you think E.T. will arrive?"
3. correct
4. "This film," exclaimed Granny, "is more explicit than *National Geographic!*"
5. As the *Globe and Mail* put it, "The Canadian dollar went on a roller coaster ride yesterday."
6. It was the philosopher Ludwig Feuerbach who first said, "Man is what he eats," and we here at Big Boy restaurants certainly agree with that.
7. correct
8. "Your every whim will be catered to," stated the Sybaritic Spas brochure.
9. correct
10. "If not," I asked my friend, "why should we spend $800 for a weekend in Collingwood?"

2

1. "Oswaldo has flown the coop again," they told her.
2. correct
3. "Unless you pay us by Friday," the letter threatened, "you'd better start wearing knee pads."
4. Each of the students made the same comment about the instructor: "He'd be a good teacher if he'd show up for class once in a while."
5. Is it Daffy Duck or Porky Pig who says, "Tha-tha-that's all, folks" at the end of the cartoon?
6. correct
7. "Anyone with any brains at all," sniffed Bugs, "knows it's Foghorn Leghorn."
8. At the gates of the Sunny Buff Nudist Colony, we were greeted by a huge sign that read, "Have a Good Time . . . Or Else!"
9. correct
10. Griselda persuaded us to proceed. "Well, we've been looking for the perfect tan," she said. "Let's try it."

3

1. The *Guinness Book of World Records* claims that the oldest living thing is the California bristlecone pine tree, which is almost 5,000 years old.
2. "Did you see the strange look on his face?" asked Roderick.
3. correct
4. "Of course," she answered, usually willing to oblige.
5. "Have you read my new essay, 'Dreaming Your Way to an Energized Future'?" Dr. Piffle asked his numbed audience. "It's in my next book entitled *Upscale Networking in a Self-Actualized Cosmos.*"

6. The fellow to my left hissed, "I'd sooner be horsewhipped; where do they find these guys?"
7. I forget whether it was John Paul Jones or George Chuvalo who said, "I have not yet begun to fight."
8. The vice-president had bad news for the staff: "Due to lack of funds and excessive vandalism at the parking gates, you're all terminated."
9. correct
10. "Wow!" I said. "That's amazing!"

4

Kezia stood on the bench and pulled down three bearskins, marred with bulletholes. A rank and musty smell arose in the cold. She considered the find gravely.

"You take them," Mr. Mears said gallantly. "I shall be quite all right."

"You'll be dead by morning, and so shall I," she answered vigorously, "if you don't do what I say. We've got to roll up in these."

"Together?" he cried in horror.

"Of course! To keep each other warm. It's the only way."

She spread the skins on the floor, hair uppermost, one overlapping another, and dragged the flustered young man down beside her, clutched him in her arms, and rolled with him, over, and over again, so that they became a single shapeless heap in the corner farthest from the draft between door and chimney.

"Put your arms around me," commanded the new Kezia, and he obeyed.

"Now," she said, "you can pray. God helps those that help themselves."

Chapter 16: The Colon

I

1. incorrect
2. incorrect
3. correct
4. incorrect
5. incorrect
6. correct
7. incorrect
8. correct
9. incorrect
10. correct

2

1. incorrect
2. incorrect
5. correct
6. correct
7. incorrect
3. correct
4. incorrect
8. incorrect
9. correct
10. incorrect

3

1. correct
2. Unless you work consistently throughout the term and prepare thoroughly for your final exam, you will achieve only one result: failure.
3. There are several troublesome implications of biological engineering, but one in particular is frightening to most people: the cloning of human beings.
4. Their credit consultant asked them an important question after their bankruptcy: "Why don't you cut up your credit cards?"
5. Only one thing prevents me from pulverizing you: the Masked Marvel, who is standing behind you.
6. correct
7. The bulk of Canada's population is worn out and exhausted at the end of a long, hard winter, but most people console themselves with one thought: spring will arrive sometime in May or June.
8. There are a number of activities that will improve physical fitness: swimming, tennis, jogging, even brisk walking.
9. Melanie is trying very hard to accomplish two things: a significant weight loss and success as a restaurant critic.
10. Several of the animals on the endangered species list are native to Canada: the wood bison, the Northern kit fox, and the whooping crane.

4

1. The three people having trouble with their nursing techniques course are Tanya, Eddy, and Rufus.
2. There are three people having trouble with their nursing techniques course: Tanya, Eddy, and Rufus.
3. correct
4. The only thing we lacked was money.
5. Our friends are certain to remain loyal if we treat them with courtesy, kindness, and honesty.
6. correct
7. Two places I wouldn't want to visit are Tuscaloosa and Saskatoon.
8. correct
9. I often attend the film festival, but this year I'm broke.
10. correct

5

1. Four of my favourite TV characters are Fred, Wilma, Barney, and Betty.
2. Whom do you trust? No one at all.
3. correct
4. Everyone wants to hire her for her looks and brains.
5. correct
6. correct
7. The economy was battered by crushing interest rates, sagging production, and continued inflation.

8. Tim picked up a new skill in Kingston Penitentiary: terrorizing weaker inmates.
9. correct
10. Roderick's needs in life were sex, drugs, and rock 'n roll.

Chapter 17: The Comma

1

1. Be sure to pick up gin, tonic, limes(,) and ice.
2. correct
3. Labatts, Molson's(,) and O'Keefe are major breweries and patrons of sport and culture.
4. I am going to hire a cleaning man to clean floors, dust furniture, scour the oven(,) and wash clothes.
5. We're tired of watching pretty faces belonging to people who can't act: Burt Reynolds, Tom Selleck, Warren Beatty(,) and Woody Allen.
6. correct
7. We are going to see *The Tempest, Julius Caesar*(,) or *The Merry Wives of Windsor* this weekend.
8. correct
9. Tim stomped into the room, threw himself into a chair, drained a six-pack of Budweiser(,) and crushed the cans against his forehead.
10. Three things that can hinder your relaxation at a cottage are rainy weather, black flies(,) and unwanted guests.

2

1. What's it all about, Alfie?
2. The cheetah is, of course, the fastest animal on earth.
3. correct
4. Malcolm Lowry, an alcoholic British expatriate, wrote *Under the Volcano*, perhaps the finest novel ever written in Canada.
5. When everyone joins in, cleaning up isn't difficult, it seems.
6. Do you know, class, what is the largest city in Canada in terms of area?
7. It is, believe it or not, Whitehorse, with 162 square miles.
8. Many children in this school, it seems, are coming in the morning without having had an adequate breakfast.
9. Phil Esposito, who played for the Boston Bruins, scored 100 points or more in six different seasons.
10. The lead singer, in a bid for notoriety, bit the head off a bat during the performance.

3

1. I refuse to wear that turkey costume to the party, nor will I go as a horse's rear end.
2. Yesterday he broke up with her, but today he is begging for forgiveness.
3. The whole class knows what the teacher is up to, so we are going to surprise him by studying for the final exam.

4. correct
5. The boss told him to stop leering at the ladies, or she would fire him.
6. Felix searched and searched for the perfect accessories, for he has sophisticated taste.
7. The day was clear and warm, so we spent the afternoon on our sailboat.
8. Susan and Sarah have left for Prince Albert, and David is going to Rainy River.
9. Waving a red flag in front of a bull is supposed to enrage him, yet experiments have shown that bulls are colour blind.
10. She bit into the taco and burst into tears, for the jalapeña peppers were far too hot for her gringo taste buds.

4

1. Esmeralda, please leave those plants on the table.
2. Third, insert your finger into the electrical socket.
3. Overwhelmed by the generous offer, we spent the evening watching Paul's home movies.
4. On her way into the Governor General's awards ceremony, Ruth was stopped by security guards.
5. By the way, young man, your account is overdue.
6. With the water running, the plumber will be unable to repair the faucet.
7. For your convenience, deposit your clothes with the attendant.
8. If you work for an airline, company policy states you are entitled to one free trip a year.
9. In addition, your next of kin is entitled to reduced fares.
10. Unless you learn to use commas properly, your writing will lack sophistication and polish.

5

1. Caffeine, which is present in coffee, tea(,) and cola, stimulates the heart and raises blood pressure.
2. If a thing is worth doing, it is worth doing badly. (G.K. Chesterton)
3. The agency interviewed, tested, investigated(,) and rejected thirty applicants.
4. That man is, in my opinion, guilty and should be convicted of murder.
5. Roger checked his parachute carefully before take off, but he forgot to pull his rip cord after he jumped out of the plane.
6. Fortunately, he landed in a tree and, later that afternoon, was found dangling helplessly.
7. Unfortunately, he had some very nasty contusions and developed an entirely justifiable fear of flying.
8. correct
9. Having left my wallet at home, I am unable to buy lunch.
10. correct

6

1. We are pleased with your résumé, and we are offering you an interview this week.
2. correct
3. As a receptionist, your duties are to greet clients, type reports, file correspondence(,) and answer the phone.

4. The Maple Leafs, acknowledging inferiority and lack of determination, gave up on or about December 1.
5. Computing the interest is his job, but collecting the debts is hers.
6. correct
7. Oswald would have nothing to do with his wife, or her mother(,) or her lawyers.
8. I have striven not to laugh at human actions, nor to weep at them, nor to hate them, but to understand them. (Baruch Spinoza)
9. Although Tim begged, his girlfriend refused to wear a tattooed heart with his name in the middle.
10. correct

7

1. Fascinating, challenging, high-paying jobs are available to the people who transfer to our exciting Beirut branch office.
2. Oswald, your lawyers agreed to work with you, not against you, didn't they?
3. Our guard dog, a Doberman pinscher, caught an intruder and maimed him for life.
4. Unfortunately, my Uncle Ladislaw was the intruder, and he intends to sue us for every penny we have.
5. correct
6. All warm-blooded animals that give live birth and suckle their young are classified as mammals, but no one knows how to classify the warm-blooded, egg-laying, chick-nursing platypus.
7. correct
8. correct
9. While he was eating, his dog stood beside him.
10. Igor asked, "May I show you to your quarters, or would you prefer to spend the night in the dungeon?"

8

For the past ten years, oil-consuming nations have been struggling with the "energy crisis" or, more specifically, the "oil crisis." Everyone is familiar with the problems the crisis has created: ever-increasing prices, higher taxes(,) and political conflict, to name only a few. Many solutions, ranging from the practical to the fantastic, have been proposed. Almost every magazine or newspaper we read contains at least one article on the exciting possibilities of solar power, tidal power, biomass(,) or wind power. Despite the optimism of the writers, however, most readers do not find such articles very reassuring. All the solutions proposed can be realized in the future; the problem confronts us here, now, today.

What is needed immediately is not new sources of electric power: we have time to develop those. What is needed immediately is a new source of fuel. The ideal fuel would be, first, one that could be manufactured from an inexhaustible Canadian resource. Second, the ideal fuel would be one that could be used to power existing cars, trucks, buses, planes(,) and other transit vehicles, without major mechanical alterations. Third, the ideal fuel must be safe, powerful(,) and nonpolluting. One possible fuel that meets these requirements is hydrogen, the most abundant element in the universe. According to Roger Billings, who is the leading expert on hydrogen-powered automobiles, almost any internal-combustion engine that runs on gasoline can be converted to run on hydrogen.

9

"The world is changing," my friends in data processing courses told me. They maintained that I, a harmless English teacher, would be unable to cope without the skills necessary to run a microcomputer. They assured me that ominous blinking machines with deceptively cute names like Amiga and Apple would relieve me of the repetitive tasks of teaching commas, colons, semicolons(,) and spelling to reluctant students. I would be free, my friends maintained, to teach the things that really mattered. In the cybernetic world of the future, people would come up with the ideas, and the machines would handle the mechanics. By looking at other enthusiastic descriptions of the microcomputer revolution, I learned that silicon chips would, in the near future, do my cooking, balance my chequebook(,) and go shopping for me, yet could they ever, I wondered dreamily, be programmed to change the cat litter?

Nevertheless, commas, colons, cooking(,) and chequebooks were enough for me, and so despite my lifelong distrust of blinking machines, I enrolled in a course called "Your Friendly Computer." I must admit the little demon seemed friendly, quickly establishing itself on a first name basis with me, but the bewildering array of disks, data bases, inputs, outputs, bugs, bytes, backups(,) and buffers soon left me in a microdaze. My friendly computer, attempting to beguile me with fun and games, allowed me to pick off Pacmans, blast Rasters(,) and incinerate Invaders; dots, gobblers(,) and rocket ships appeared on my screen with annoying rapidity. Ever cheerful, the affable machine consoled me for my pitiful scores: "Nice try," it blinked, but my hand-eye co-ordination was obviously unequal to the demands of video games. Feeling somewhat more comfortable in the slower world of punctuation, I tried a program on commas and semicolons. Now, I thought happily, I'm really hands-on, online(,) and programmed. Alas, my machine, friendly no more, flashed "BDOS ERROR. REBOOT." It had found me out, detecting my fear and loathing of all things electronic. Defeated, I left the glowering machine behind me and went home to change the cat litter.

10

I sometimes wonder what our ancestors, were they able to observe us now, would think of some of the activities we take for granted. I'm sure that breakdancing would seem peculiar to them, as would surfing, water-skiing(,) and hang-gliding. However, I suspect that our forebears would find even those strange activities understandable, perhaps even enjoyable, compared to jogging. The sight of otherwise perfectly reasonable people decked out in various types of colourful underwear, doggedly puffing and sweating along every pathway, road(,) and trail would, I am convinced, put The Fear into Great Grandad and send him scurrying back whence he had come.

All kinds of people jog: there are short joggers, tall joggers, fat joggers, thin joggers; serious joggers, light-hearted joggers, fashionable joggers(,) and practical joggers; joggers with outfits of every hue from black to white and every shade in between. In fact, there may be more people who jog than don't!

I gave up jogging some years ago with the excuse that, although I adored distance running, an old basketball injury prevented me from measuring up to my own expectations. This pitiful story, together with a wistful sigh for lost youth, usually gets me off the hook. While my friends claim to be fit and keen, I take satisfaction in quoting Satchel Paige, the famous baseball player, who, at age 60, pitched three scoreless innings in the major leagues. In his "Six Rules for a Long Life," Satch warns, "On no account, run." This is sound advice, and I intend to live by this sensible and energy-efficient rule.

Chapter 18: The Semicolon

1

1. correct
2. incorrect
3. incorrect
4. incorrect
5. incorrect

6. correct
7. incorrect
8. incorrect
9. incorrect
10. incorrect

2

1. incorrect
2. incorrect
3. correct
4. incorrect
5. incorrect

6. correct
7. incorrect
8. incorrect
9. incorrect
10. incorrect

3

1. correct
2. I'd like to meet your friend, so bring him to the party tonight.
3. We've eaten all the goodies; it's time to go home.
4. There's a storm on the way; let's head for shelter.
5. We're seeing a wave of 60s nostalgia; for example, miniskirts have made a comeback.
6. correct
7. The Argos are my favourite team; I always buy season tickets.
8. Your instructor would like to pass you; however, there may be a small fee involved.
9. Florence is going to Hollywood; she wants to appear on "Let's Make A Deal."
10. We knew that the party was a huge success: Uncle Morty tap-danced across the top of the piano; Aunt Madeline did her Big Bird imitation; and Tim ignited two of his cousins.

4

1. Many people dislike hockey because some of the players act like goons rather than athletes.
2. Orville tried and tried, but he couldn't get the teacher's attention.
3. correct
4. I'd like to take a southern vacation this year; however, I don't think I can afford it.
5. The car sped quickly past the spectators; for a moment the driver could see their

faces.
6. correct
7. First, we'll have a cool drink; then we'll see if we can find a way to start this car.
8. Dudley left his clothes by the pool, so it's no wonder people in the lounge are looking at him strangely.
9. Electrical plugs come in both male and female versions, so you can raise your own.
10. Uranus is Rudolf's favourite planet; therefore, he is making preparations to live there someday.

5

1. Mrs. Reagan had a message for the unemployed: "There is no hunger in America; let them eat Kraft Dinner."
2. Lionel hates country music; therefore, he brought his earplugs to the Dolly Parton concert.
3. Unless everyone here is lying, UFOs are flying.
4. Most computer languages have been developed for a specific purpose; for example, COBOL is used in business while FORTRAN is used for mathematics, science, and engineering.
5. Some sociobiologists believe that human beings have evolved socially because female humanoids learned to barter sex for food and protection; however, this theory is controversial in academic circles.
6. Native land claims are a very complex issue; nevertheless, many of the Indian and Inuit groups are in the process of negotiating these claims with federal and local governments.
7. Andy, Pat, Annah, and Maggie are four of my favourite people who can always have fun with the rest of us.
8. Louis Riel led a Métis rebellion in Manitoba in 1885, but he was defeated, tried, and executed the same year. His death caused a deep rift between English and French Canada.
9. The house was ridden with termites, sagging from age, littered with garbage, and bereft of charm, yet the owner was asking $260,000 because of its location.
10. correct

6

1. The entire town is in an uproar; it seems Rudolf has been missing since yesterday.
2. Of course, everyone knows Rudolf is a bit wacky; he's been very strange since his close encounter of the fourth kind.
3. He claims that a hamburger-shaped, chrome-coloured, smoke-belching UFO pinned him under its wheels, and its inhabitants kept him prisoner for several hours.
4. The creatures spoke to him through little slits; however, Rudolf says he got a good look at them.
5. According to him, the aliens looked like a cross between Bonzo the Chimp and Sylvester Stallone.

6. The creatures told Rudolf many secrets; one thing they told him was that they had searched the universe for a perfect specimen like him.
7. correct
8. In fact, Rudolf later told us he is under the aliens' control; perhaps this explains why he talks like Donald Duck.
9. But now everyone is beginning to worry; there's an unexplained burned spot in Rudolf's yard, and he's been gone since yesterday.
10. correct

7

1. One dark, windy, stormy night, I settled myself into bed and almost immediately fell into a deep sleep; suddenly a dreadful noise jolted me awake.
2. My door swung open, and a hideous howling beast leapt into my room and ran over to my bed.
3. Frozen with panic, I could hear it snarling and snorting beside me; it was huge, doglike, and fierce.
4. correct
5. As I made a lunge for the bat, the beast leapt on my back; then it inflicted a dozen or so savage bites.
6. Screaming in pain, I thought I was going to die, but just then my trusty Great Dane, Hrothgar, ran into the room.
7. correct
8. My attacker was finished; I was able to attend to my wounds.
9. If it hadn't been for Hrothgar, the bloody pulp on the floor would have been me instead of the vicious beast who had stalked me.
10. I patted the Great Dane gratefully; "Hrothgar, my friend," I said, "I owe you several juicy steak bones above and beyond your daily ration of Burger Bits."

8

Two young women we'll call Linda and Meredith began college in September; both were nineteen, high school graduates(,) and eager to succeed in their educational careers. By December and the end of the first term, Linda had enjoyed her courses and passed with A's and B's; however, Meredith had fallen badly behind, failed four or five courses(,) and decided to leave college permanently. What caused this difference between two people's college experience? Some of the reasons may originate in the subtle but important distinctions between high school and college.

Both Linda and Meredith were exhilarated by what they saw as the freedom of college studies; no one forced them into classes, checked up on them(,) or phoned parents to verify absences. Linda appreciated this but made sure that she attended classes regularly. Meredith took this freedom as a licence to skip numerous classes or to come late. Teaching methods were different; instructors never hounded students for assignments and often did not provide the lecture notes as high school teachers had. Linda made sure she turned in all assignments promptly and took care to prepare her own notes; however, Meredith was slack about assignments and rarely took notes in class. By the end of November, the workload had increased to a level unprecedented in high school. Linda felt pressured, but she was able to cope and do well because she was on top of her work. Meredith was hopelessly behind and unable to complete her work despite frantic, last-minute efforts. Understanding the nature of college studies is crucial to success; high school work does not always provide this understanding. Consistent effort, discipline(,) and responsibility for oneself are absolutely essential if a person is going to make the most of a college education.

9

1. I have grown fond of semicolons in recent years. The semicolon tells you that there is still some question about the preceding full sentence; something needs to be added.
2. It is almost always a greater pleasure to come across a semicolon than a period. The period tells you that that is that; if you didn't get all the meaning you wanted or expected, you got all the writer intended to parcel out and now you have to move along.
3. But with a semicolon there, you get a pleasant little feeling of expectancy; there is more to come; read on; it will get clearer.
4. Colons are a lot less attractive, for several reasons: firstly, they give you the feeling of being rather ordered around, or at least having your nose pointed in a direction you might not be inclined to take if left to yourself, and, secondly, you suspect you're in for one of those sentences that will be labelling the points to be made: firstly, secondly, and so forth, with the implication that you haven't enough sense to keep track of a sequence of notions without having them numbered.
5. correct

Chapter 19: Capital Letters

1

1. Joanna is a regular princess.
2. Why on earth would you buy a Toyota?
3. We need to get rid of some of our high school habits when we start college.
4. The Depression is a period that has been on everyone's mind during the present hard times.
5. Have you read Dr. Ernie L. Piffle's new book, *I'm OK — You're Fat: A Self-Help Guide to Fitness Fascism*?
6. The English language has its roots in northern European Germanic tongues.
7. Montague will be staying at the Harbour Castle Hilton this summer.
8. The Loyalists were considered patriots to inhabitants of Upper Canada but traitors to people in the United States.
9. The upper classes often resent economic schemes that attempt to redistribute wealth.
10. Garth Drabinsky has produced numerous Canadian horror films; *Shivers* is one of his most famous.

2

1. I didn't do very well in my fluid power course; maybe I'd better switch to culinary arts.
2. When I grow up, I'd like to be a duchess or at least a movie star.
3. Well, look who's here; it's Mr. Olympics.

4. Take a right at Yonge Street, a left at Lawrence Avenue, and a right at Avenue Road.
5. My English teacher also teaches French to Asian immigrants.
6. Marcia's father, being conservative in his tastes, disapproved of Ronald's leather jacket and Harley-Davidson 750.
7. Neither was he amused when Marcia ran off with Ron's rock group, The Stoned Angels.
8. The French were very much a part of Canada for more than a century before the English became its rulers.
9. My guess is that this artifact dates back to the Bronze Age.
10. Can you tell me whether the Roughriders are from Ottawa and the Rough Riders from Saskatchewan, or is it the other way around?

3

1. Several psychiatrists in California are developing computer programs to treat patients with mild forms of depression or neurosis.
2. They envision computer therapy programs within the next fifteen years that will diagnose the patient's problem (to be confirmed by a psychiatrist) and select a treatment program.
3. The computer would interact with the patient and switch to various subprograms to analyse his mental problems.
4. A TV camera could view the patient to see if he exhibits signs of stress, nervousness, or lying.
5. correct
6. Most psychiatrists are against such unorthodox treatment methods, but proponents of computer therapy argue that it has many advantages.
7. These advantages include low cost and convenience: the computer would function as a cheap psychiatrist, available on weekends and holidays, summer or winter.
8. Other advantages are the long-term total memory of the computer and its appearance of honesty and objectivity.
9. Personally, I am surprised that anyone in the medical profession takes such a proposal seriously; treatment of complex human problems by machine seems perverse to me.
10. Taking my own personal depressions, fears, and phobias to a VDT would be likely to trigger a massive anxiety attack.

4

By this time I was in high school. I resisted my mother's plan to send me to a private girls' school, where the pupils wore kilts and little plaid ties. Ever since Brownies I'd been wary of any group composed entirely of women, especially women in uniforms. So instead I went to the nearest high school, which was second-best in my mother's opinion but not as bad as it might have been, since by now we were living in a respectable neighbourhood. The catch was that the children of the families my mother viewed as her peers and models were sent to the kind of private school she wanted to send me to, so the high school got mostly the leftovers from the smaller houses around the fringes of the area, the brash new apartment buildings which had been opposed by the established residents, and even worse, the flats above the stores on the commercial streets. Some of my classmates were not at all what she had in mind, though I didn't tell her this as I didn't want to be forced into uniform.

6

1. What kind of fool am I?
2. Mary Wollstonecraft makes an interesting comparison in *A Vindication of the Rights of Woman* (1792): "The divine right of husbands, like the divine right of kings, may, it is hoped, in this enlightened age, be contested without danger."
3. There are three kinds of body type: ectomorph, mesomorph, and endomorph.
4. I wonder whether I'll remain an endomorph forever.
5. Unless everyone donates some money, we won't have enough for the trip, and the children will be disappointed.
6. The Bible, the Torah, the Koran, and the Upanishads are all sacred texts.
7. Jacob said, "You, Roderick, are my very best friend."
8. I understand that the regulations do not allow us to increase salaries more than 8 percent; however, the fact remains that inflation is running at 11 percent.
9. The English course you take in college is sure to be different from the English courses you took in high school.
10. The necessary steps for a successful building are to plan and design carefully, to purchase and order carefully, and to build and construct wisely.

7

Coureurs de bois are Frenchmen who were either born in Canada or who came to settle there. They are always young men in the prime of life, for older men cannot endure the hardships of this way of life. Some are of good social standing; others are merely farmers or sons of farmers; others still have no occupation.

Since all of Canada is a vast and trackless forest, it is impossible for them to travel by land. They travel by lake and river in canoes usually occupied by three men.

Since little time is required to carry out this trade, the life of the *coureur de bois* is spent in idleness and dissolute living. They sleep, smoke, drink brandy, no matter what the cost. Gambling, drinking, and women often consume all their money and the profits of their voyages. They live in complete independence and account to no one for their actions.

8

Many studies have been done on the changing sex roles in Western society in the late twentieth century, yet no one is quite sure what these changes mean. What are the implications of women pursuing careers, having smaller families, and of men assuming more responsibility for childrearing? Some people say that these changes will free both men and women from hidebound, restrictive, inflexible traditions. Women, they say, will become more independent and productive; moreover, men will benefit from closer ties with their offspring. On the other hand, some people maintain that there are numerous destructive effects of changing sex roles: broken families, neglected children, and lonely people. Proponents of this view argue that selfish and aggressive instincts flourish in an unstable society where no one is sure what is expected of him or her and pursues only self-gratification. The arguments will continue, for the answers are as yet unclear. But there is no doubt that the changes will continue and even accelerate.

Chapter 20: Finding Something to Write About

1

1. Not specific. It's far too large a topic.
2. Not specific. What kind of alienation?
3. Not significant. Unless it's a particularly exotic one, who cares?
4. Not single. Do you mean war heroes, political heroes, discoverers, pioneers, etc.?
5. Not single or specific. This topic would require a book.
6. Not supportable. How do we have any way of knowing?
7. Not significant.
8. Not single.
9. Not specific or supportable.
10. Not single or specific.

2

1. Possible. Make it single.
2. Possible. Again, it isn't a single topic.
3. Impossible. Hopelessly vague.
4. Possible. But this topic will have to become much more specific.
5. Impossible. This one is not supportable given the rate of technological change.
6. Possible. This subject isn't single as it stands, though.
7. Impossible. Insignificant.
8. Impossible. Though a perennial favourite, this topic isn't specific or single and usually leads to vague expressions of incoherent opinion.
9. Possible. However, this one needs careful narrowing; it is far from being a single topic.
10. Impossible. Vague, unspecific, unsupportable in its present form.

6

1. intramural sports (not significant enough)
2. opera (not pop music)
3. good quality paper
4. privacy; freedom
5. stories (overlaps with fiction)
6. more dates; look better
7. more spaces for children
8. Canadian system (not a "feature"); president is elected (not true)

7

1. lack of financial stability; (overlap with first point)
2. career training; knowledge (both kinds of institutions provide these)
3. poetry and drama (not reasons)
4. downhill (part of Alpine); speed (not a kind); cross-country (part of Nordic)
5. choose a satisfactory topic (overlap with first point)
6. Reformed (a branch of Protestantism); Judaism (not a Christian religion)
7. increases vocabulary; improves general knowledge (these are not detrimental effects)
8. depression (not related to parapsychology)

9

Subject	Order		Main Points
1. learning to drive a car	chronological	3	taking lessons
		4	taking road test
		2	obtaining permit
		5	driving on one's own
		1	studying manual
2. why free public education through high school is essential	climactic	3	the education of all young people is crucial to a society
		2	poor as well as rich children must be educated
		1	every child needs an education
3. breaking a bad habit	chronological	2	substituting other activities
		1	recognizing the bad habit
		3	eliminating the bad habit completely
4. causes of college failure	logical	5	student drops out
		3	student misses classes
		1	student lacks basic skills
		2	student is unable to comprehend course material
		4	student fails courses
5. why hockey violence must be curtailed	climactic	3	violence jeopardizes entire future of the sport
		1	individual players may be injured
		2	children are encouraged to play hockey at too young an age
6. why economic recessions occur	logical	2	buying of consumer goods decreases
		4	unemployment causes general economic slowdown
		1	inflation causes fear and decreases consumer confidence
		3	lowered demand for consumer goods causes widespread unemployment

7. how to change a tire	chronological	_6_	loosen nuts completely and remove wheel
		_5_	raise the car until tire clears ground
		_2_	block the wheels
		_8_	lower vehicle and re-tighten nuts
		_1_	park on flat ground
		_4_	slightly loosen wheel nuts
		_3_	put the jack under the car's frame
		_7_	install spare and retighten nuts

8. problems associated with alcoholism	climactic	_2_	being socially ostracized
		_4_	having poor health
		_3_	losing one's job
		_1_	making a fool of oneself
		_5_	endangering one's own and other people's lives as a drinking driver

Chapter 21: Writing the Thesis Statement

I

1. There are four kinds of driver who cause accidents on expressways: road hogs, tailgaters, speed demons, and Sunday drivers.
2. Cigarette smoking is a habit to be avoided at all costs, for it detracts from appearance, diminishes finances, and threatens health.
3. The five steps for reading assigned material efficiently consist of previewing chapter headings, reading the assignment carefully, taking careful notes, looking up unfamiliar terms, and reviewing the material thoroughly.
4. Einstein's general theory of relativity fundamentally changed the way we think about the nature of matter, the extent of the cosmos, and the fate of the universe.
5. Because owning and maintaining a home involves considerable amounts of money, time, and work, one should carefully consider the decision to buy a house.
6. The principles of dealing with handicapped children include accepting their limitations, understanding their development, allowing them to take some risks, and encouraging them to develop to their fullest potential.
7. In British aristocracy, the five ranks of peer, or title holder in the peerage, are in ascending order, barons, viscounts, earls, marquises, and dukes.
8. It is by the goodness of God that in our country we have those three unspeakably precious things: freedom of speech, freedom of conscience, and the prudence never to practice either of them. (Mark Twain)

9. <u>Getting the job you want</u> requires that you <u>prepare a flawless résumé</u>, <u>research the firm you are interested in</u>, <u>respond intelligently at the interview</u>, and <u>follow up the interview in an appropriate manner</u>.
10. The most prevalent types of crime fiction are <u>detective stories</u>, in which particular private eyes take part; "<u>whodunits</u>", in which a criminal is identified; <u>mystery stories</u>, in which supernatural elements may intervene; and <u>puzzle mysteries</u>, in which clues, not characters, are all-important.

2

1. d. left
2. d. kindness
3. c. joyful
4. c. in the car
5. b. learning to accept disappointment

6. a. unfair
7. c. witlessly
8. b. book-lined den
9. d. diminish our intelligence
10. c. the best restaurant whenever you want good food

3

1. not parallel
2. not parallel
3. not parallel
4. parallel
5. not parallel

6. not parallel
7. parallel
8. parallel
9. not parallel
10. not parallel

4

1. It's important that every college student have enough time to study, sleep, work, and socialize.
2. They like to hang-glide, parachute, and skydive.
3. The downtown streets were dirty, noisy, hot and humid.
4. correct
5. Lucinda will always be remembered for her insane jealousy, venomous tongue, charmless personality, and complete craziness.
6. Before every flight he took, Maxwell rewrote his will, said a prayer, and got really drunk.
7. correct
8. correct
9. After a big party like that one, people always help us to clean up the living room, dining room, den, yard, and to count the empties.
10. That's the last time I go to a croquet tournament, because the fans are inevitably wild, riotous, and beastly.

5

1. The chief characteristics of a good parent are kindness, firmness, and consistency.
2. Frequent causes of failure in college are lack of responsibility, lack of discipline, and lack of basic skills.
3. Organization, expression, and revision are the three keys to good writing.
4. The celebrity fund raiser featured the greats of rock, the elite of sport, the stars of film, and the giants of television.

5. Being unemployed, broke, and alone all contribute to depression.
6. Moving to a rural environment is attractive to some people, because of the slower pace, cleaner air, and the closely knit communities.
7. A first-class baseball team must have a superb pitching staff, a top-notch hitting line-up, and a speedy outfield.
8. There are two important questions about the burgeoning high technology field: will it remain a fast-track industry and will Canada have a part in it?
9. To be an effective manager, an administrator or executive must ensure that he or she is maintaining open lines of communication, allowing a free exchange of ideas, encouraging input from subordinates, and giving them opportunities for achieving greater responsibility.
10. Though both Canadians and Americans are part of a highly affluent society, Canadians seem to be more obsessed with life insurance, pension plans, and savings.

6

1. Children of working parents sometimes suffer from inferior day-care arrangements, insufficient after-school supervision, and insufficient time with their parents.
2. Over the years, boycotts of consumer goods have proved to be effective political tools. Among the goods that people have refrained from buying are lettuce from California, grapes from Chile, and wines from South Africa.
3. Among my favourite works of drama are Shakespeare's plays of the sixteenth century, Sheridan's plays of the eighteenth century, and O'Neill's plays of the twentieth century.
4. It will be many generations before human beings will even understand, let alone benefit from, quarks, black holes, or antimatter.
5. The new Charter of Rights precludes discrimination on the grounds of sex, age, race, or religion.
6. Though their elder sisters and brothers may have been interested in changing the world, today's college students seem primarily interested in having a secure job and a good salary.
7. Newcomers to Canada who come from warm climates with no snow often find themselves depressed by the drizzly autumns, freezing winters, and non-existent springs.
8. We are constantly being bombarded with messages in the forms of oral, written, and visual communication.
9. When I can afford it, I will choose among a Jaguar for its prestige, a Porsche for its speed, and a Mercedes for its reliability.
10. Writing a clear, coherent paper is guaranteed if you are very careful about finding a subject, writing the thesis statement, writing the paragraphs, and revising the essay.

Chapter 22: Writing the Outline

1

A good business letter is concise, clear, and courteous.
I.   conciseness
   A.   don't waste time with irrelevant personal details
   B.   cut out all unnecessary words
II.   clarity
   A.   use an accepted business-letter format
   B.   include all information your reader might need
      1.   include file number or other reference number, if possible
      2.   include specific information such as names, dates, product numbers
III.   courteousness
   A.   avoid sarcasm and insults
   B.   politely request what action you want the reader to take

Notice that we've omitted number 6, "always type your letter." It isn't relevant to any of our main points (nor is it always possible).

2

"The Dimensions of a Complete Life"
Introduction
     Attention-getter: paragraphs 1 and 2
     Statement of subject: paragraph 3
I.   (paragraphs 5 to 8)
   A.   paragraph 5
   B.   (paragraphs 6 and 7)
      1.   paragraph 6
      2.
         a. ⎫ paragraph 7
         b. ⎭
   C.   paragraph 8
II.   (paragraphs 9 to 13)
   A.   paragraph 9
   B.   (paragraphs 10 to 13)
      1.   paragraphs 10 and 11
      2.
         a. ⎫ paragraph 12
         b. ⎭
      3.
         a. ⎫
         b. ⎰ paragraph 13
         c. ⎭
III   (paragraphs 14 to 18)
   A.   paragraph 14
   B.   paragraph 15
   C.   (paragraphs 16 and 17)
      1. ⎫
      2. ⎬ paragraph 16
      3. ⎭
      4.   paragraph 17

    D. paragraph 18
Conclusion
    Summary: paragraph 19
    Memorable statement: paragraph 20

3

I. What makes a good teacher
    A. definition: a good teacher is someone who inspires and motivates students, and who shares in their learning
    B. characteristics of a good teacher
        1. has a variety of interests outside the classroom
        2. relates to students as people
        3. enjoys learning

II. What makes a good course
    A. what a good course does *not* require
        1. an outstanding teacher
        2. undemanding content: ''bird'' courses are like junk food
    B. definition: a good course is one that supplies information, not trivia; one that offers practical principles and leaves students free to apply them
    C. characteristics of a good course
        1. clear organization
        2. fair and appropriate evaluation method
        3. interesting presentation of material

Chapter 23: Writing the Paragraphs

I

paragraph 2: In reflecting on my career as a student I realize that I have learned a great deal.

paragraph 3: A *good* teacher is someone who does all this and at the same time inspires, motivates, and participates in the learning of his or her students.

paragraph 5: An unavoidable part of any course is evaluation.

paragraph 6: And I believe the same principles will apply in any other career I enter.

7

1. examples, details
2. examples, details
3. definition
4. comparison and quotation
5. examples
6. comparison, definition, details
7. examples
8. specific details
9. examples
10. examples

10

I can't understand how anyone could like gardening. In fact, it's such a pointless hobby, I don't know where to begin listing the reasons I dislike it. Flowers grow perfectly well in the wild, so why force them into rows and beds? Some people claim working in the garden is relaxing, but I know one man who got a hernia from lifting manure and another who developed ulcers because his dahlias died. Even inside the house, plants are a hazard. They attract insects, aggravate allergies, poison pets, and spread dirt. In short, gardening is a dangerous activity, one that sensible people avoid.

12

Anyone who enjoys baseball must be a masochist! It is the dullest game ever invented. Let me give you some examples of how boring baseball is. First, the batter swings at every third pitch, on average, which means that the fielders are totally inactive for the greater part of the game. Second, the fielding team does come to life when there's a hit ... an event that occurs about fifteen times per game. Allowing thirty seconds of action per hit, this means that the players actually do something for seven and one half minutes out of an entire afternoon. Even home runs are dull: one man trots around the bases while everyone else stands still and watches. I've come to the conclusion that anyone who enjoys baseball must be a pretty boring person!

Chapter 27: Wordiness

1

1. Even then corpses were treated with respect, just as they now are by civilized nations.
2. I think as you do about the value of Bargain Barry's sale items.
3. Despite being small and being surrounded by children he didn't know, the brave seven-year-old took on the class bully.
4. Again the sergeant said to the new recruits, "I'll call you at 5:30 in the morning. Circle the barracks on the double until 5:45. At 6 o'clock, report to the barracks mess for breakfast."
5. The new recruits called a secret meeting after the 7 o'clock breakfast to discuss their revenge on a sergeant who woke them up one hour early.

6. Believing the sergeant would play his dirty trick every day, they planned an appropriate response.
7. Their plan was to get the sergeant very drunk in the evening and put him to bed at about 4:30 A.M. in the bunkhouse next to the officers' quarters.
8. I thought it was a great idea.
9. They had made sure the sergeant would believe, in the morning, that he was in his own bunkhouse; they bribed their friends who lived in that bunkhouse to leave it empty and decorate it like the sergeant's.
10. At 5:30 A.M., true to his promise that nothing would prevent his wake-up call, the sergeant staggered into the bunkhouse next to his and blasted with bugle and voice. He never did a 5:30 reveille again.

Chapter 28: Abusages

I

1. Nell should have gone with us to the beach; now she can't go anywhere.
2. Many of us thought he might be prejudiced, but actually he turned out to be a really nice man.
3. I'm supposed to see whether the reason for the delay is that it's raining.
4. They are supposed to get the ball themselves, regardless of where it is when they come off the field.
5. Because I won't lend her my homework, she thinks I'm showing prejudice, but she was supposed to do her own homework.
6. If you don't do anything about boarding the windows, you'll have pieces of glass everywhere in the house.
7. It's very sad to see signs of prejudice in young children, who must have been influenced by their parents.
8. It is irrelevant whether she fell or was pushed off her bicycle; she is disqualified anyway.
9. They should have finished the race even though they were behind, since every entrant is supposed to finish unless disqualified or injured.
10. I didn't talk to anyone about seeing one cyclist cheat, since the judges don't consider a spectator's remarks to be relevant.

2

1. correct
2. He and I can't push this car any farther than you and she could.
3. She and I did a really stupid thing.
4. He is a better cook than she, and she plays snooker better than he.
5. You and I can use the Caravan passports all week, and you and she can use them on the weekend when I'm not here.
6. As we walked along Bloor Street, we saw Marie and him going into Toby's restaurant.
7. The police stopped him and me at the door of our apartment building.
8. correct
9. We and they are not very good friends anymore.
10. No one is happier than I that you got the job.

3

The 1987 Rendezvous at Thunder Bay would have been the best party he and I had ever attended if the weather had only been better. The Rendezvous is an annual event that brings together many folks who come dressed as voyageurs and fur traders. People are supposed to wear canvas and leather and wool. No polyester or nylon is allowed, regardless of how wet it gets. The reason is that everyone is supposed to dress exactly the way people did in the eighteenth century. But canvas doesn't hold out water, and the rain couldn't have come down harder. You wouldn't have believed how soaked we got.

Then the people of Thunder Bay came out to Old Fort William with food and drink and threw a party for us in the shelter of a huge barn. We quickly forgot our sodden clothing as we found ourselves laughing and dancing with our new friends. The party was a huge success, and the reason was that the people of Thunder Bay showed such generosity and friendship that even the torrential rains couldn't spoil our stay.

To the owner of this book:

We are interested in your reaction to **The Bare Essentials Form B**, Second Edition by Sarah Norton and Brian Green.

1. What was your reason for using this book?

_____ university course _____ continuing education course
_____ college course _____ personal interest
_____ other (specify)

2. In which school are you enrolled? _____

3. Approximately how much of the book did you use?

_____ 1/4 _____ 1/2 _____ 3/4 _____ all

4. What is the best aspect of the book?

5. Have you any suggestions for improvement?

6. Is there anything that should be added?

Fold here

43652

POSTAGE WILL BE PAID BY
  SUSAN LILHOLT
  Publisher
College Editorial Department
HOLT, RINEHART AND WINSTON
  OF CANADA, LIMITED
55 HORNER AVENUE
TORONTO, ONTARIO
M8Z 9Z9

Tape shut